Bring on the Apocalypse

Bring on the Apocalypse
Essays on Self-Destruction

George Monbiot

Anchor Canada

Library and Archives Canada Cataloguing in Publication

Monbiot, George, 1963-

Bring on the Apocalypse : essays on self-destruction / George
Monbiot.

Compilation of author's previously published columns.

Includes bibliographical references.

ISBN 978-0-385-66304-5

1. History, Modern—21st century—Miscellanea. 2. World
politics—21st century—Miscellanea. 3. Popular culture—
Miscellanea. I. Title.

CB430.M654 2008   909.83'1   C2007-907224-0

This book is printed on paper that is ancient forest-friendly
(100% post consumer recycled) and chlorine free.

Cover image: *Oxford Tire Pile No. 8, Westley, California 1999.*
Photograph by Edward Burtynsky,
Courtesy of Nicholas Metivier Gallery, Toronto.

Printed and bound in Canada

Published in Canada by Anchor Canada, a division of
Random House of Canada Limited

Visit Random House of Canada Limited's website:
www.randomhouse.ca

10   9   8   7   6   5   4   3   2   1

Contents

Arguments With Money

Arguments With Culture

Notes

Bring on the Apocalypse

Introduction

Four Missed Meals Away from Anarchy

I am writing this on a train rattling slowly down the Dyfi Valley in Wales. It is April and the oaks are twitching into life. A moment ago I saw a lamb that had just been born. Afterbirth still trailed from the ewe like scarlet bunting. The Dyfi is lower than it should be at this time of year; its pale shoulders have been exposed. On its banks is the debris of the winter storms: sticks and leaves trapped in the branches of the sallows; trees like the picked skeletons of whales dumped in the grass. It is hard to believe that the river could have mustered such force.

It has not taken me long to adjust to my new home. When I travel to London, I can think only of the rivers and the hills. It is strangely peaceful here, almost as if the cruelty of nature has been suspended. But so, in its way, is every landscape I have travelled through. The houses lining the railway canyon north of Euston look like prisons, but no one riots. In the West Midlands the demolition of our industry takes place without ceremony or panic. Machines stack and sift the rubble; property developers park their Audis and stroll around the remains. There are no mobs; no fires; only the occasional bomb. The country is slumbering through a deep and unremarked peace.

By peace, I mean not just an absence of war. I also mean an absence of the competition for resources encountered in any place or at any time in which the necessities of life are short. Whenever I read about the fighting in Iraq or the massacres in Congo and Darfur, or the torture and repression in Burma or Uzbekistan, or the sheer bloody misery of life in Malawi or Zambia, I am reminded that our peace is a historical and geographical anomaly.

It results primarily from a surplus of energy. A lasting surplus of useful energy is almost unknown to ecologists. Trees will crowd out the sky until no sunlight reaches the forest floor. Bacteria will multiply until they have consumed their substrate. A flush of prey will be followed by a flush of predators, which will proliferate until the prey is depleted. But we have so far been able to keep growing without constraint. By extracting fossil fuels, we can mine the ecological time of other eras. We use the energy sequestered in the hush of sedimentation – the infinitesimal rain of plankton on to the ocean floor, the spongy settlement of fallen trees in anoxic swamps – compressed by the weight of succeeding deposits into concentrated time. Every year we use millions of years accreted in other ages. The gift of geological time is what has ensured, in the rich nations, that we have not yet reached the point at which we must engage in the struggle for resources. We have been able to expand into the past. Fossil fuels have so far exempted us from the violence that scarcity demands.

There are a few exceptions. Some of the troops sent abroad to secure and control other people's energy supplies will die. Otherwise we have outsourced the killing. Other people kill each other on our behalf; we simply pay the victors for the spoils. Oil wars have been waged abroad ever since petroleum became a common transport fuel. Columbite-tantalite, a mineral of whose very existence we are ignorant but upon which much of our post-industrial growth depends, has been one of the main causes of a conflict that has led to some 4 million deaths in the Democratic Republic of Congo. We pay not to fight.

One phrase, picked up in the rhythm of the train, keeps chugging through my head. "Every society is four missed meals away from anarchy." I heard it at a meeting a fortnight ago.[1] Our peace is as transient and contingent as the water level in the Dyfi river.

Some of the accounts of the violence in New Orleans following Hurricane Katrina were exaggerated, but not all of them. The slightest disruption in the supply of essential goods, coupled with the state's failure to assert its monopoly of violence, is sufficient to persuade people to rob, threaten, even to kill. A violent response to scarcity affects even those who are in no danger of starvation. Look at what happens on the first day of the Harrods sale. Prosperous people, aware that bargains are in short supply, shove, elbow, scramble, sometimes exchange blows, in their effort to obtain one of a small number of dinner services or carriage clocks or other such symbols of refinement. Civilisation, so painfully maintained by their hypocritical British manners at other times, disintegrates like the china they tussle over at the first hint of competition. We take our peace for granted only because we fail to understand what sustains it.

Order, in such circumstances, can be quickly restored through the superior force of arms. But order in times of scarcity is not the same as order in times of plenty. It is harsher and less flexible; the realities of power are more keenly felt. There have been instances where the superior force intervenes to try to ensure a fair distribution of resources. This happened, for example, in Britain during the Second World War. More commonly, it intervenes to protect those who still possess supplies from those who do not. It is not always the state that performs this role: the rich also arrange their own security, paying other people to fight.

Look at the compounds and condominiums in Johannesburg, Nairobi, Rio de Janeiro, Buenos Aires, Mumbai and Jakarta. The rich live behind razor wire, broken glass, dogs and armed guards. It is, to my eyes, a hideous existence. But only one thing is worse than living in a gated community in these cities: not living in a gated community. Without guards, you sleep with one ear tuned to the breaking of your door.

Yet even here there is, most of the time, no absolute shortage of any essential resource. In all these places you can buy whatever you want. There is no shortage of food or fuel or clean water or any other commodity, if you have money. Money is the limiting factor the absence of which keeps people hungry. But the situations I would like you to consider are those in which not money but the resources themselves become the constraint.

There are three major commodities whose supply, in many countries, could become subject to absolute constraints during our lifetimes: liquid fuels, fresh water, and food. Over the past three years there has, at last, been some public discussion about "peak oil", the point at which global petroleum supplies peak and then go into decline. I have come to believe that some predictions of its imminent arrival have been exaggerated, but it is clear that it will happen sooner or later, and probably within the next 30 years. In a sense, the date of peaking is irrelevant. Once infrastructure that depends on the consumption of petroleum has been established, demand for this commodity is inelastic: if you live in a distant suburb, you cannot get to work or to the shops or to school without it. This means that absolute scarcity can occur before oil peaks, as demand outstrips supply. Some of the likely consequences are discussed in the essay Crying Sheep.

The greater purchasing power of the rich nations means that they will be the last to be affected by an absolute shortage. They will pay far more for petroleum, but they will still be able to buy it. In poorer countries, by contrast, it will become a scarce and precious commodity, and a constant source of conflict.

Supplies of both fresh water and food are threatened by climate change. Scientists at the UK's Meteorological Office believe that a temperature rise of just 2.1ºC above pre-industrial levels will expose between 2.3 and 3 billion people to the risk of water shortages.[2] The glaciers and snowpack that supply many cities are melting rapidly. Rising sea levels threaten coastal aquifers. In many places, rainfall is decreasing. One study suggests that, on current trends, by 2090 the land area subject to extreme drought will increase thirtyfold.[3] This also affects food supply. Initially, while food production falls in many hot nations with increasing temperatures, it rises in temperate places. This causes regional suffering, but total global food supplies are sustained. But beyond a certain level of warming – perhaps 4°C or so – there is a danger of an overall decline in production, even as the human population continues to rise. At that point, to use the mild term employed by ecologists, an "adjustment" must occur. This means that hundreds of millions must die to bring population into line with food supply.

All over the rich world, where we have forgotten what collective suffering means, there are people who appear to be perversely determined to accelerate these processes, and to shatter the peace we have become too comfortable to enjoy. The most obvious examples are the politicians, noisily assisted by their court journalists, who forced us into war with Iraq. It was as obvious in 2002 as it is today that they decided to go to war before they had developed a justification for it. As two of the essays in this collection show (Thwart Mode and Dreamers and Idiots), they deliberately shut down the opportunities for peace. Whenever Saddam Hussein offered to negotiate, they slapped his hand away. The same approach was used against the Taliban in Afghanistan (as Dreamers and Idiots also shows). When politicians have achieved elected office by scaring the living daylights out of the electorate, they correctly perceive an outbreak of peace as a threat to their interests. Journalists support them partly because they celebrate power regardless of its complexion and partly because war makes better copy than peace.

There are also those who perceive war as a desirable end in itself, irrespective of any political advantage it might confer. These are the people whose story is told in the first essay in this book, Bring on the Apocalypse. It is a remarkable and chilling tale, which shows how strange a world you can create for yourself when you are insulated (by your wealth and the force of your government's arms) from reality.

But all of us appear to some extent to be willing these catastrophes to happen. The extreme examples come from the United States. People arrive on the beaches of Florida in enormous motor homes. These disgorge a pair of sports utility vehicles, which are then raced across the sand. The environmental writer Clive Hamilton reports that people in Texas have begun to install log fires in order to make their homes seem cosy. To enjoy them, they must turn up the air conditioning.[4] But these examples simply represent an exaggeration of the way we all live. The central quest of our lives appears to be to find new ways to use fossil fuels.

The enhanced efficiency of our machines makes no difference to our consumption: we use any savings we make to power some other delightful toy. The internal combustion engine is far more efficient than it was a century ago, when the Model T Ford travelled 25 miles on a gallon of petrol.[5] Yet average fuel economy in the United States today is 21mpg.[6] Greater efficiency has been used to enhance the engine's performance, to carry more weight, to power more gadgets. We exchange our light bulbs for less hungry models, then buy a flatscreen TV almost as wide as the house.

The environmental activist George Marshall has a term for this behaviour: "reactive denial". It is as if, by enhancing our consumption of energy even as we become more aware of the dangers of climate change and peak oil, we are persuading ourselves that these problems cannot be real ones. If they were, surely someone would stop us?

I wish we knew the value of peace. I wish it were a daily marvel to us, as it must be to people who have just emerged from conflict. I wish we understood that without it everything else we value is at risk. I wish we possessed the imagination to grasp the horror of war. But because peace is an absence of events, it is not felt. We throw it away before we have understood what it is worth. I hope that some of the essays in this book will encourage people to consider the alternative.

Arguments With God

Bring On the Apocalypse

To understand what is happening in the Middle East, you must first understand what is happening in Texas. To understand what is happening there, you should read the resolutions passed at the state's Republican party conventions last month. Take a look, for example, at the decisions made in Harris County, which covers much of Houston.[1]

The delegates began by nodding through a few uncontroversial matters: homosexuality is contrary to the truths ordained by God; "any mechanism to process, license, record, register or monitor the ownership of guns" should be repealed; income tax, inheritance tax, capital gains tax and corporation tax should be abolished; and immigrants should be deterred by electric fences.[2] Thus fortified, they turned to the real issue: the affairs of a small state 7000 miles away. It was then, according to a participant, that the "screaming and near fistfights" began.

I don't know what the original motion said, but apparently it was "watered down significantly" as a result of the shouting match. The motion they adopted stated that Israel has an indivisible claim to Jerusalem and the West Bank, that Arab states should be pressured to absorb refugees from Palestine, and that Israel should do whatever it wishes in seeking to eliminate terrorism.[3] Good to see that the extremists didn't prevail, then.

But why should all this be of such pressing interest to the people of a state that is seldom celebrated for its fascination with foreign affairs? The explanation is slowly becoming familiar to us, but we still have some difficulty in taking it seriously.

In the United States, several million people have succumbed to an extraordinary delusion. In the 19th century, two immigrant preachers cobbled together a series of unrelated passages from the Bible to create what appears to be a consistent narrative, stating that Jesus will return to earth when certain preconditions have been met.[4] The first of these is the establishment of a state of Israel. The next involves Israel's occupation of the rest of its "Biblical lands" (most of the Middle East), and the rebuilding of the Third Temple on the site now occupied by the Dome of the Rock and Al-Aqsa mosques. The legions of the Antichrist will then be deployed against Israel and their war will lead to a final showdown in the valley of Armageddon. The Jews will either burn or convert to Christianity, and the Messiah will return to earth.

What makes the story so appealing to Christian fundamentalists is that before the big battle begins, all "true believers" (ie those who believe what *they* believe) will be lifted out of their clothes and wafted up to heaven during an event called the Rapture. Not only do the worthy get to sit at the right hand of God, but they will be able to watch, from the best seats, their political and religious opponents being devoured by boils, sores, locusts and frogs, during the seven years of Tribulation that will follow.

The true believers are now seeking to bring all this about. This means staging confrontations at the old temple site (in 2000 three US Christians were deported for trying to blow up the mosques there,[5] sponsoring Jewish settlements in the occupied territories, demanding ever more US support for Israel, and seeking to provoke a final battle with the Muslim world/Axis of Evil/United Nations/European Union/France, or whoever the legions of the Antichrist turn out to be.

The believers are convinced that they will soon be rewarded for their efforts. The Antichrist is apparently walking among us, in the guise of Kofi Annan, Javier Solana, Yasser Arafat, or, more plausibly, Silvio Berlusconi.[6] The Wal-Mart corporation is also a candidate (in my view a very good one), because it wants to radio-tag its stock, thereby exposing humankind to the Mark of the Beast.[7] By clicking on www.raptureready.com you can discover how close you might be to flying out of your pyjamas. The infidels among us should take note that the Rapture Index currently stands at 144, just one point below the critical threshold, beyond which the sky will be filled with floating nudists. Beast Government, Wild Weather, and Israel are all trading at the maximum five points (the EU is debating its constitution, there was a freak hurricane in the South Atlantic, Hamas has sworn to avenge the killing of its leaders), but the Second Coming is currently being delayed by an unfortunate decline in drug abuse among teenagers and a weak showing by the Antichrist, both of which score only two.

We can laugh at these people, but we should not dismiss them. That their beliefs are bonkers does not mean they are marginal. American pollsters believe that between 15 and 18% of US voters belong to churches or movements that subscribe to these teachings.[8] A survey in 1999 suggested that this figure included 33% of Republicans.[9] The best-selling contemporary books in the United States are the 12 volumes of the Left Behind series, which provide what is usually described as a "fiction-alised" account of the Rapture (this, apparently, distinguishes it from the other one), with plenty of dripping details about what will happen to the rest of us. The people who believe all this don't believe it just a little; for them, it is a matter of life eternal and death.

And among them are some of the most powerful men in America. John Ashcroft, the attorney general, is a true believer, so are several prominent senators and the House majority leader, Tom DeLay. Mr DeLay (who is also the co-author of the marvellously named DeLay-Doolittle Amendment, postponing campaign finance reforms) travelled to Israel last year to tell the Knesset that "there is no middle ground, no moderate position worth taking".[10]

So here we have a major political constituency, representing much of the current president's core vote, in the most powerful nation on earth, which is actively seeking to provoke a new world war. Its members see the invasion of Iraq as a warm-up act, as Revelation 9:14–15 maintains that four angels "which are bound in the great river Euphrates" will be released "to slay the third part of men". They batter down the doors of the White House as soon as its support for Israel wavers. When Bush asked Ariel Sharon to pull his tanks out of Jenin in 2002 he received 100,000 angry emails from Christian fundamentalists, and never mentioned the matter again.[11]

The electoral calculation, crazy as it appears, works like this. Governments stand or fall on domestic issues. For 85% of the US electorate, the Middle East is a foreign issue and therefore of secondary interest when they enter the polling booth. For 15% of the electorate, the Middle East is not just a domestic matter, it's a personal one: if the president fails to start a conflagration there, his core voters don't get to sit at the right hand of God. Bush, in other words, stands to lose fewer votes by encouraging Israeli aggression than he stands to lose by restraining it. He would be mad to listen to these people. He would also be mad not to.

April 20 2004

The Virgin Soldiers

The flame of sexual liberation may soon have to be kept alive by us geriatric delinquents. A US evangelical group has announced that next month it will be recruiting British teenagers to its campaign against sex before marriage. In the United States, over a million have taken the pledge. "Great Britain", the organiser insists, "is fascinated with the idea of sexual abstinence."[1] In my day the fellow would have been horse-whipped. Yet young people are flocking to him. Is there no end to the depravity of today's youth?

Not if the US government can help it. The abstinence campaign that hopes to corrupt the morals of our once-proud nation – a group called the Silver Ring Thing – has so far received $700,000 from George Bush, as part of his campaign to replace sex education with Victorian values.[2] This year he doubled the federal budget for virginity training, to $270m.[3] In terms of participation, his programme is working. In every other respect, it's a catastrophe.

No one could dispute that thousands of teenagers in Britain and the United States are suffering as a result of sex before marriage. Teenage pregnancies are overwhelmingly concentrated at the bottom of the social scale; the teenage daughters of unskilled manual labourers are ten times as likely to become pregnant as middle-class girls.[4] According to the United Nations agency Unicef, women born into poverty are twice as likely to stay that way if they have their children too soon. They are more likely to be unemployed, to suffer from depression, and to become dependent on alcohol or drugs.[5]

The prevalence of both teenage pregnancy and venereal disease in this country and the US is generally blamed on lax morals and a permissive welfare state. Teenagers are in trouble today, the conservatives who dominate this debate insist, because of the sexual liberation of the 1960s and 70s, and the willingness of the state to support single mothers. On Sunday, Ann Widdecombe maintained that sex education has "failed"; those who promote it should now "shut up" and leave the welfare of our teenagers to the virginity campaigners.[6] Denny Pattyn, the founder of the Silver Ring Thing, calls this "the Cesspool Generation – suffering the catastrophic effects of the sexual revolution".[7] These people have some explaining to do.

Were we to accept the conservatives' version, we would expect the nations in which sex education and access to contraception are most widespread to be those that suffer most from teenage pregnancy and sexually transmitted diseases. The truth is the other way around.

The two western countries at the top of the disaster league; the United States and the United Kingdom, are those in which conservative campaigns are among the strongest and sex education and access to contraception are among the weakest. The United States, the UN

Population Fund's figures show, is the only rich nation stuck in the middle of the Third World bloc, with 53 births per 1000 teenagers – a worse record than India, the Philippines and Rwanda.[8] The United Kingdom comes next, at 20 births per 1000. The nations the conservatives would place at the top of the list are clumped at the bottom. Germany and Norway produce 11 babies per 1000 teenagers, Finland eight, Sweden and Denmark seven, and the Netherlands five.[9]

Unicef's explanation is pretty unequivocal. Sweden, for example, radically changed its sex education policies in 1975. "Recommendations of abstinence and sex-only-within-marriage were dropped, contraceptive education was made explicit, and a nationwide network of youth clinics was established specifically to provide confidential contraceptive advice and free contraceptives to young people ... Over the next two decades, Sweden saw its teenage birth rate fall by 80 per cent."[10] Sexually transmitted diseases, in contrast to rising rates in the UK and US, declined in Sweden by 40% in the 1990s.[11]

"Studies of the Dutch experience", Unicef continues, "have concluded that the underlying reason for success has been the combination of a relatively inclusive society with more open attitudes towards sex and sex education, including contraception." Requests for contraceptives there "are not associated with shame or embarrassment" and "the media is willing to carry explicit messages" about them which are "designed for young people".[12] This teeming cesspool has among the lowest abortion and teenage birth rates on earth.

The US and the UK, by contrast, are "less inclusive societies" in which "contraceptive advice and services may be formally available, but in a 'closed' atmosphere of embarrassment and secrecy". The UK has a higher teenage pregnancy rate not because there is more sex or more abortion here, but because of "lower rates of contraceptive use".[13]

The catastrophe afflicting so many teenagers in Britain and America, in other words, has been caused not by liberal teachers, liberated parents, Marie Stopes International and the Guardian, but by George Bush, Ann Widdecombe and the Daily Mail. They campaign against early sex education, discourage access to contraceptives and agitate against the social inclusion (economic equality, the welfare state) which offers young women better prospects than getting knocked up. Abstinence campaigns like the Silver Ring Thing do delay the onset of sexual activity, but when their victims are sucked into the cesspool (nearly all eventually are), they are around one third less likely to use contraceptives (according to a study by researchers at Columbia University), as they are not "prepared for an experience that they have promised to forgo".[14] The result, a paper published in the British Medical Journal shows, is that abstinence programmes are "associated with an increase in number of pregnancies among partners of young male participants".[15] You read that right: abstinence training increases the rate of teenage pregnancy.

If all this were widely known, the conservatives and evangelicals would never dare to make the claims they do. So they must ensure that we don't find out. In January, the Sunday Telegraph claimed that Europeans "look on in envy" at the US record on teenage pregnancies.[16] It supported this extraordinary statement by deliberately fudging the figures: running the teenage birth rate per 1000 in the US against the total teenage birth rate in the UK, so leaving its readers with no means of comparison.

Breathtaking as this deception is, it's not half as bad as what Bush has been up to. When his cherished abstinence programmes failed to reduce the teenage birth rate, he instructed the US Centers for Disease Control to stop gathering data.[17] He also forced them to drop their project to identify the sex education programmes that work, after they found that none of the successful ones were "abstinence-only".[18] Bush should also hope that we don't look too closely at his record as governor of Texas. He spent $10m on abstinence campaigns there, with the result that Texas has the fourth-highest rate of HIV infection in the Union, and the slowest decline of any state in the birth rate among 15–17-year-olds.[19]

So when this bunch of johnny-come-lately foreigners arrives here next month with their newfangled talk about "virginity" and "abstinence",

I urge you chaps to lock up your daughters and send them on their way. It's up to the older generation to keep our young whippersnappers off the straight and narrow.

May 11 2004

Is the Pope Gay?

"What a man believes upon grossly insufficient evidence", Bertrand Russell wrote, "is an index to his desires – desires of which he himself is often unconscious."[1] The Vatican's current obsession with homosexuality suggests that something interesting might be going on. Are some of the church's most powerful cardinals struggling with their sexuality? Could Pope John Paul II himself be gay?

On Sunday, the Holy Father launched his fiercest attack on gays, insisting that the World Pride festival in Rome was "an offence to [the] Christian values" of the city.[2] Homosexuality, he maintained, is "objectively disordered" and "contrary to natural law".

Last year, the Congregation for the Doctrine of the Faith (CDF), the Church's sinister enforcement agency, run by Cardinal Joseph Ratzinger, forbade a priest and a nun from ministering to gays in the United States after they refused to sign a statement testifying that "homosexual acts are always objectively evil".[3] Gays, the Vatican believes, bring their misfortunes upon themselves. "When civil legislation is introduced to protect behaviour to which no one has any conceivable right," the CDF asserts, "neither the church nor society at large should be surprised when ... violent reactions increase."[4] Gay rights campaigners maintain that between 150 and 200 gay men are murdered in Italy every year.[5]

For this reason, if for no other, we should take this papal bull seriously. So let us examine the two main themes of the Vatican's edicts: homosexuality, it maintains, is both immoral and unnatural.

Morality is surely meaningless unless it refers to the impact we have on other people. Interestingly, even the Vatican appears unable to point to any ill-effects of safe sex between consenting gay adults, other than to suggest that its acceptance might "deprave" or "corrupt" other people. What this appears to mean is that they might be led away from the teachings of the church. Heterosexuality is quite another matter. Reproduction among prosperous people has a demonstrable impact on the welfare of others. Thanks to the depletion of resources and the effects of climate change, every child born to the rich deprives children elsewhere of the means of survival. In a world of diminishing assets, being gay is arguably more moral than being straight.

The claim that homosexuality is "unnatural" is more interesting. This could mean one of two things. Perhaps the Pope is suggesting that it lies beyond the scope of "normal" human behaviour. If so, this has uncomfortable implications for an association of old men who wear dresses and hear voices.

Alternatively, he might be suggesting that homosexual behaviour is at variance with that of the non-human world. Here, too, the church has a problem. Biological Exuberance, a book by the science writer Bruce Bagemihl, documents homosexuality in no fewer than 470 animal species.[6] He shows how groups of manatees carouse in gay orgies; how male giraffes start "necking" and end up fornicating, how female Japanese macaques will pair off for weeks at a time, fondling each other and having sex.

As New Scientist magazine records, at the beginning of the last century the embarrassed keepers of Edinburgh Zoo had repeatedly to rechristen their penguins, after they found that the loving couples they observed were not all that they seemed.[7] Female roseate terns sometimes mate with each other for life, allowing themselves to be fertilised by males, but making nests and bringing up their young together. I would hesitate to describe what pygmy chimpanzees, orang-utans or long-eared hedgehogs get up to, even in a liberal newspaper. The world's wildlife, in other words, is depraved. But we would be hard put to call it unnatural. Self-enforced celibacy, by contrast, is all but unknown among other animal species. If any sexual behaviour is out of tune with the natural world, it is surely that of the priesthood.

My guess is that the Pope is not gay, but that he has found in homosexuals a necessary enemy, an external threat that allows the Holy See to justify its iron grip on the lives of the faithful. Though some brave priests and bishops have sought to resist its excesses, for centuries the Vatican has picked on the victims of existing prejudice and persecution. It is no longer allowed to burn heretics and witches at the stake, so now it preys instead upon homosexuals and pregnant women, exposing gays to violent abuse, seeking to prevent even the rape victims of Kosovo from taking the morning-after pill.

Homosexuality is surely both natural and moral. Can the same be said of the Pope?

July 13 2000

A Life With No Purpose

All is not lost in America. When President George Bush came out a couple of weeks ago in favour of teaching "intelligent design" – the new manifestation of creationism – the press gave him a tremendous kicking. The Christian Taliban have not yet won.

But they are gaining on us. So far there have been legislative attempts in 13 states to have intelligent design added to the school curriculum.[1] In Kansas, Texas and Philadelphia, it already has a foot in the door. In April a new "museum of earth history" opened in Arkansas, which instructs visitors that "dinosaurs and humans did coexist", and that juvenile dinosaurs, though God forgot to mention it, hitched a ride on Noah's Ark.[2] Similar museums are being built in Texas and Kentucky. According to a Gallup poll last year, 45% of Americans believe that "human beings did not evolve, but instead were created by God ... essentially in their current form about 10,000 years ago".[3]

And it's not just in America. Last month the Catholic archbishop of Vienna, Cardinal Christoph Shönborn, asserted that "any system of thought that denies or seeks to explain away the overwhelming evidence for design in biology is ideology, not science".[4] He appears to have the support of the new Pope.[5] Last week the Australian education minister, Brendan Nelson, announced that "if schools also want to present students with intelligent design, I don't have any difficulty with that".[6] In the UK, the head of one of Prime Minister Blair's new business-sponsored academies claims that evolution is merely a "faith position"[7].

The controversy fascinates me. This is partly because of its similarity to the dispute about climate change. Like the climate change deniers, the advocates of intelligent design cherry-pick the data that appear to support their case. They ask for evidence, then ignore it when it's presented to them. They invoke a conspiracy to explain the scientific consensus, and are unembarrassed by their own scientific illiteracy. In an article published in the American Chronicle on Friday, the journalist Thomas Dawson asserted that "all of the vertebrate groups, from fish to mammals appear [in the fossil record] at one time" and that if evolution "were true, there would be animal life fossils of particular animals without vision and others with varying degrees of eye development ... Such fossils do not exist."[8] The first fish and the first mammals are in fact separated by some 300 million years, and the fossil record has more eyes, in all stages of development, than the CIA.

But it fascinates me also because natural selection is such a barren field for the fundamentalists to till. For 146 years Darwinian evolution has seen off all-comers. There is a massive accumulation of evidence – from the fossil record, genetics and direct observation – that appears to support it. Were they to concentrate instead on the questions now assailing big bang theory,[9] or on the failure so far to reconcile gravity with quantum physics, or on the stubborn non-appearance of the Higgs boson and the abiding mystery of the phenomenom of mass, the Christian conservatives would be much harder to confront. Why pick on Darwin?

It is surely because as soon as you consider the implications, you must cease to believe that either Life or life are affected by purpose. As G Thomas Sharp, chairman of the Creation Truth Foundation, admitted to the Chicago Tribune, "if we lose Genesis as a legitimate scientific and historical explanation for man, then we lose the validity of Christianity. Period."[10]

We lose far more than that. Darwinian evolution tells us that we are incipient compost: assemblages of complex molecules that, for no greater purpose than to secure sources of energy against competing claims, have developed the ability to speculate. After a few score years, the molecules disaggregate and return whence they came. Period.

As a gardener and ecologist, I find this oddly comforting. I like the idea of literal reincarnation: that the molecules of which I am composed will, once I have rotted, be incorporated into other organisms. Bits of me will be pushing through the growing tips of trees, will creep over them as caterpillars, will hunt those caterpillars as birds. When I die, I would like to be buried in a fashion that ensures that no part of me is wasted. Then I can claim to have been of some use after all.

Is this not better than the awful lottery of judgment? Is a future we can predict not more comforting than one committed to the whims of inscrutable authority? Is eternal death not a happier prospect than eternal life? The atoms of which we are composed, which we have borrowed momentarily from the ecosphere, will be recycled until the universe collapses. This is our continuity, our eternity. Why should anyone want more?

Two days ago, I would have claimed that the demand for more was universal – that every society has or had its creation story and, as Joseph Campbell put it, "it will always be the one, shape-shifting yet marvellously constant story that we find."[11] But yesterday I read a study by the anthropologist Daniel Everett of the language of the Piraha people of the Brazilian Amazon, published in the latest edition of Current

Anthropology.[12] Its findings could scarcely be more disturbing, or more profound.

The Piraha, Everett reveals, possess "the most complex verbal morphology I am aware of [and] are some of the brightest, pleasantest, most fun-loving people that I know". Yet they have no numbers of any kind, no terms for quantification (such as all, each, every, most and some), no colour terms, and no perfect tense. They appear to have borrowed their pronouns from another language, having previously possessed none. They have no "individual or collective memory of more than two generations past", no drawing or other art, no fiction, and "no creation stories or myths".

All this, Everett believes, can be explained by a single characteristic: "Piraha culture constrains communication to non-abstract subjects which fall within the immediate experience of [the speaker]." What can be discussed, in other words, is what has been seen. When it can no longer be perceived, it ceases, in this realm at least, to exist. After struggling with one grammatical curiosity, he realised that the Piraha were "talking about liminality – situations in which an item goes in and out of the boundaries of their experience. [Their] excitement at seeing a canoe go around a river bend is hard to describe; they see this almost as travelling into another dimension." The Piraha, still living, watch the sparrow flit in and out of the banqueting hall.[13]

"Happy the hare at morning," WH Auden and Christopher Isherwood wrote, "for she cannot read / The Hunter's waking thoughts. Lucky the leaf / Unable to predict the fall ... But what shall man do, who can whistle tunes by heart, / Know to the bar when death shall cut him short, like the cry of the shearwater?"[14]

It seems to me that we are the happy ones: we, alone among organisms, who perceive eternity, and know that the world will carry on without us.

August 16 2005

America the Religion

"The death of Uday and Qusay", the commander of the ground forces in Iraq told reporters on Wednesday, "is definitely going to be a turning point for the resistance."[1] Well, it was a turning point, but unfortunately not of the kind he envisaged. On the day he made his announcement, Iraqi insurgents killed one US soldier and wounded six others. On the following day, they killed another three; over the weekend they assassinated five and injured seven. Yesterday they slaughtered one more and wounded three. This has been the worst week for US soldiers in Iraq since George Bush declared that major combat operations there were over.

Few people believe that the resistance in that country is being coordinated by Saddam Hussein and his noxious family, or that it will come to an end when those people are killed. But the few appear to include the military and civilian command of the United States armed forces. For the hundredth time since the US invaded Iraq, the predictions made by those with access to intelligence have proved less reliable than the predictions made by those without. And, for the hundredth time, the inaccuracy of the official forecasts has been blamed on "intelligence failures".

The explanation is wearing a little thin. Are we really expected to believe that the members of the US security services are the only people who cannot see that many Iraqis wish to rid themselves of the US army as fervently as they wished to rid themselves of Saddam Hussein? What is lacking in the Pentagon and the White House is not intelligence (or not, at any rate, of the kind we are considering here), but receptivity. Theirs is not a failure of information, but a failure of ideology.

To understand why this failure persists, we must first grasp a reality that has seldom been discussed in print. The United States is no longer just a nation. It is now a religion. Its soldiers have entered Iraq to liberate its people not only from their dictator, their oil and their sovereignty, but also from their darkness. As George Bush told his troops on the day he announced victory: "Wherever you go, you carry a message of hope – a message that is ancient and ever new. In the words of the prophet Isaiah, 'To the captives, "come out", and to those in darkness, "be free".'"[2]

So American soldiers are no longer merely terrestrial combatants; they have become missionaries. They are no longer simply killing enemies; they are casting out demons. The people who reconstructed the faces of Uday and Qusay Hussein carelessly forgot to restore the pair of little horns on each brow, but the understanding that these were opponents from a different realm was transmitted nonetheless. Like all those who send missionaries abroad, the high priests of America cannot conceive that the infidels might resist through their own free will; if they refuse to convert, it is the work of the devil, in his current guise as the former dictator of Iraq.

As Clifford Longley shows in his book Chosen People, published last year, the founding fathers of the USA, though they sometimes professed otherwise, sensed that they were guided by a divine purpose.[3] Thomas Jefferson argued that the Great Seal of the United States should depict the Israelites, "led by a cloud by day and a pillar of fire by night".[4] George Washington claimed, in his inaugural address, that every step towards independence was "distinguished by some token of providential agency".[5] Longley argues that the formation of the American identity was part of a process of supersession. The Catholic church claimed that it had supplanted the Jews as the elect, as the Jews had been repudiated by God. The English Protestants accused the Catholics of breaking faith, and claimed that they had become the beloved of God. The American revolutionaries believed that the English, in turn, had broken their covenant; the Americans had now become the chosen people, with a divine duty to deliver the world to God's dominion. Six weeks ago, as if to show that this belief persists, George Bush recalled a remark of Woodrow Wilson's. "America", he quoted, "has a spiritual energy in her which no other nation can contribute to the liberation of mankind."[6]

Gradually this notion of election has been conflated with another, still more dangerous idea. It is not just that the Americans are God's chosen people; America itself is now perceived as a divine project. In his farewell presidential address, Ronald Reagan spoke of his country as a "shining city on a hill", a reference to the Sermon on the Mount.[7] But what Jesus was describing was not a temporal Jerusalem, but the kingdom of heaven. Not only, in Reagan's account, was God's kingdom to be found in the United States of America, but the kingdom of hell could also now be located on earth: the "evil empire" of the Soviet Union, against which His holy warriors were pitched.

Since the attacks on New York, this notion of America the divine has been extended and refined. In December 2001, Rudy Giuliani, the mayor of that city, delivered his last mayoral speech in St Paul's Chapel, close to the site of the shattered twin towers. "All that matters", he claimed, "is that you embrace America and understand its ideals and what it's all about. Abraham Lincoln used to say that the test of your Americanism was . . . how much you believed in America. Because we're like a religion really. A secular religion."[8] The chapel in which he spoke had been consecrated not just by God, but by the fact that George Washington had once prayed there. It was, he said, now "sacred ground to people who feel what America is all about".[9] The United States of America no longer needs to call upon God; it is God, and those who go abroad to spread the light do so in the name of a celestial domain. The flag has become as sacred as the Bible; the name of the nation as holy as the name of God. The presidency is turning into a priesthood.

So those who question George Bush's foreign policy are no longer merely critics; they are blasphemers, or "anti-Americans". Those foreign states that seek to change this policy are wasting their time: you can negotiate with politicians; you cannot negotiate with priests. The US has a divine mission, as Bush suggested in January, "to defend . . . the hopes of all mankind",[10] and woe betide those who hope for something other than the American way of life.

The dangers of national divinity scarcely require explanation. Japan went to war in the 1930s convinced, like George Bush, that it possessed a heaven-sent mission to liberate Asia and extend the realm of its divine imperium. It would, the fascist theoretician Kita Ikki predicted, "light the darkness of the entire world".[11] Those who seek to drag heaven down to earth are destined only to engineer a hell.

July 29 2003

Arguments With Nature

Junk Science

For the past three weeks, a set of figures has been working a hole in my mind. On April 16, New Scientist published a letter from the British botanist and television personality David Bellamy. Many of the world's glaciers, he claimed, "are not shrinking but in fact are growing . . . 555 of all the 625 glaciers under observation by the World Glacier Monitoring Service in Zurich, Switzerland, have been growing since 1980."[1] His letter was instantly taken up by climate change deniers. And it began to worry me. What if Bellamy was right?

He is a scientist, formerly a senior lecturer at the University of Durham. He knows, in other words, that you cannot credibly cite data unless it is well sourced. Could it be that one of the main lines of evidence for the impact of global warming – the retreat of the world's glaciers – is wrong?

The question could scarcely be more important. If man-made climate change is happening, as the great majority of the world's climatologists claim, it could destroy the conditions that allow human beings to remain on the planet. The effort to cut greenhouse gases must come before everything else. This won't happen unless we can be confident that the science is right. Because Bellamy is president of the Conservation Foundation, the Wildlife Trusts, Plantlife International and the British Naturalists' Association, his statements carry a great deal of weight. When, for example, I challenged the Society of Motor Manufacturers and Traders over climate change, its spokesman cited Bellamy's position as a reason for remaining sceptical.[2]

So last week I telephoned the World Glacier Monitoring Service and read out Bellamy's letter. I don't think the response would have been published in Nature, but it had the scientific virtue of clarity. "This is complete bullshit."[3] A few hours later, they sent me an email.

"Despite his scientific reputation, he makes all the mistakes that are possible." He had cited data that was simply false, failed to provide references, completely misunderstood the scientific context, and neglected current scientific literature.[4] The latest studies show unequivocally that most of the world's glaciers are retreating.[5]

But I still couldn't put the question out of my mind. The figures Bellamy cited must have come from somewhere. I emailed him to ask for his source. After several requests, he replied to me at the end of last week. The data, he said, came from a website called www.iceagenow.com.

Iceagenow.com was constructed by a man called Robert W Felix to promote his self-published book about "the coming ice age". It claims that sea levels are falling, not rising; that the Asian tsunami was caused by the "ice age cycle"; and that "underwater volcanic activity – not human activity – is heating the seas".

Is Felix a climatologist, a vulcanologist, or an oceanographer? Er, none of the above. His biography describes him as a "former architect".[6] His website is so bonkers that I thought at first it was a spoof. Sadly, he appears to believe what he says. But there indeed was all the material Bellamy cited in his letter, including the figures – or something resembling the figures – he quoted. "Since 1980, there has been an advance of more than 55% of the 625 mountain glaciers under observation by the World Glacier Monitoring group in Zurich."[7] The source, which Bellamy also cited in his email to me, was given as "the latest issue of 21st Century Science and Technology".

21st Century Science and Technology? It sounds impressive, until you discover that it is published by Lyndon Larouche. Lyndon Larouche is the American demagogue who in 1989 received a 15-year sentence for conspiracy, mail fraud and tax code violations.[8] He has claimed that the British royal family is running an international drugs syndicate,[9] that Henry Kissinger is a communist agent,[10] that the British government is controlled by Jewish bankers,[11] and that modern science is a conspiracy against human potential.[12]

It wasn't hard to find out that this is one of his vehicles. Larouche is named on the front page of the magazine's website, and the edition Bellamy cites contains an article beginning with the words "We in LaRouche's Youth Movement find ourselves in combat with an old enemy that destroys human beings . . . it is empiricism."[13]

Oh well, at least there is a source for Bellamy's figures. But where did 21st Century Science and Technology get them from? It doesn't say. But I think we can make an informed guess, for the same data can be found all over the internet. They were first published online by Professor Fred Singer, one of the very few climate change deniers who has a vaguely relevant qualification (he is, or was, an environmental scientist). He posted them on his website, www.sepp.org, and they were then reproduced by the appropriately named junk-science.com, by the Cooler Heads Coalition, the National Center for Public Policy Research, and countless others.[14] They have even found their way into the Washington Post.[15] They are constantly quoted as evidence that manmade climate change is not happening. But where did they come from? Singer cites half a source: "a paper published in *Science* in 1989".[16] Well, the paper might be 16 years old, but at least, and at last, there is one. Surely?

I went through every edition of Science published in 1989, both manually and electronically. Not only did it contain nothing resembling those figures; throughout that year there was no paper published in this journal about glacial advance or retreat.

So it wasn't looking too good for Bellamy, or Singer, or any of the people who have cited these figures. But there was still one mystery to clear up. While Bellamy's source claimed that 55% of 625 glaciers are advancing, Bellamy claimed that 555 of them, or 89%, are advancing. This figure appears to exist nowhere else. But on the standard English keyboard, 5 and % occupy the same key. If you try to hit %, but fail to press shift, you get 555 instead of 55%. This is the only explanation I can produce for his figure. When I challenged him, he admitted that there had been "a glitch of the electronics".[17]

So, in Bellamy's poor typing, we have the basis for a whole new front in the war against climate science. The 555 figure is now being cited as definitive evidence that global warming is a "fraud", a "scam", a "lie". I phoned New Scientist to ask if he had requested a correction. He had not been in touch.[18]

It is hard to convey just how selective you have to be to dismiss the evidence for climate change. You must climb over a mountain of evidence to pick up a crumb – a crumb that then dissolves in your palm. You must ignore an entire canon of science, the statements of the world's most eminent scientific institutions, and thousands of papers published in the foremost scientific journals. You must, if you are David Bellamy, embrace instead the claims of an eccentric former architect, which are based on what appears to be a non-existent data set. And you must do all this while calling yourself a scientist.

May 10 2005

Mocking Our Dreams

It is now mid-February, and already I have sown eleven species of vegetable. I know, though the seed packets tell me otherwise, that they will flourish. Everything in the UK – daffodils, primroses, almond trees, bumblebees, nesting birds – is a month ahead of schedule. And it feels wonderful. Winter is no longer the great grey longing of my childhood. The freezes this country suffered in 1982 and 1963 are, unless the Gulf Stream stops, unlikely to recur. Our summers will be long and warm.

Across most of the upper northern hemisphere, climate change, so far, has been kind to us.

And this is surely one of the reasons why we find it so hard to accept what the climatologists are now telling us. In our mythologies, an early spring is a reward for virtue. "For, lo, the winter is past," Solomon, the beloved of God, exults. "The rain is over and gone; / The flowers appear on the earth; the time of the singing of birds is come".[1] How can something that feels so good result from something so bad?

Tomorrow, after 13 years of negotiation, the Kyoto protocol on climate change comes into force. No one believes that this treaty alone, which commits 30 developed nations to reduce their greenhouse gas emissions by 5.2%, will solve the problem. It expires in 2012 and, thanks to US sabotage, so far there has been no progress towards a replacement.[2] It paroles the worst offenders – the United States and Australia – and imposes no limits on the gases produced by developing countries. The cuts it enforces are at least an order of magnitude too small to stabilise greenhouse gas concentrations at anything approaching a safe level.[3] But even this feeble agreement is threatened by our complacency about the closing of the climatic corridor down which we walk.

Why is this? Why are we transfixed by terrorism, yet relaxed about the collapse of the conditions that make our lives possible? One reason is surely the disjunction between our expectations and our observations. If climate change is to introduce horror into our lives, we would expect, because throughout our evolutionary history we survived by finding patterns in nature, to see that horror beginning to unfold. It is true that a few thousand people in the rich world have died as a result of floods and heatwaves. But the overwhelming sensation, experienced by all of us, almost every day, is that of being blessed by our pollution.

Instead, the consequences of our gluttony are visited on others. The climatologists who met at the government's conference in Exeter this month heard that a rise of just 2.1°C – almost certain to happen this century – will confront as many as 3 billion people with water stress.[4]

This, in turn, is likely to result in tens of millions of deaths. But the same calm voice that tells us that climate change means mild winters and early springs informs us, in countries like the UK, that we will be able to buy our way out of trouble. While the price of food will soar as the world goes into deficit, those who are rich enough to have caused the problem will, for a couple of generations at least, be among the few who can afford to ignore it.

Another reason is that there is a well-funded industry whose purpose is to reassure us, and it is granted constant access to the media. We flatter its practitioners with the label "sceptics". If this were what they are, they would be welcome. Scepticism (the Latin word means "inquiring" or "reflective") is the means by which science advances. Without it we would still be rubbing sticks together. But most of those we call sceptics are nothing of the kind. They are PR people, the loyalists of Exxon Mobil (by whom most of them are paid), who have been commissioned to begin with a conclusion and then devise arguments to justify it.[5] Their presence on outlets such as BBC radio's flagship current affairs show Today might be less objectionable if every time a rocket goes into orbit the Flat Earth Society was invited to explain that it could not possibly have happened. As it is, our most respected media outlets give Exxon Mobil what it has paid for; they create the impression that a significant scientific debate exists, when it does not.

But there's a much bigger problem here. The denial of climate change, while out of tune with the science, is consistent with – even necessary for – the outlook of almost all the world's economists. The continuous growth prescribed by modern economics, whether informed by Marx or Keynes or Hayek, depends on the notion that the planet has an infinite capacity to supply us with wealth and absorb our pollution. In a finite world, this is impossible. Pull this rug from under the dominant economic theories, and the whole system of thought collapses.

And this, of course, is beyond contemplation. It mocks the dreams of both left and right, of every child and parent and worker. It destroys all notions of progress. If the engines of progress – technology and its amplification of human endeavour – have merely accelarated our rush to the brink, then everything we thought was true is false. Brought up to believe that it is better to light a candle than to curse the darkness, we are now discovering that it is better to curse the darkness than to burn your house down.

Our economists are exposed by climatologists as utopian fantasists, the leaders of a millenarian cult as mad as, and far more dangerous than, any religious fundamentalism. But their theories govern our lives, so those who insist that physics and biology still apply are ridiculed by a global consensus founded on wishful thinking.

And this leads us, I think, to a further reason for turning our eyes away. When terrorists threaten us, it shows that we must count for something, that we are important enough to kill. They confirm the grand narrative of our lives, in which we strive through thickets of good and evil towards an ultimate purpose. But there is no glory in the threat of climate change. The story it tells us is of yeast in a barrel, feeding and farting until it is poisoned by its own waste. It is too squalid an ending for our anthropocentric conceit to accept.

The challenge of climate change is not, primarily, a technical one. It is possible greatly to reduce our environmental impact by investing in energy efficiency, though as the Exeter conference concluded, "energy efficiency improvements under the present market system are not enough to offset increases in demand caused by economic growth."[6] It is possible to generate far more of the energy we consume by benign means. But if our political leaders are to save the people rather than the people's fantasies, then the way we see ourselves must begin to shift. We will succeed in tackling climate change only when we accept that we belong to the material world.

February 14 2005

Preparing for Take-Off

I suppose I should be flattered. In a speech to fellow airline bosses a few days ago, Martin Broughton, the chief executive of British Airways, announced that the primary challenge for the industry is to "isolate the George Monbiots of this world".[1] That shouldn't be difficult. For a terrifying spectre, I'm feeling pretty lonely. Almost everyone in politics appears to want to forget about flying's impact on the environment.

On Wednesday, the secretary of state for communities launched a bold plan to make new homes more energy-efficient. She claims it will save 7 million tonnes of carbon.[2] On Thursday, Douglas Alexander, the British transport secretary, announced that he would allow airports to keep growing; by 2030 the number of passengers will increase from 228 million to 465 million.[3] As a result, according to a report commissioned by the environment department, carbon emissions will rise by between 22 and 36 million tonnes.[4] So much for joined-up government.

The government says it will cut carbon dioxide emissions by 60% between 1990 and 2050. Last month it promised to introduce a climate change bill, which will make this target legally binding. Douglas Alexander's decision ensures that the new law will be broken.

A 60% cut means that our emissions by 2050 must amount to no more than 65 million tonnes of carbon (MtC). The "best case" figures produced by the Department for Transport would see emissions from air transport rising from 4.6 to 15.7MtC, or 24% of the target for the whole economy. According to the House of Commons Environmental Audit Committee, "this is likely to be a very substantial understatement".[5]

The Tyndall Centre for Climate Change Research estimates that the UK's aeroplane emissions are more likely to amount to 32MtC by 2050, or 49% of the target.[6] The report produced for the environment department, by researchers at Manchester Metropolitan University, calculates that they will rise to between 29.8 and 44.4MtC, or 46–68% of the target.[7] This, they say, is an underestimate, as they don't include non-scheduled flights.

None of these calculations takes into account the other greenhouse gases aircraft produce. According to the Intergovernmental Panel on Climate Change, these create a global warming effect 2.7 times as great as the carbon dioxide alone.[8] Nor do they recognise the fact that 70% of people flying out of the United Kingdom live in this country; all the estimates give the UK a 50% share of the flights landing or taking off here, rather than 70%.[9] Throw these numbers into the equation and you discover that aviation will account for between 91% and 258% of all the greenhouse gases the United Kingdom will be permitted, under the new law, to produce in 2050.

So how does the government navigate this contradiction? It's simple. It doesn't include international aircraft emissions in its target. Whatever their impact on the world's atmosphere might be, they don't officially exist.

No one now pretends that the industry can design its way out of this. The Department for Transport's wildly optimistic figure (a mere 91% of the UK's target) assumes improvements in efficiency that most observers believe will be impossible to realise. After a 70% reduction in the fuel consumed by jet engines over the past 40 years, they have pretty well reached their limits, while radical new aircraft designs and new fuels are, at best, several decades away from commercialisation. Even Martin Broughton admits that the airlines' fuel efficiency gains "are likely to be outweighed by future growth".[10] So the government relies on two other mechanisms, taxation and trading. It knows that neither of them will work.

Gordon Brown, the British finance minister, announced two weeks ago that he will double air passenger duty, from £5 to £10.[11] This merely reverses the cut he made in 2001. In its White Paper on aviation, the transport department investigated the effect of a bigger levy – a 100% fuel tax. This, it found, would increase the airlines' prices by 10%.[12] But the growth of the no-frills carriers would be sufficient to offset it, ensuring that there was no suppression of demand.[13] Air passenger duty might begin to bite at 10 times its current level. Is there anyone in government who has the guts to make that happen?

Brown's pathetic levy is counteracted by subsidies that he has managed, so far, to keep mostly hidden from public view. It turns out that the government has been authorising "route development funds" to establish "new links from regional airports".[14] European rules permit governments to provide up to 50% of the start-up costs for regional airports and their new connections.[15] Last week, for example, the Guardian reported that Derry City Council has been secretly giving Ryanair £1.3m a year.[16] Our money is being used to subsidise climate change.

Tomorrow, the European Union will wave its wand and make the airlines carbon emissions magically disappear. It will incorporate them into the European emissions trading scheme. According to Douglas Alexander, this is "the most efficient and cost-effective way to ensure that the sector plays its part in tackling climate change".[17] The airlines can keep growing, he argues, as long as they buy carbon permits from other industries, which can cut their output more cheaply. All that counts is that the European economy as a whole is reducing its emissions – it doesn't matter how they are distributed.

So how is this going to work, if aviation accounts for 258% of all the greenhouse gases the target permits us to produce? Or even 91%? Again, there is sleight of hand involved. The other greenhouse gases don't count; the trading scheme recognises only carbon. But even if we were to accept its restricted terms, why should aviation force the rest of the European economy to reduce its emissions much faster than the average? Is flying more important than heating and lighting?

You can shuffle carbon between different industries when the overall reduction you are trying to achieve is just 8% and still stay within the cap. But when you go much beyond that point, as the EU must in 2012, almost every industry will have to start making cuts of its own. So what

happens when the growth in flights outstrips the cuts the other industries can make? How will the airlines cut their emissions in order to
stay within the scheme? If the government knows, it hasn't told us.

Douglas Alexander knows as well as I do that emissions trading is
a red herring. In his new report is a table showing what would happen
if trading raised the price of carbon to the government's upper estimate of £140 per tonne by 2030 (this is 32 times the current price).[18]
It would mean that instead of 465 million tickets sold in 2030, there
would be 455 million.[19] That sorts it out, then.

The only certain means by which the growth of flights can be
curtailed is by restricting the capacity of our airports. Aviation expands
to fill the available landing space. Unless the government's decision to
double the size of the UK's airports is reversed, the rest of its climate
change programme is a waste of time.

Come on out British Airways, Virgin, Ryanair, easyJet, BMI, the British
government, the opposition, and most of Middle England. I've got you
surrounded.

December 19 2006

A Lethal Solution

It used to be a matter of good intentions gone awry. Now it is plain
fraud. The governments using biofuel to tackle global warming know
that it causes more harm than good. But they plough on regardless.

In theory, fuels made from plants can reduce the amount of carbon
dioxide emitted by cars and trucks. Plants absorb carbon as they grow;
it is released again when the fuel is burnt. By encouraging oil companies to switch from fossil plants to living ones, governments on both
sides of the Atlantic claim to be "decarbonising" our transport networks.

In the budget last week, Gordon Brown announced that he would
extend the tax rebate for biofuels until 2010. From next year, all

suppliers in the UK will have to ensure that 2.5% of the fuel they sell is made from plants; if not, they must pay a penalty of 15p per litre. The obligation rises to 5% in 2010.[1] By 2050, the government hopes that 33% of our fuel will come from crops.[2] Last month, George Bush announced that he would quintuple the US target for biofuels:[3] by 2017 they should be supplying 24% of the nation's transport fuel.[4]

So what's wrong with these programmes? Only that they are a formula for environmental and humanitarian disaster. In 2004 this column warned that biofuels would set up a competition for food between cars and people. The people would necessarily lose: those who can afford to drive are, by definition, richer than those who are in danger of starvation. It would also lead to the destruction of rainforests and other important habitats.[5] I received more abuse than I've had for any other column, except when I attacked the 9/11 conspiracists. I was told my claims were ridiculous, laughable, impossible. Well, in one respect I was wrong. I thought these effects wouldn't materialise for many years. They are happening already.

Since the beginning of last year, the price of maize has doubled.[6] The price of wheat has also reached a 10-year high, while global stockpiles of both grains have reached 25-year lows.[7] Already there have been food riots in Mexico, and reports that the poor are feeling the strain all over the world. The US Department of Agriculture warns that "if we have a drought or a very poor harvest, we could see the sort of volatility we saw in the 1970s, and if it does not happen this year, we are also forecasting lower stockpiles next year."[8] According to the UN Food and Agriculture Organisation, the main reason is the demand for ethanol, the alcohol used for motor fuel, which can be made from both maize and wheat.[9]

Farmers will respond to better prices by planting more, but it is not clear that they can overtake the booming demand for biofuel. Even if they do, they will catch up only by ploughing virgin habitat.

Already we know that biofuel is worse for the planet than petroleum. The UN has just published a report suggesting that 98% of the natural rainforest in Indonesia will be degraded or gone by 2022.[10] Just five years ago, the same agencies predicted that this wouldn't happen until 2032. But they reckoned without the planting of palm oil to turn into biodiesel for the European market. This is now the main cause of deforestation there, and it is likely soon to become responsible for the extinction of the orang utan in the wild. But it gets worse. As the forests are burnt, both the trees and the peat they sit on are turned into carbon dioxide. A report by the Dutch consultancy Delft Hydraulics shows that every tonne of palm oil results in up to 33 tonnes of carbon dioxide emissions, or up to 10 times as much as petroleum produces.[11] I feel I need to say that again. Biodiesel from palm oil causes *10 times* as much climate change as ordinary diesel.

There are similar impacts all over the world. Sugar cane producers are moving into rare scrubland habitats (the cerrado) in Brazil, and soya farmers are ripping up the Amazon rainforests. As President Bush has just signed a biofuel agreement with President Lula, it's likely to become a lot worse. Indigenous people in South America, Asia and Africa are starting to complain about incursions on to their land by fuel planters. A petition launched by a group called biofuelwatch, begging western governments to stop, has been signed by campaigners from 250 groups.[12]

The British government is well aware that there's a problem. On his blog last year the environment secretary David Miliband noted that palm oil plantations "are destroying 0.7% of the Malaysian rainforest each year, reducing a vital natural resource (and in the process, destroying the natural habitat of the orang utan). It is all connected."[13] Unlike government policy.

The reason governments are so enthusiastic about biofuels is that they don't upset drivers. They appear to reduce the amount of carbon from our cars, without requiring new taxes. It's an illusion sustained by the fact that only the emissions produced at home count towards our national total. The forest clearance in Malaysia doesn't increase our official impact by a gram.

In February, the European Commission was faced with a straight choice between fuel efficiency and biofuels. It had intended to tell car companies that the average carbon emission from new cars in 2012 would be 120 grams per kilometre. After heavy lobbying by German Chancellor Angela Merkel on behalf of her car manufacturers, it caved in and raised the limit to 130 grams. It announced that it would make up the shortfall by increasing the contribution from biofuel.[14]

The British government says it "will require transport fuel suppliers to report on the carbon saving and sustainability of the biofuels they supply".[15] But it will not require them to do anything. It can't; its consultants have already shown that if it tries to impose wider environmental standards on biofuels, it will fall foul of world trade rules.[16] And even "sustainable" biofuels merely occupy the space that other crops now fill, displacing them into new habitats. It promises that one day there will be a "second generation" of biofuels, made from straw or grass or wood. But there are still major technical obstacles.[17] By the time the new fuels are ready, the damage will have been done.

We need a moratorium on all targets and incentives for biofuels, until a second generation of fuels can be produced for less than it costs to make fuel from palm oil or sugar cane. Even then, the targets should be set low and increased only cautiously. I suggest a five-year freeze.

This would require a huge campaign, tougher than the one that helped to win a five-year freeze on growing genetically modified crops in the UK. That was important – GM crops give big companies unprecedented control over the food chain. But most of their effects are indirect, while the devastation caused by biofuel is immediate and already visible.

This is why it will be harder to stop. Encouraged by government policy, vast investments are now being made by farmers and chemical companies. Stopping them requires one heck of a battle. But it has to be fought.

March 27 2007

Giving Up On Two Degrees

The rich nations seeking to cut climate change have this in common: they lie. You won't find this statement in the draft of the new report by the Intergovernmental Panel on Climate Change, which was leaked to the Guardian last week. But as soon as you understand the numbers, the words form before your eyes. The governments making genuine efforts to tackle global warming are using figures they know to be false.

The British government, the European Union and the United Nations all claim to be trying to prevent "dangerous" climate change. Any level of climate change is dangerous for someone, but there is a broad consensus about what this word means: 2°C of warming above pre-industrial levels. It is dangerous because of its direct impacts on people and places – it could, for example, trigger the irreversible melting of the Greenland ice sheet[1] and the collapse of the Amazon rainforest[2] – and because it is likely to stimulate further warming, as it encourages the world's natural systems to start releasing greenhouse gases.

The aim of preventing more than 2°C of warming has been adopted overtly by the UN[3] and the European Union,[4] and implicitly by the British, German and Swedish governments. All of them say they are hoping to confine the concentrations of greenhouse gases in the atmosphere to a level that would prevent 2°C from being reached. And all of them know that they have set the wrong targets, based on outdated science. Fearful of the political implications, they have failed to adjust to the levels the new research demands.

This isn't easy to follow, but please bear with me, as you cannot understand the world's most important issue without grappling with some numbers. The average global temperature is affected by the concentration of greenhouse gases in the atmosphere. This concentration is usually expressed as "carbon dioxide equivalent". It is not an exact science – you cannot say that a certain concentration of gases will lead to a precise increase in temperature – but scientists discuss the relationship in terms of probability. A paper published last year by the climatologist Malte Meinshausen suggests that if greenhouse gases reach a concentration of 550 parts per million (ppm) carbon dioxide equivalent, there is a 63–99% chance (with an average value of 82%) that global warming will exceed 2°C.[5] At 475 ppm the average likelihood is 64%. Only if concentrations are stabilised at 400 ppm or below is there a low chance (an average of 28%) that temperatures will rise by over 2°C.

The IPCC's draft report contains similar figures. A concentration of 510 ppm gives us a 33% chance of preventing more than 2°C of warming. A concentration of 590 ppm gives us a 10% chance.[6] You begin to understand the scale of the challenge when you discover that the current level of greenhouse gases in the atmosphere (using the IPCC's formula) is 459ppm.[7] We have already exceeded the safe level. To give ourselves a high chance of preventing dangerous climate change, we will need a programme so drastic that greenhouse gases in the atmosphere end up below the current concentrations. The sooner this happens, the greater the chance of preventing 2°C of warming.

But no government has set itself this task. The European Union and the Swedish government have established the world's most stringent target. It is 550 ppm, which gives us a near certainty of an extra 2°C. The British government makes use of a clever conjuring trick. Its target is also "550 parts per million", but 550 parts of carbon dioxide alone. When you include the other greenhouse gases, this translates into 666 ppm carbon dioxide equivalent (a fitting figure).[8] According to the Stern Report, at 650 ppm there is a 60–95% chance of 3°C of warming.[9] The government's target, in other words, commits us to a very dangerous level of climate change.

The British government has been aware that it has set the wrong target for at least four years. In 2003 the environment department found that "with an atmospheric CO_2 stabilisation concentration of 550 ppm, temperatures are expected to rise by between 2°C and 5°C".[10] In March last year it admitted that "a limit closer to 450 ppm or even lower, might be more appropriate to meet a 2°C stabilisation limit."[11] Yet the target has not changed. Last October, I challenged the environment secretary, David Miliband, over this issue on Channel 4 News. He responded as if he had never come across it before.

The European Union is also aware that it is using the wrong figures. In 2005 it found that "to have a reasonable chance to limit global warming to no more than 2°C, stabilisation of concentrations well below 550 ppm CO_2 equivalent may be needed".[12] But its target hasn't changed either.

Embarrassingly for the government and for leftwingers like me, the only large political entity that seems able to confront this is the British Conservative Party. In a paper published a fortnight ago, it called for an atmospheric stabilisation target of 400–450 ppm carbon dioxide equivalent.[13] Will this become policy? Does Cameron have the guts to do what his advisers say he should?

In my book Heat I estimate that to avoid 2°C of warming we require a global emissions cut of 60% per capita between now and 2030.[14] This translates into an 87% cut in the United Kingdom. This is a much stiffer target than the British government's – which requires a 60% cut in the UK's emissions by 2050. But my figure now appears to have been an underestimate. A recent paper in the journal Climatic Change emphasises that the sensitivity of global temperatures to greenhouse gas concentrations remains uncertain. But if we use the average figure, to obtain a 50% chance of preventing more than 2°C of warming requires a global cut of 80% by 2050.[15]

This is a cut in total emissions, not in emissions per head. If the population were to rise from 6 to 9 billion between now and then, we would need an 87% cut in global emissions per person. If carbon emissions are to be distributed equally, the greater cut must be made by the biggest polluters: rich nations like us. The UK's emissions per capita would need to fall by 91%.

But our governments appear quietly to have abandoned their aim of preventing dangerous climate change. If so, they condemn millions to death. What the IPCC report shows is that we have to stop treating climate change as an urgent issue. We have to start treating it as an international emergency.

We must open immediate negotiations with China, which threatens to become the world's biggest emitter of greenhouse gases by November this year,[16] partly because it manufactures many of the products we use. We must work out how much it would cost to decarbonise its growing economy, and help to pay. We need a major diplomatic offensive – far more pressing than it has been so far – to persuade the United States to do what it did in 1941 and turn the economy around on a dime. But above all we need to show that we remain serious about fighting climate change, by setting the targets the science demands.

May 1 2007

Crying Sheep

Are global oil supplies about to peak? Are they, in other words, about to reach their maximum and then go into decline? There is a simple answer to this question: no one has the faintest idea.

Consider these two statements: 1. "Last year Saudi Aramco made credible claims that as much as 500 billion–700 billion barrels remain to be discovered in the kingdom." 2. "Saudi Arabia clearly seems to be nearing or at its peak output and cannot materially grow its oil production."

The first comes from a report by Energy Intelligence, a consultancy used by the major oil companies.[1] The second comes from a book by Matthew Simmons, an energy investor who advises the Bush administration.[2] Whom should we believe? I have now read 4000 pages of reports on global oil supply, and I know less about it than I did before I started. The only firm conclusion I have reached is that the people sitting on the world's reserves are liars.

In 1985, Kuwait announced that it possessed 50% more oil than it had previously declared. Had it just discovered a new field? Had it developed a new technology, which could extract more oil from the old fields? No. OPEC, the price-fixing cartel to which it belongs, had decided to allocate production quotas to its members based on the size of their reserves. The bigger your stated reserve, the more you were allowed to produce.[3] The other states soon followed Kuwait, adding a total of 300 billion barrels to their reserves[4] – enough, if it existed, to supply the world for 10 years. And their magic oil never runs out. Though extraction has long outstripped discovery, Kuwait posts the same reserves today as it claimed in 1985.[5]

So we turn to the US Geological Survey for an answer, and find that its estimates of global oil supply are as reliable as the Pentagon's assessments of Iraqi weapons of mass destruction. In 1981 it said we possessed 1719 billion barrels of oil.[6] In 2000, 2659.[7] Yet the discovery of major oil fields peaked in 1964.[8] Where has it come from?

It is true to say that oil reserves are not fixed. As technology improves or the price increases, oil that was formerly too expensive to extract becomes available. But the oil geologist Jean Laherrere points out that the Geological Survey's estimate "implies a five-fold increase in discovery rate and reserve addition, for which no evidence is presented. Such an improvement in performance is in fact utterly implausible, given the great technological achievements of the industry over the past twenty years, the worldwide search, and the deliberate effort to find the largest remaining prospects."[9]

The current high oil prices are the result of a shortage of refineries, exacerbated by the hurricanes in the Gulf of Mexico, rather than a global shortage of crude. But behind that problem lurks another. Last week, Chris Vernon of the organisation PowerSwitch published figures showing that while total global oil production has risen since 2000, the production of light sweet crude, the kind that is easiest to refine into motor fuels, has fallen by 2 million barrels a day.[10] This grade, he claims, has already peaked. The refinery crisis results partly from this constraint: there aren't enough plants capable of processing the heavier grades.

And next in the queue? Who knows? All I can say is that Bush himself does not appear to share the Geological Survey's optimism. "In terms of world supply," he said in March, "I think if you look at all the statistics, demand is outracing supply, and supplies are getting tight."[11] What has he seen that we haven't?

If the figures have been fudged, we're stuffed. That might sound extreme, but it is not my conclusion. It is that of the consultants hired by the US Department of Energy. In February this year, the department released a report called "Peaking of World Oil Production: Impacts, Mitigation, & Risk Management".[12] I say "released", for it was never properly published. For several months the only publicly available copy was lodged on the website of the Hilltop High School in Chula Vista, California.[13]

The department's consultants, led by the energy analyst Robert L. Hirsch, concluded that "without timely mitigation, the economic, social, and political costs will be unprecedented". It is possible to reduce demand and to start developing alternatives, but this would take "10–20 years" and "trillions of dollars". "Waiting until world oil production peaks before taking crash program action leaves the world with a significant liquid fuel deficit for more than two decades", which would cause problems "unlike any yet faced by modern industrial society".[14]

Of course, we have been here before. Oil analysts and environmentalists have warned of disappearing reserves ever since drilling began, and they have always been proved wrong. According to people like the Danish statistician Bjorn Lomborg, this is because the industry is self-regulating. "High real prices deter consumption and encourage the development of other sources of oil and non-oil energy supplies," he says. "Since searching costs money, new searches will not be initiated too far in advance of production. Consequently, new oil fields will be continuously added as demand rises ... we will stop using oil when other energy technologies provide superior benefits."[15]

It is beginning to look as if he is wrong on all counts. As the Economist magazine pointed out on September 10, "demand for petrol is pretty inelastic in the short term",[16] because people still have to go to work, however much it costs. According to the analyst it cites, "it would take a doubling of petrol prices to reduce American petrol consumption by just 5%."[17] Lomborg's idea that companies can just go out and find new oil when demand rises suggests that he believes geology is as malleable as statistics. One day, or so we should hope, a superior technology will certainly emerge, but cheap alternatives to liquid fuels are currently decades away. Yes, the pessimists have been crying wolf for almost a century. But better that, perhaps, than crying "sheep" when the wolves appear.

The Hirsch report has no truck with those who believe in the magic of the markets. "High prices do not a priori lead to greater production. Geology is ultimately the limiting factor."[18] There are plenty of oil shales, tar sands and coal seams available for turning into liquid fuels, but it would take years and a massive investment before enough came online. Hirsch compares the projections of the oil optimists to those of the gas optimists in the late 1990s, who promised "growing supply at reasonable prices for the foreseeable future" in the US and Canada. Today the same people are bemoaning the deficit. "The North American natural gas market is set for the longest period of sustained high prices in its history, even adjusting for inflation . . . Gas production in the United States (excluding Alaska) now appears to be in permanent decline."[19]

"The bottom line", Hirsch says, "is that no one knows with certainty when world oil production will reach a peak, but geologists have no doubt that it will happen." Our hopes of a soft landing rest on just two propositions: that the oil producers' figures are correct, and that governments act before they have to. I hope that reassures you.

September 27 2005

Feeding Frenzy

If these animals lived on land there would be a global outcry. But the great beasts roaming the savannahs of the open seas summon no such support. Big sharks, giant tuna, marlin and swordfish should have the conservation status of the giant panda or the snow leopard. Yet still we believe it is acceptable for fishmongers to sell them and celebrity chefs to teach us how to cook them.

A study in this week's edition of Science reveals the disastrous collapse of the ocean's megafauna. The great sharks are now wobbling on the edge of extinction. Since 1972 the number of blacktip sharks has fallen by 93%, tiger sharks by 97%, and bull sharks, dusky sharks and smooth hammerheads by 99%.[1] Just about every population of major predators is now in freefall. Another paper, published in Nature four years ago, shows that over 90% of large predatory fishes throughout the global oceans have gone.[2]

You respond with horror when you hear of Chinese feasts of bear paws and tiger meat. But these are no different, as far as conservation is concerned, from eating shark's fin soup or swordfish or steaks from rare species of tuna. One practice is considered barbaric in Europe and North America. The other is promoted in restaurant reviews and recipes in the colour supplements of respectable newspapers.

In terms of its impact on both ecology and animal welfare, shark fishing could be the planet's most brutal industry. While some sharks are taken whole, around 70 million are caught every year for their fins.[3] In many cases the fins are cut off and the shark is dumped, alive, back into the sea. It can take several weeks to die. The longlines and gillnets used to catch them snare whales, dolphins, turtles and albatrosses. The new paper shows that shark catching also causes a cascade of disasters through the foodchain. Since the large sharks were removed from coastal waters in the western Atlantic, the rays they preyed on have multiplied 10-fold and have wiped out all the main commercial species of shellfish.[4]

Much of this trade originates in East Asia, where shark's fin soup, which sells for up to £100 a bowl, is a sign of great wealth and rank, like caviar in Europe. The global demand for shark fins is rising by about 5% a year.[5] But if you believe that this is yet another problem for which the Chinese can be blamed and the Europeans absolved, consider this: the world's major importer (and presumably re-exporter) of sharks is Spain.[6] Its catches have increased ninefold since the 1990s[7] and it has resisted, in most cases successfully, every European and global effort to conserve its prey.

The Spanish defend their right to kill rare sharks as fiercely as the Japanese defend their right to kill rare whales. The fishing industry, traditionally dominated by Galician fascists, exerts an extraordinary degree of leverage over the socialist government. The Spanish government, in turn, usually gets its way in Europe. The European Union, for example, claims to have banned the finning of sharks. But the ratio it sets for the weight of fins to the weight of bodies landed by fishermen is 5%. As edible fins make up only 2% of the shark's body weight,[8] this means that two and a half finless sharks can be returned to the water for every one that comes ashore. Even this is not enough for the Spanish, whose MEPs have been demanding that the percentage be raised.[9]

Northern European civilisation doesn't come out of this very well either. In 2001 the British government promised to protect a critically endangered species called the angel shark, whose population in British waters was collapsing. It ducked and dithered until there was no longer a problem: the shark is now extinct in the North Sea.[10]

Why do we find it so hard to stand up to fishermen? This tiny industrial lobby seems to have governments in the palm of its hand. Every year, the European Union sets catch limits for all species way above the levels its scientists recommend. Governments know that they are allowing the fishing industry to destroy itself and to destroy the ecosystem on which it depends. But nothing is sacred, as long as it is underwater. In November, the United Nations failed even to produce a resolution urging a halt to trawling on the sea mounts at the bottom of the ocean. These ecosystems, which are only just beginning to be explored, harbour great forests of deepwater corals and sponges, in which thousands of unearthly species hide. But we can't summon the will to stop the handful of boats that are ripping them to shreds.

The power of the fishermen's lobby explains the lack of protection for marine predators. Though fish species far outnumber mammal species, the Convention on International Trade in Endangered Species protects 654 kinds of mammal and just 77 kinds of fish. Trade in only nine of these is subject to a complete ban.[11]

The rules that do get passed are ignored by both fishermen and governments. On Sunday I stood with a fisheries manager on the banks of a famous sea trout river in Wales. Perhaps I should say a famous former sea trout river in Wales. For the past four years, scarcely any fish – sea trout or salmon – have appeared. He was not sure why, but he told me that trawlers in the Irish Sea land boxes of what appear to be bass; hidden under the top layer are salmon and sea trout. No one seems to care enough to stop them: government monitoring appears to be non-existent. The pressure group Oceana walks into European ports whenever there's a public holiday and finds hundreds of miles of illegal drift nets stowed on the boats.[12] Where are the official inspectors?

Of course, governments plead poverty. Which makes you wonder why they decided last year to allocate €3.8 billion to the destruction of the marine environment. This is what you and I are now paying in subsidies to keep the ocean wreckers afloat. The money buys new engines, and boats for young fishermen hoping to expand their business.[13] For the same cost you could put a permanent inspector on every large fishing vessel in European waters.

If we don't act, we know what will happen. Another paper published in Science suggests that on current trends we'll see the global collapse of all the species currently caught by commercial fishermen by 2048. Yet, if we catch the ecosystems in time, with temporary fishing bans and the creation of large marine reserves, they can recover with remarkable speed.[14] I hope British ministers, now drafting a new marine bill, have read this study.

But beyond a certain point, the collapse is likely to be permanent. Off the coast of Namibia, where the fishery has crashed as a result of overharvesting, we have a glimpse of the future. A paper in Current Biology reports that the ecosystem is approaching a "trophic dead-end".[15] As the fish have been mopped up, they have been replaced by jellyfish, which now outweigh them by three to one. The jellyfish eat the eggs and larvae of the fish, so the switch is probably irreversible. We have entered, the paper tells us, the "era of jellyfish ascendancy".

It's a good symbol. The jellyfish represents the collapse of the ecosystem and the spinelessness of the people charged with protecting it.

April 3 2007

Natural Aesthetes

The world, if the biologists' projections turn out to be correct, will soon begin to revert to the fourth day of creation. There will be grass and "herb yielding seed" and "the fruit tree yielding fruit". But "the moving creature that hath life", the "fowl that may fly above the earth", or the "great whales, and every living creature that moveth" may one day be almost unknown to us.[1] Last week the journal Nature published a report suggesting that by 2050 around a quarter of the world's animal and plant species could die out as a result of global warming.[2] To these we must add the millions threatened by farming, logging, hunting, fishing and introduced species. The future is beginning to look a little lonely.

Does it matter? To most of those who govern us, plainly not. To most of the rest of us, the answer seems to be yes, but we are not quite sure why. We have little difficulty in recognising the importance of other environmental issues. Climate change causes droughts and floods, ozone depletion gives us skin cancer, diesel pollution damages our lungs. But while most people feel that purging the world of its diversity of animals and plants is somehow wrong, the feeling precedes a rational explanation. For the past 30 years, the conservation movement has been trying to provide one. Its efforts have, for the most part, failed.

The problem conservationists face is this: that by comparison to almost all other global issues, our concerns about biodiversity seem effete and self-indulgent. If we are presented with a choice between growing food to avert starvation and protecting an obscure forest frog, the frog loses every time. If climate change is going to make life impossible for hundreds of millions of human beings, who cares about what it might do to Boyd's forest dragon?

So they have sought to confront utilitarianism with utilitarianism. If the rainforests are destroyed, they argue, we may never find the cure for cancer. If the wild relatives of our crop plants die out, we might lose the genes that could be used to breed new pest-resistant strains. Many of the world's indigenous people depend upon a wide range of species for their survival. An impoverished environment is likely to be less stable, and so less productive, than a diverse one.

All this may be true, but it doesn't solve the problem of justification. Most of us don't need biodiversity to survive. The farmers who produce our food try to keep the ecosystem as impoverished as possible. A utilitarian approach, long favoured by communists as well as capitalists, would integrate indigenous people into the mainstream economy, drag almost all the population of the countryside out of its "rural idiocy", and turn every productive acre of the earth over to crops.

Utilitarianism also suggests that the value of biodiversity is exhausted once it ceases to be useful to us. When a rainforest has been screened for pharmaceutical compounds, it offers, according to this doctrine, no further benefits. We can grow the useful species in plantations, or produce the compounds they contain in the lab, and junk the rest. By arguing for biodiversity on the grounds of human need, in other words, conservationists play into the hands of their enemies.

The lovers of fine art or rare books don't feel the need to set this trap for themselves. They never suggest that money and effort should be spent on restoring old masters because one day someone might want to eat them. They can defend the things they value, even while accepting that there may be a conflict between their protection and other social needs. We could solve London's housing crisis by levelling its historic buildings, grubbing up the parks and building high-rise homes in their place. But the aesthetes can confidently assert that the lives of its people would scarcely be improved by those means.

The special problem confronting the conservationists of nature is that in many parts of the world their cause has been used as an excuse for the maintenance of a colonial model of exclusion. Nothing has done more harm to conservation than the work of people like Richard Leakey, Joy Adamson and Diane Fossey.[3] To white tourists, who now have more or less exclusive access to the places they helped to protect, these people are heroes. To local people they are villains, and the wildlife they protected is perceived as a threat. If every time a public gallery were built, thousands of us were kicked out of our homes to make way for it, then told we could enter only by paying the equivalent of our annual income, we would feel the same way about art.

This legacy of exclusion makes conservation look harder to justify on the grounds of aesthetics. But it seems to me that this is the only sensible argument that can be made. It is surely sufficient to say that wildlife should be preserved because it is wonderful.

But, somehow, most conservationists can't quite bring themselves to do so. Even those who admit that they want to protect it because they love it can't leave it at that, but insist on seeking some higher justification. It used to be God; now they claim to be acting for "the sake of the planet" or "the ecosystem" or "the future".

As far as the planet is concerned, it is not concerned. It is a lump of rock. It is inhabited by clumps of self-replicating molecules we call life forms, the purpose of which is to reverse entropy for as long as possible, by capturing energy from the sun or from other life forms.

The ecosystem is simply the flow of captured energy between these life forms. It has no values, no wishes, no demands. It neither offers nor recognises cruelty or kindness.

Like other life forms, we exist only to replicate ourselves. We have become so complex only because that enables us to seize more energy. One day, natural selection will shake us off the planet. Our works won't even be forgotten. There will be nothing capable of remembering.

But a curious component of our complexity is that, in common with other complex forms, we have evolved a capacity for suffering. We suffer when the world becomes a less pleasant and fascinating place. We suffer because we perceive the suffering of others. It seems to me that the only higher purpose we could possibly possess is to seek to relieve suffering: our own and that of other people and other animals. This is surely sufficient cause for any project we might attempt. It is sufficient cause for the protection of fine art or rare books. It is sufficient cause for the protection of rare wildlife.

Biodiversity, in other words, matters because it matters. If we are to protect wildlife, we must do it for ourselves. We need not pretend that anything else is bidding us to do so. We need not pretend that anyone depends upon the king protea or the golden toad or the silky sifaka for their survival. But we can say that, as far as we are concerned, the world would be a poorer place without them.

January 13 2004

Bring Them Back

It hardly compares in importance to the invasion of Iraq, or the fall of the dollar, or the outcome of the next election. But in some ways the decision we are being asked to make will say more about us and the world we choose to inhabit than any of the grand political themes.

Last week a man called Paul Lister held a conference in Scotland.

He explained that, if his plans are accepted by the public, within five years he will be able to reintroduce the wolf, the bear, the Eurasian lynx, the wild boar and the European bison to the Highlands. Similar claims have been made before, but Lister is the first enthusiast who can make it happen. He has millions of pounds and a 23,000 acre estate. He wants his land to become the core of a much larger conservation area. Another landowner, Paul van Vlissingen, has volunteered to add his 81,000 acres to the scheme. As animals like wolves and lynxes are smart and agile enough to escape from almost any large enclosure, this is, in effect, a proposal to repopulate Britain with its extinct native wildlife.

Two days later, we discovered that the mammals had pre-empted them. A herd of wild boar, the fourth to have established itself in this country, has emerged from the Forest of Dean, having escaped, it seems, from a farm. The government must decide whether or not to let it survive. The big wild animals are returning. It is an attractive idea, with unattractive implications.

Though the advocates of reintroduction sometimes seek to deny it, four out of five of the species they hope to bring back are dangerous to humans. A couple of years ago Mr van Vlissingen told The Times that there have been no known cases of a wolf killing a person in Europe during the last 100 years.[1] If this were true, then the objections to reintroduction would be harder to sustain. But it is not. Twenty-one people were attacked by healthy wolves in Europe between 1950 and 2000, and four of them were killed.[2] Five others (though this should not be an issue in Britain) were killed by wolves with rabies.[3] Lynx won't hurt anyone, but European brown bears, though less aggressive than North American grizzlies, killed 36 people in the twentieth century.[4] Though only a few hundred boar are living in the British countryside, several people have already been chased by them.[5] The boar aren't half as scary as the bison, as the photos in this month's BBC Wildlife magazine testify: a herd in Poland appears to be playing volleyball with a wild boar it has gored to death.

An admiration for large wild animals often appears to be linked with a contempt for human life. "And I think in this empty world there was room for me and a mountain lion", D. H. Lawrence wrote. "And I think in the world beyond how easily we might spare a million or two of humans / And never miss them."[6] John Aspinall and Joy Adamson would have nodded vehemently. There is a certain kind of ill-adjusted person who seems to project himself into the mind of a predator, roaming across a world without people.

The risk of being attacked by one of these beasts is tiny by comparison with almost any of the other hazards we confront. In Canada, where bears occasionally prey on people, you are 67 times more likely to be killed by a domestic dog, and 374 times as likely to be killed by lightning.[7] But it's a risk that those who would introduce these animals impose on other people, with or without their consent. It is hard to argue with the verse with which anyone who picks up a shotgun is instructed: "All the pheasants ever bred / Won't repay for one man dead." If we believe that human lives are more important than animal lives, and if even one person is killed by a wild animal deliberately reintroduced into this country, is that not too great a price to pay for the purely aesthetic benefit of restoring our native wildlife?

I am not convinced that it is. If every tree that grows close to a road or a house were felled, dozens of human lives could be saved; but you would be hard put to find anyone who thinks this is a good idea. The French government ran into massive opposition when it tried to clear the famous avenues that line its country roads. A few extra deaths are considered, by most French people, to be a fair exchange for the preservation of some flickering shade. When a city council in Britain proposed to cut down a row of horse chestnut trees because children might be hurt when collecting conkers, or might hurt someone else when throwing sticks and stones into the branches, it caused a national outcry. Similarly, we use public money, which could be spent on the National Health Service, to support galleries, museums and parks. In all these cases, aesthetic concerns are weighed against human life, and permitted by society to win.

There is, of course, a moral difference between failing to eliminate existing risks and introducing new ones. But, in permitting public bodies to plant new trees or dig new ponds, we commission them to trade human survival against a diffuse social pleasure. Unlike the businessmen who want to be allowed to expose their workers to dangerous industrial practices in order to boost their profits, the tree planters give us something in return for the risk they impose on us.

This might make sense even in terms of moral arithmetic: people who live in unstimulating places are more likely to become depressed, and people who become depressed are more likely to kill themselves. Dramatic but mildly dangerous life forms – or just the excitement of knowing that they are out there somewhere – might even save lives.

And the vision of those who would deny room in this empty world for large wild animals is surely as misanthropic as D. H. Lawrence's. When Norwegian hunters set out to eliminate the wolves that kill a few dozen sheep in that country each year, or when, as they did last month, French hunters shoot the last female Pyrenean brown bear, we are rightly outraged. We see in them an intolerance of diversity, of contingency, of unruliness. They would reduce the world to a money-making monoculture, a bland, controlled, mechanical place that is as hostile to the needs of humans as it is to the needs of animals.

I want to live in a land in which wolves might prowl. In which, as I have done in eastern Poland, I can follow a bend in a forest path and come face to face with a bison. In which, as I have done in the Pyrenees, I can stumble across a pair of wild boar sleeping under a bush. I am prepared to exchange a small risk to my life for the thrill of encountering that which lies beyond it. This is a romantic proposition, I admit. But is it not also a rational one?

December 7 2004

Seeds of Distraction

The question is as simple as this: do you want a few corporations to monopolise the global food supply? If the answer is yes, you should welcome the announcement the government is expected to make today, that the commercial planting of a genetically modified crop in Britain can go ahead. If the answer is no, you should regret it. The principal promotional effort of the genetic engineering industry is to distract us from this question.

GM technology permits companies to ensure that everything we eat is owned by them. They can patent the seeds and the processes that give rise to them. They can make sure that crops can't be grown without their patented chemicals. They can prevent seeds from reproducing themselves. By buying up competing seed companies and closing them down, they can capture the food market, the biggest and most diverse market of all.

No one in his right mind would welcome this, so the corporations must persuade us to focus on something else. At first they talked of enhancing consumer choice, but when the carrot failed, they switched to the stick. Now we are told that unless we support the deployment of GM crops in Britain, our science base will collapse. And that, by refusing to eat GM products in Europe, we are threatening the developing world with starvation. Both arguments are – shall we say? – imaginative, but in public relations cogency counts for little. All that matters is that you spin the discussion out for long enough to achieve the necessary result. And that means recruiting eminent figures to make the case on your behalf.

Last October, 114 scientists, many of whom receive funding from the biotech industry, sent an open letter to the prime minister claiming that Britain's lack of enthusiasm for GM crops "will inhibit our ability to contribute to scientific knowledge internationally".[1] Scientists specialising in this field, they claimed, were being forced to leave the country to find work elsewhere.

Now, forgive me if you've heard this before, but it seems to need repeating. GM crops are not science. They are technological products of science. To claim, as Tony Blair and several senior scientists have done, that those who oppose GM are "anti-science" is like claiming that those who oppose chemical weapons are anti-chemistry. Scientists are under no greater obligation to defend GM food than they are to defend the manufacture of Barbie dolls.

This is not to say that the signatories were wrong to claim that some researchers, who have specialised in the development of engineered crops, are now leaving Britain to find work elsewhere. As the public has rejected their products, the biotech companies have begun withdrawing from this country, and they are taking their funding with them. But if scientists attach their livelihoods to the market, they can expect their livelihoods to be affected by market forces. The people who wrote to Blair seem to want it both ways: commercial funding, insulated from commercial decisions.

In truth, the biotech companies' contribution to research in Britain has been small. Far more money has come from the government. Its Biotechnology and Biological Sciences Research Council, for example, funds 26 projects on GM crops and just one on organic farming.[2] If scientists want a source of funding that's unlikely to be jeopardised by public concern, they should lobby for this ratio to be reversed.

But the plight of the men in white coats isn't much of a tear-jerker. A far more effective form of emotional blackmail is the one deployed in the Guardian last week by Lord Taverne, the founder of the Prima PR consultancy. "The strongest argument in favour of developing GM crops", he wrote, "is the contribution they can make to reducing world poverty, hunger and disease."[3]

There's little doubt that some GM crops produce higher yields than some conventional crops, or that they can be modified to contain more nutrients, though both of these developments have been over-hyped. Two projects have been cited everywhere: a sweet potato being engineered in Kenya to resist viruses, and vitamin A-enhanced rice. The first scheme has just collapsed. Despite $6m of funding from Monsanto, the World Bank and the US government, and endless hype in the press, it turns out to have produced no improvement in virus resistance, and a decrease in yield.[4] Just over the border in Uganda, a far cheaper conventional breeding programme has almost doubled sweet potato yields. The other, never more than a concept, now turns out not to work even in theory: malnourished people appear not to be able to absorb vitamin A in this form.[5] But none of this stops Lord Taverne, or George Bush, or the Nuffield Council on Bioethics, from citing them as miracle cures for global hunger.

But some trials of this kind are succeeding, improving both yield and nutritional content. Despite the best efforts of the industry's boosters to confuse the two ideas, however, this does not equate to feeding the world.

The world has a surplus of food, but still people go hungry. They go hungry because they cannot afford to buy it. They cannot afford to buy it because the sources of wealth and the means of production have been captured, and in some cases monopolised, by landowners and corporations. The purpose of the biotech industry is to capture and monopolise the sources of wealth and the means of production.

Now, in some places governments or unselfish private researchers are producing GM crops that are free from patents and not dependent on the application of proprietary pesticides, and these could well be of benefit to small farmers in the developing world. But Taverne and the other propagandists are seeking to persuade us to approve a corporate model of GM development in the rich world, in the hope that this will somehow encourage the opposite model to develop in the poor world.

Indeed, it is hard to see what on earth the production of crops for local people in poor nations has to do with consumer preferences in Britain. Like the scientists who wrote to Blair, the emotional blackmailers want to have it both ways: these crops are being grown to feed starving people, but the starving people won't be able to eat them unless, er ... they can export this food to Britain.

And here we encounter the perpetually neglected truth about GM crops. The great majority are not being grown to feed local people. In fact, they are not being grown to feed people at all, but to feed livestock, the meat, milk and eggs from which are then sold to the world's richer consumers. The GM maize the government is expected to approve today is no exception. If in the next 30 years there is a global food crisis, it will be partly because the arable land that should be producing food for humans is instead producing feed for animals.

The biotech companies are not interested in whether or not science is flourishing or people are starving. They simply want to make money. The best way to make money is to control the market. But before you can control the market, you must first convince people that there's something else at stake.

March 9 2004

Arguments With War

Thwart Mode

There is little that those of us who oppose the coming war with Iraq can now do to prevent it. George Bush has staked his credibility on the project; he has mid-term elections to consider, oil supplies to secure and a flagging war on terror to revive. Our voices are as little heeded in the White House as the singing of the birds.

Our role is now, perhaps, confined to the modest but necessary task of demonstrating the withdrawal of our consent, while seeking to undermine the moral confidence that could turn the attack on Iraq into a war against all those states perceived to offend US strategic interests. No task is more urgent than to expose the two lies contained in George Bush's radio address on Saturday, namely that "the United States does not desire military conflict, because we know the awful nature of war", and "we hope that Iraq complies with the world's demands".[1] Mr Bush appears to have done everything in his power to prevent Iraq from complying with the world's demands, while ensuring that military conflict becomes inevitable.

On July 4 this year, Kofi Annan, the secretary general of the United Nations, began negotiating with Iraq over the return of UN weapons inspectors. Iraq had resisted UN inspections for three and a half years, but now it felt the screw turning and appeared to be on the point of capitulation. On July 5, the Pentagon leaked its war plan to the New York Times. The US, a Pentagon official revealed, was preparing "a major air campaign and land invasion", to "topple President Saddam Hussein".[2] The talks immediately collapsed.

Ten days ago, they were about to resume. Hans Blix, the head of the UN inspections body, was due to meet Iraqi officials in Vienna to discuss the practicalities of re-entering the country. The US air force launched bombing raids on Basra, in southern Iraq, destroying a radar system. As the Russian government pointed out, the attack could scarcely have been better designed to scupper the talks.[3] But this time the Iraqis, mindful of the consequences of excluding the inspectors, kept talking. Last Tuesday, they agreed to let the UN back in. The State Department immediately announced, with more candour than elegance, that it would "go into thwart mode".[4]

It wasn't bluffing. The following day, it leaked the draft resolution on inspections that it was placing before the UN Security Council.[5] This resembles nothing so much as a plan for unopposed invasion. The decisions about which sites should be inspected would no longer be made by the UN alone, but also by "any permanent member of the Security Council", such as the United States. The people inspecting these sites could also be chosen by the US, and they would enjoy "unrestricted rights of entry into and out of Iraq" and "the right to free, unrestricted and immediate movement" within Iraq, "including unrestricted access to presidential sites". They would be permitted to establish "regional bases and operating bases throughout Iraq", where they would be "accompanied . . . by sufficient US security forces to protect them". They would have the right to declare exclusion zones, no-fly zones and "ground and air transit corridors". They would be allowed to fly and land as many planes, helicopters and surveillance drones in Iraq as they want, to set up "encrypted communication" networks, and to seize "any equipment" they chose to lay hands on.

The resolution, in other words, could not have failed to remind Iraq of the alleged infiltration of the UN team in 1996. Both the Iraqi government and the former inspector Scott Ritter maintain that the weapons inspectors were joined that year by CIA covert operations specialists, who used the UN's special access to collect information and encourage the Republican Guard to launch a coup. On Thursday, Britain and the

United States instructed the weapons inspectors not to enter Iraq until the new resolution has been adopted.

As Milan Rai's new book, War Plan Iraq, documents, the US has been undermining disarmament for years.[6] The UN's principal means of persuasion was paragraph 22 of the Security Council's resolution 687, which promised that economic sanctions would be lifted once Iraq ceased to possess weapons of mass destruction. But in April 1994, Warren Christopher, the US Secretary of State, unilaterally withdrew this promise, removing Iraq's main incentive to comply. Three years later his successor, Madeleine Albright, insisted that sanctions would not be lifted while Saddam remained in power.

The US government maintains that Saddam Hussein expelled the UN inspectors from Iraq in 1998, but this is not true. On October 30 1998, the US rejected a new UN proposal by again refusing to lift the oil embargo if Iraq disarmed. On the following day, the Iraqi government announced that it would cease to cooperate with the inspectors. In fact it permitted them to continue working, and over the next six weeks they completed around 300 operations. On December 14, Richard Butler, the head of the inspection team, published a curiously contradictory report. The body of the report recorded that over the past month "the majority of the inspections of facilities and sites under the ongoing monitoring system were carried out with Iraq's cooperation", but his well-publicised conclusion was that "no progress" had been made.[7] Russia and China accused Butler of bias. On December 15, the US ambassador to the UN warned him that his team should leave Iraq for its own safety. Butler pulled out, and on the following day the US started bombing Iraq.

From that point on, Saddam Hussein refused to allow UN inspectors to return. At the end of last year, Jose Bustani, the head of the Organisation for the Prohibition of Chemical Weapons, proposed a means of resolving the crisis. His organisation had not been involved in the messy business of 1998, so he offered to send in his own inspectors and complete the job the UN had almost finished. The US responded by demanding Bustani's dismissal. The other member states agreed to depose him only after the United States threatened to destroy the organisation if he stayed.[8] Now Hans Blix, the head of the new UN inspectorate, may also be feeling the heat. On Tuesday he insisted that he would take his orders only from the Security Council. On Thursday, after an hour-long meeting with US officials, he agreed with the Americans that there should be no inspections until a new resolution had been approved.[9]

For the past eight years, the US, with Britain's help, appears to have been seeking to prevent a resolution of the crisis in Iraq. It is almost as if Iraq has been kept on ice, as a necessary enemy to be warmed up whenever the occasion demands. Today, as the economy slides and Bin Laden's latest mocking message suggests that the war on terrorism has so far failed, an enemy that can be located and bombed is more necessary than ever. A just war can be pursued only when all peaceful means have been exhausted. In this case, the peaceful means have been averted.

October 8 2002

One Rule for Us

Suddenly, the government of the United States has discovered the virtues of international law. It may be waging an illegal war against a sovereign state; it may be seeking to destroy every treaty that impedes its attempts to run the world, but when five of its captured soldiers were paraded in front of the Iraqi television cameras on Sunday, Donald Rumsfeld, the US defence secretary, immediately complained that "it is against the Geneva convention to show photographs of prisoners of war in a manner that is humiliating for them".[1]

He is, of course, quite right. Article 13 of the third convention, concerning the treatment of prisoners, insists that they "must at all

times be protected . . . against insults and public curiosity".[2] This may
number among the less heinous of the possible infringements of the
laws of war, but the conventions, ratified by Iraq in 1956, are non-
negotiable. If you break them, you should expect to be prosecuted for
war crimes.

This being so, Rumsfeld had better watch his back. For this enthusiastic convert to the cause of legal warfare is, as head of the Department
of Defense, responsible for a series of crimes sufficient, were he ever
to be tried, to put him away for the rest of his natural life.

His prison camp in Guantanamo Bay, in Cuba, where 641 men
(nine of whom are British citizens) are held, breaches no fewer than
15 articles of the third convention. The US government broke the first
of these (article 13) as soon as the prisoners arrived, by displaying
them, just as the Iraqis have done, on television. In this case, however,
they were not encouraged to address the cameras. They were kneeling
on the ground, hands tied behind their backs, wearing blacked-out
goggles and earphones. In breach of article 18, they had been stripped
of their own clothes and deprived of their possessions. They were
then interned in a penitentiary (against article 22), where they were
denied proper mess facilities (article 26), canteens (article 28), religious
premises (article 34), opportunities for physical exercise (article 38),
access to the text of the convention (article 41), freedom to write to
their families (articles 70 and 71), and parcels of food and books
(article 72).[3]

They were not "released and repatriated without delay after the cessa-
tion of active hostilities" (article 118), because, the US authorities say,
their interrogation might, one day, reveal interesting information about
al-Qaida. Article 17 rules that captives are obliged to give only their name,
rank, number and date of birth. No "coercion may be inflicted on prisoners of war to secure from them information of any kind whatever".
In the hope of breaking them, however, the authorities have confined
them to solitary cells and subjected them to what is now known as
"torture lite": sleep deprivation and constant exposure to bright light.[4]

Unsurprisingly, several of the prisoners have sought to kill themselves, by smashing their heads against the walls or trying to slash their wrists with plastic cutlery.[5]

The US government claims that these men are not subject to the Geneva Conventions, as they are not "prisoners of war", but "unlawful combatants". The same claim could be made, with rather more justice, by the Iraqis holding the US soldiers who illegally invaded their country. But this redefinition is itself a breach of article 4 of the third convention, under which people detained as suspected members of a militia (the Taliban) or a volunteer corps (al-Qaida) must be regarded as prisoners of war.

Even if there is doubt about how such people should be classified, article 5 insists that they "shall enjoy the protection of the present Convention until such time as their status has been determined by a competent tribunal".[6] But when, earlier this month, lawyers representing 16 of them demanded a court hearing, the US Court of Appeals ruled that as Guantanamo Bay is not sovereign US territory, the men have no constitutional rights. Many of these prisoners appear to have been working in Afghanistan as teachers, engineers or aid workers. If the US government either tried or released them, its embarrassing lack of evidence would be brought to light.

You would hesitate to describe these prisoners as lucky, unless you knew what had happened to some of the other men captured by the Americans and their allies in Afghanistan. On November 21 2001, around 8000 Taliban soldiers and Pashtun civilians surrendered at Konduz to the Northern Alliance commander General Abdul Rashid Dostum. Many of them have never been seen again. As Jamie Doran's film Afghan Massacre – Convoy of Death records, some hundreds, possibly thousands, of them were loaded into container lorries at Qala-i-Zeini, near the town of Mazar-i-Sharif, on November 26 and 27.[7] The doors were sealed and the lorries were left to stand in the sun for several days. At length, they departed for Sheberghan prison, 120 kilometres away. The prisoners, many of whom were dying of thirst and asphyxiation, started banging on the sides of the trucks. Dostum's men stopped the convoy and machine-gunned the containers. When they arrived at Sheberghan, most of the captives were dead.[8]

The US special forces running the prison watched the bodies being unloaded. They instructed Dostum's men to "get rid of them before satellite pictures can be taken".[9] Doran interviewed a Northern Alliance soldier guarding the prison. "I was a witness when an American soldier broke one prisoner's neck. The Americans did whatever they wanted. We had no power to stop them."[10] Another soldier alleged, "They took the prisoners outside and beat them up and then returned them to the prison. But sometimes they were never returned and they disappeared."[11]

Many of the survivors were loaded back into the containers with the corpses, then driven out to a place in the desert called Dasht-i-Leili. In the presence of between 30 and 40 US special forces, both the living and the dead were dumped into ditches. Anyone who moved was shot. The German newspaper Die Zeit investigated the claims and concluded that "No one doubted that the Americans had taken part. Even at higher levels there are no doubts on this issue."[12] The US group Physicians for Human Rights visited the places identified by Doran's witnesses and found that they "all . . . contained human remains consistent with their designation as possible gravesites."[13]

It should not be necessary to point out that hospitality of this kind also contravenes the third Geneva convention, which prohibits "violence to life and person, in particular murder of all kinds, mutilation, cruel treatment and torture", as well as extrajudicial execution. Donald Rumsfeld's department, assisted by a pliant media, has done all it can to suppress Jamie Doran's film,[14] while General Dostum has begun to assassinate his witnesses.[15]

It is not hard, therefore, to see why the US government fought first to prevent the establishment of the International Criminal Court and then to ensure that its own citizens are not subject to its jurisdiction. The five soldiers dragged in front of the cameras yesterday should thank their lucky stars that they are prisoners not of the American forces fighting for civilisation, but of the "barbaric and inhuman" Iraqis.

March 25 2003

Dreamers and Idiots

Those who would take us to war must first shut down the public imagination. They must convince us that there is no other means of preventing invasion, or conquering terrorism, or even defending human rights. When information is scarce, imagination is easy to control. As intelligence gathering and diplomacy are conducted in secret, we seldom discover, until it is too late, how plausible the alternatives may be.

So those of us who called for peace before the wars with Iraq and Afghanistan were mocked as effeminate dreamers. The intelligence our governments released suggested that Saddam Hussein and the Taliban were immune to diplomacy or negotiation. Faced with such enemies, what would we do? the hawks asked, and our responses felt timid beside the clanking rigours of war. To the columnist David Aaronovitch, we were "indulging . . . in a cosmic whinge".[1] To the Daily Telegraph, we had become "Osama bin Laden's useful idiots".[2]

Had the options been as limited as the western warlords and their bards suggested, this may have been true. But, as many of us suspected at the time, we were lied to. Most of the lies are now familiar: there appear to have been no weapons of mass destruction, and no evidence to suggest that, as President Bush claimed in March, Saddam had "trained and financed . . . al Qaeda".[3] Bush and Blair, as their courtship of the president of Uzbekistan reveals, appear to possess no genuine concern for the human rights of foreigners.

But a further, and even graver, set of lies is only now beginning to come to light. Even if all the claims Bush and Blair made about their enemies and their motives had been true, and all their objectives had been legal and just, there may still have been no need to go to war. For, as we discovered last week, Saddam Hussein proposed to give Bush and Blair almost everything they wanted before a shot had been fired.[4] Our governments appear both to have withheld this information from the public and to have lied to us about the possibilities for diplomacy.

Over the four months before the coalition forces invaded Iraq, Saddam Hussein's government made a series of increasingly desperate offers to the United States. In December, the Iraqi intelligence services approached Vincent Cannistraro, the CIA's former head of counter-terrorism, with an offer to prove that Iraq was not linked to the September 11 attacks, and to permit several thousand US troops to enter the country to look for weapons of mass destruction.[5] If the object was regime change, then Saddam, the agents claimed, was prepared to submit himself to internationally monitored elections within two years.[6] According to Mr Cannistraro, these proposals reached the White House, but were "turned down by the president and vice president".[7]

By February, Saddam's negotiators were offering almost everything the US government could wish for: free access to the FBI to look for weapons of mass destruction wherever it wanted, support for the US position on Israel and Palestine, even rights over Iraq's oil.[8] Among the people they contacted was Richard Perle, the security adviser who for years had been urging a war with Iraq. He passed their offers to the Central Intelligence Agency. Last week he told the New York Times that the CIA had replied: "Tell them that we will see them in Baghdad."[9]

Saddam Hussein, in other words, appears to have done everything possible to find a diplomatic alternative to the impending war, and the US government appears to have done everything necessary to frustrate it. This is the opposite to what we were told by George Bush and Tony Blair. On March 6, 13 days before the war began, Bush said to journalists: "I want to remind you that it's his choice to make as to whether or not we go to war. It's Saddam's choice. He's the person that can make the choice of war and peace. Thus far, he's made the wrong choice."[10] Ten days later, Blair told a press conference: "We have provided the right diplomatic way through this, which is to lay down a clear ultimatum to Saddam: cooperate or face disarmament by force . . . all the way through we have tried to provide a diplomatic solution."[11] On March 17, Bush claimed that "Should Saddam Hussein choose confrontation, the American people can know that every measure has been taken to avoid war."[12] All these statements are false.

The same thing happened before the war with Afghanistan. On September 20 2001, the Taliban offered to hand Osama bin Laden to a neutral Islamic country for trial if the US presented them with evidence that he was responsible for the attacks on New York and Washington.[13] The US rejected the offer. On October 1, six days before the bombing began, the Taliban repeated it, and their representative in Pakistan told reporters "we are ready for negotiations. It is up to the other side to agree or not. Only negotiation will solve our problems."[14] Bush was asked about this offer at a press conference the following day. He replied: "There's no negotiations. There's no calendar. We'll act on our time [sic]." [15]

On the same day, Tony Blair, in his speech to the Labour party conference, ridiculed the idea that we could "look for a diplomatic solution". "There is no diplomacy with Bin Laden or the Taliban regime . . . I say to the Taliban: surrender the terrorists; or surrender power. It's your choice."[16] Well, they had just tried to exercise that choice, but George Bush had rejected it.

Of course, neither Bush nor Blair had any reason to trust the Taliban or Saddam Hussein: these people were, after all, negotiating under duress. But neither did they have any need to trust them. In both cases they could have presented their opponents with a deadline for meeting the concessions they had offered. Nor could the allies argue that the offers were not worth considering because they were inadequate: both the Taliban and Saddam Hussein were attempting to open negotiations, not to close them; there appeared to be plenty of scope for bargaining. In other words, peaceful resolutions were rejected before they were attempted. What this means is that even if all the other legal tests for these wars had been met (they had not), both would still have been waged in defiance of international law. The charter of the United Nations specifies that "the parties to any dispute . . . shall, first of all, seek a solution by negotiation."[17]

None of this matters to the enthusiasts for war. That these conflicts were unjust and illegal, that they killed or maimed tens of thousands of civilians, is irrelevant, as long as their aims were met. So the hawks should ponder this. Had a peaceful resolution of these disputes been attempted, Osama bin Laden might now be in custody, Iraq might be a pliant and largely peaceful nation finding its own way to democracy, and the prevailing sentiment within the Muslim world might be sympathy for the United States, rather than anger and resentment. Now, who are the dreamers and the useful idiots, and who the prag-matists?

November 11 2003

The Moral Myth

It is no use telling the hawks that bombing a country in which al-Qaida was not operating was unlikely to rid the world of al-Qaida. It is no use arguing that had the billions spent on the war with Iraq been used instead for intelligence and security, atrocities such as last week's attacks in Istanbul may have been prevented. As soon as one argument for the invasion and occupation of Iraq collapses, they switch to another. Over the past month, almost all the warriors – Bush, Blair, and the belliger-ents in both the conservative and the liberal press – have fallen back on the last line of defence, the argument we know as "the moral case for war".

Challenged in the Commons by the MP Pete Wishart on Wednesday over those devilishly uncooperative weapons of mass destruction, for example, Tony Blair dodged the question. "What everyone should realise is that if people like the honourable gentleman had had their way, Saddam Hussein, his sons and his henchmen would still be terrorising people in Iraq. I find it quite extraordinary that he thinks that that would be a preferable state of affairs."[1]

I do believe that there was a moral case for deposing Saddam Hussein, who was one of the world's most revolting tyrants, by violent means. I also believe that there was a moral case for not doing so, and that this case was the stronger. That Saddam is no longer president of Iraq is, without question, a good thing. But against this we must weigh the killing or mutilation of thousands of people; the possibility of civil war in Iraq; the anger and resentment the invasion has generated throughout the Muslim world and the creation, as a result, of a more hospitable environment in which terrorists can operate; the reassertion of imperial power; and the vitiation of international law. It seems to me that these costs outweigh the undoubted benefit.

But the key point, overlooked by all those who have made the moral case for war, is this: that a moral case is not the same as a moral reason. Whatever the argument for toppling Saddam Hussein on humanitarian grounds may have been, this is not why Bush and Blair went to war.

A superpower does not have moral imperatives. It has strategic imperatives. Its purpose is not to sustain the lives of other people, but to sustain itself. Concern for the rights and feelings of others is an impediment to the pursuit of its objectives. It can make the moral case, but that doesn't mean that it is motivated by the moral case.

Writing in the Observer recently, David Aaronovitch argued in favour of US intervention, while suggesting that it could be improved by means of some policy changes. "Sure, I want them to change. I want more consistency. I want Bush to stop tolerating the nastystans of Central Asia, to tell Ariel where to get off, to treat allies with more respect, to dump the hubristic neo-cons . . ."[2] So say we all. But the White House is not a branch of Amnesty International. When it suits its purposes to append a moral justification to its actions, it will do so. When it is better served by supporting dictatorships like Uzbekistan's, expansionist governments like Ariel Sharon's, and organisations that torture and mutilate and murder, like the Colombian army and (through it) the paramilitary AUC, it will do so. It armed and funded Saddam Hussein when it needed to, it knocked him down when it needed to. In neither case did it act because it cared about the people of his country. It acted because it cared about its own interests. The US, like all superpowers, does have a consistent approach to international affairs. But it is not morally consistent; it is strategically consistent.

It is hard to see why we should expect anything else. All empires work according to the rules of practical advantage, rather than those of kindness and moral decency. In Arthur Koestler's Darkness at Noon, Rubashov, the fallen hero of the revolution, condemns himself for "having followed sentimental impulses, and in so doing to have been led into contradiction with historical necessity. I have lent my ear to the laments of the sacrificed, and thus became deaf to the arguments which proved the necessity to sacrifice them."[3] "Sympathy, conscience, disgust, despair, repentance and atonement", his interrogator reminds him, "are for us repellent debauchery".[4]

Koestler, of course, was describing a different superpower, but these considerations have always held true. During the Cold War, the two empires supported whichever indigenous leaders advanced their interests. They helped them to seize and retain power by massacring their own people, then flung them into conflicts in which millions were killed. One of the reasons why the US triumphed was that it possessed the resources to pursue that strategy with more consistency than the Soviet Union could. Today the necessity for mass murder has diminished. But those who imagine that the strategic calculus has somehow been overturned are deceiving themselves.

There were plenty of hard-headed reasons for the United States to go to war with Iraq. As Paul Wolfowitz, the deputy defense secretary, has admitted, the occupation of that country permits the US to retain its presence in the Middle East while removing "almost all of our forces from Saudi Arabia".[5] The presence of "crusader forces on the holy land"[6] was, he revealed, becoming ever less sustainable. (Their removal, of course, was Osama bin Laden's first demand. Who said that terrorism does not work?) Retaining troops in the Middle East permits the US to continue to exercise control over its oil supplies, and thus to hold China, its new economic and political rival, to ransom. The bombing of Iraq was used by Bush to show that his war on terror had not lost momentum. And power, as anyone who possesses it appreciates, is something you use or lose. Unless you flex your muscles, they wither away.

We can't say which of these motives was dominant, but we can say that they are realistic reasons for war. The same cannot be said of a concern for the human rights of foreigners. This is merely the cover under which one has to act in a democracy.

But in debating the war, those of us who opposed it find ourselves drawn into this fairy tale. We are obliged to argue about the relative moral merits of leaving Saddam in place or deposing him, while we know, though we are seldom brave enough to say it, that the moral issue is a distraction. The genius of the hawks has been to oblige us to accept a fiction as the reference point for debate.

Of course, it is possible for empires to do the right thing for the wrong reasons, and upon this possibility the hawks may hang their last best hopes of justification. But the wrong reasons, consistently applied, lead, at the global level, to the wrong results. Let us argue about the moral case for war by all means; but let us do so in the knowledge that it had nothing to do with the invasion of Iraq.

November 25 2003

The Lies of the Press

So Andrew Gilligan, the BBC reporter who claimed that the government had sexed up the intelligence about Iraq's weapons of mass destruction, was mostly right. Much of the rest of the media, which took the doctored intelligence at face value, was wrong. The reward for getting it right was public immolation and the sack. The punishment for getting it wrong was the usual annual bonus. No government commissions inquiries to discover why reporters reproduce the government's lies.

All journalists make mistakes. When deadlines are short and subjects are complicated, we are bound to get some things wrong. But the falsehoods reproduced by the media before the invasion of Iraq were massive and consequential; it is hard to see how Britain could have gone to war if the press had done its job. If the newspapers have any interest in putting the record straight, they should surely each be commissioning an inquiry of their own.

Unlike the government's, it should be independent, consisting perhaps of a lawyer, a media analyst and an intelligence analyst. Its task would be to assess the paper's coverage of Iraq, decide what it got right and what it got wrong, discover why the mistakes were made and what should be done to prevent their repetition. Its report should be published in full by the paper.

No British newspaper is likely to emerge unharmed from such an inquiry. The Independent, Independent on Sunday and the Guardian, which were the most sceptical about the claims made by the government and intelligence agencies, still got some important things wrong.

Much of the problem here is that certain falsehoods have slipped into the political language. The Guardian, for example, has claimed on ten occasions that the weapons inspectors were expelled from Iraq in 1998. Embarrassingly, one of these claims was contained in an article called Iraq: The Myth and the Reality.[1] Even more embarrassingly, I was responsible for another one of them.[2] It's not that any of us believe this to be the case; the Guardian has published plenty of reports showing that the inspectors were withdrawn by the UN after the US insisted that they should leave Iraq for their own safety. But the lie is repeated so often by the government that it keeps seeping back into our reports. More gravely, an article published on the Guardian's website in April 2002 reproduced false claims, first carried by Vanity Fair, without sufficient caveats. The article alleged that Iraq was developing a long-range ballistic missile system capable of carrying chemical, biological and nuclear warheads.[3]

The Observer, I think, would do less well. It commissioned some brilliant investigative reporting, which exposed many of the falsehoods reproduced elsewhere in the media. But it also carried several reports that were simply wrong.

It published five articles claiming that there were "direct Iraqi links with the US hijackers" who destroyed the World Trade Center in 2001.[4] One of them suggested that "Iraqi training, intelligence and logistics were hidden behind an Islamist facade".[5] Iraq, it claimed, "ran a terrorist camp for foreign Islamists, where it taught them how to hijack planes with boxcutters".[6]

Two reports suggested that the anthrax attacks in the United States in October 2001 had "an ultimate Iraqi origin".[7] Another article maintained that Iraq "has tried to buy thousands of ... aluminium tubes, which American officials believe were intended as components of centrifuges to enrich uranium".[8] All these stories turn out to have been based on false information supplied by the Iraqi National Congress and the US and UK intelligence agencies.

Its editorials also appear to have been too willing to give Bush and Blair the benefit of the doubt. In November 2002, for example, the paper maintained that Saddam Hussein "expelled UN weapons inspectors in 1998; he subsequently built up an arsenal of weapons of mass destruction ... the real responsibility [for averting war] lies with Saddam himself".[9] The paper consistently argued that we should not go to war without an international mandate, but still supported the invasion when that mandate didn't materialise.

The Observer published plenty of stories that contradicted these reports. But a balance between true and false still averages out as partly false, and its readers were left not knowing what to believe. In May this year, the paper published an article by David Rose retracting some of the incorrect material.[10] I don't think I'm alone in believing that it provided insufficient redress. It failed to deal with the allegations of links between Iraq and al-Qaida, or of Iraq's responsibility for the anthrax attacks. And it seems wrong that one journalist should take responsibility for decisions that must have been approved elsewhere. This partial retraction contrasts uncomfortably with the comprehensive apology published by the New York Times four days before. "Editors at several levels who should have been challenging reporters and pressing for more skepticism", the NYT confessed, "were perhaps too intent on rushing scoops into the paper . . . Articles based on dire claims about Iraq tended to get prominent display, while follow-up articles that called the original ones into question were sometimes buried. In some cases, there was no follow-up at all."[11]

But the Observer's sins are minor by comparison to those of The Times, and Sunday Times and the Daily and Sunday Telegraph. They all appear to have been willing accomplices in the Pentagon's campaign of disinformation.

By far the worst of these offenders is the Sunday Telegraph. In September 2001, it claimed that "the Iraqi leader had been providing al-Qaeda . . . with funding, logistical back-up and advanced weapons training. His operations reached a "frantic pace" in the past few months".[12] In October 2001, it reported that "Saddam Hussein has relocated his chemical weapons factories after the first case of anthrax poisoning in America . . . A senior Western intelligence official said that . . . "The entire contents of their chemicals weapons factories around Baghdad have been moving through the nights to specially built bunkers."[13]

In September 2002, it reported that "Saddam Hussein is developing frightening new ways to deliver his arsenal of chemical and biological weapons, including smallpox and the deadly VX nerve agent."[14] Another report on the same day claimed that "Saddam is on the verge of possessing crude nuclear devices that could be "delivered" using "unorthodox" means such as on lorries or ships ... Saddam has the capability to assemble all the components required to make nuclear weapons."[15] In February 2003, it claimed that "Iraq's air force has advanced poison bombs".[16]

All of these stories – and many others – appear to be false. But far from retracting them, it keeps publishing new allegations, which look as dodgy as its pre-war claims. Like the Observer, it appears to have been used by black propagandists in the intelligence services and Iraqi defectors seeking to boost their credentials. Unlike the Observer, it seems happy to be duped.

So who will hold the newspapers to account? It seems to me that the only possible answer is you. You the readers must take us to task if we mislead you. Pressure groups should be bombarding us with calls and emails – you'd be amazed by the difference it makes. And if we don't respond with openness and honesty, you should cancel your subscriptions and look elsewhere for your news.

July 20 2004

War Without Rules

Did US troops use chemical weapons in Falluja? The answer is yes. The proof is not to be found in the documentary broadcast on Italian TV last week, which has generated gigabytes of hype on the internet. It's a turkey, whose evidence that white phosphorus was fired at Iraqi troops is flimsy and circumstantial."[1] But the bloggers debating it found the smoking gun.

The first account they unearthed comes from a magazine published by the US Army. In the March 2005 edition of Field Artillery, officers from the 2nd Infantry's Fire Support Element boast about their role in the attack on Falluja in November last year. On page 26 is the following text. "White Phosphorous. WP proved to be an effective and versatile munition. We used it for screening missions at two breeches and, later in the fight, as a potent psychological weapon against the insurgents in trench lines and spider holes when we could not get effects on them with HE [high explosives]. We fired 'shake and bake' missions at the insurgents, using WP to flush them out and HE to take them out."[2]

The second comes from a report in California's North County Times, by a staff reporter embedded with the Marines during the siege of Falluja in April 2004. "Gun up!" Millikin yelled ... grabbing a white phosphorus round from a nearby ammo can and holding it over the tube. 'Fire!' Bogert yelled, as Millikin dropped it. The boom kicked dust around the pit as they ran through the drill again and again, sending a mixture of burning white phosphorus and high explosives they call 'shake 'n' bake' into a cluster of buildings where insurgents have been spotted all week."[3]

White phosporus is not listed in the schedules of the Chemical Weapons Convention. It can be legally used as a flare to illuminate the battlefield, or to produce smoke to hide troop movements from the enemy. Like other unlisted substances, it may be deployed for "Military purposes ... not dependent on the use of the toxic properties of chemicals as a method of warfare".[4] But it becomes a chemical weapon as soon as it is used directly against people. A chemical weapon can be "any chemical which through its chemical action on life processes can cause death, temporary incapacitation or permanent harm".[5]

White phosphorus is fat-soluble and burns spontaneously on contact with the air. According to globalsecurity.org, "The burns usually are multiple, deep, and variable in size. The solid in the eye produces severe injury. The particles continue to burn unless deprived of atmospheric oxygen ... If service members are hit by pieces of white phosphorus, it could burn right down to the bone."[6] As it oxidises, it produces a smoke composed of phosphorous pentoxide. According to the standard US industrial safety sheet, the smoke "releases heat on contact with moisture and will burn mucous surfaces . . . Contact with substance can cause severe eye burns and permanent damage."[7]

Until last week, the US State Department maintained that US forces used white phosphorus shells "very sparingly in Fallujah, for illumination purposes. They were fired into the air to illuminate enemy positions at night, not at enemy fighters."[8] Confronted with the new evidence, on Thursday it changed its position. "We have learned that some of the information we were provided . . . is incorrect. White phosphorus shells, which produce smoke, were used in Fallujah not for illumination but for screening purposes, i.e., obscuring troop movements and, according to . . . Field Artillery magazine, "as a potent psychological weapon against the insurgents in trench lines and spider holes . . ." The article states that US forces used white phosphorous rounds to flush out enemy fighters so that they could then be killed with high explosive rounds."[9] The US government, in other words, appears to admit that white phosphorus was used in Falluja as a chemical weapon.

The invaders have been forced into a similar climbdown over the use of napalm in Iraq. In December 2004, the Labour MP Alice Mahon asked the British armed forces minister, Adam Ingram, "whether napalm or a similar substance has been used by the Coalition in Iraq (a) during and (b) since the war". "No napalm", the minister replied, "has been used by Coalition forces in Iraq either during the war-fighting phase or since."[10]

This seemed odd to those who had been paying attention. There were widespread reports that in March 2003 US Marines had dropped incendiary bombs around the bridges over the Tigris and the Saddam Canal on the way to Baghdad. The commander of Marine Air Group 11 admitted that "We napalmed both those approaches."[11] Embedded journalists reported that napalm was dropped at Safwan Hill on the border with Kuwait.[12] In August 2003, the Pentagon confirmed that the Marines had dropped "Mark 77 firebombs". Though the substance they contained was not napalm, its function, the Pentagon's information sheet said, was "remarkably similar".[13] While napalm is made from petrol and polystyrene, the gel in the Mark 77 is made from kerosene and polystyrene. I doubt it makes much difference to the people it lands on.

So, in January this year, the MP Harry Cohen refined Alice Mahon's question. He asked "whether Mark 77 firebombs have been used by Coalition forces". "The United States", the minister replied "have confirmed to us that they have not used Mark 77 firebombs, which are essentially napalm canisters, in Iraq at any time."[14] The US government had lied to him. Mr Ingram had to retract his statements in a private letter to the MPs in June.[15]

We were told that the war with Iraq was necessary for two reasons. Saddam Hussein possessed biological and chemical weapons and might one day use them against another nation. And the Iraqi people needed to be liberated from his oppressive regime, which had, among its other crimes, used chemical weapons to kill them. Tony Blair, Colin Powell, William Shawcross, David Aaronovitch, Nick Cohen, Ann Clwyd and many others referred, in making their case, to Saddam's gassing of the Kurds at Halabja in 1988. They accused those who opposed the war of caring nothing for the welfare of the Iraqis.

Given that they care so much, why has none of these hawks spoken out against the use of unconventional weapons by coalition forces? Ann Clwyd, the Labour MP who turned from peace campaigner to chief apologist for an illegal war, is, as far as I can discover, the only one of these armchair warriors to engage with the issue. In May this year she wrote to the Guardian to assure us that reports that a "modern form of napalm" had been used by US forces "are completely without foundation. Coalition forces have not used napalm – either during operations in Falluja, or at any other time."[16] How did she know? The Foreign Office minister told her. Before the invasion, Ann Clwyd travelled through Iraq to investigate Saddam's crimes against his people. She told the Commons that what she had discovered moved her to tears.

After the invasion, she took the minister's word at face value, when a thirty-second search on the internet could have told her it was bunkum. It makes you wonder whether she, or any of the other enthusiasts for war, really gave a damn about the people for whom they claimed to be campaigning.

Saddam Hussein, facing a possible death sentence, is accused of mass murder, torture, false imprisonment, the embezzlement of billions, and the use of chemical weapons. He is certainly guilty on all counts. So, it now seems, are the people who overthrew him.

November 15 2005

A War of Terror

Last week, on the day George Bush delivered his State of the Union address, the Pentagon received a visitor. A few hours before the president told the American people that "we will not permit the triumph of violence in the affairs of men",[1] General Carlos Ospina, head of the Colombian army, was shaking hands with his American counterpart. He had come to discuss the latest instalment of US military aid.

General Ospina has done well. Just four years ago, he was a lieutenant-colonel in command of the army's Fourth Brigade. He was promoted first to divisional commander, then, in August last year, to chief of the army. But let us dwell for a moment on his career as a brigadier, and his impressive contribution to the war against terror.

According to Human Rights Watch, the Fourth Brigade, under Ospina's command, worked alongside the death squads controlled by the paramilitary leader Carlos Castaño.[2] A report published three years ago summarises the results of an investigation carried out by the attorney general's office in Colombia. On October 25 1997, a force composed of Ospina's regulars and Castaño's paramilitaries surrounded a village called El Aro, in a region considered sympathetic to the country's left-wing guerrillas. The soldiers cordoned off the village while Castaño's men moved in. They captured a shopkeeper, tied him to a tree, gouged out his eyes, cut off his tongue and castrated him. The other residents tried to flee, but were turned back by Ospina's troops. The paramilitaries then mutilated and beheaded 11 of the villagers, including three children, burned the church, the pharmacy and most of the houses and smashed the water pipes. When they left, they took 30 people with them, who are now listed among Colombia's disappeared.[3]

This operation was unusual only in that it has been so well documented. Among other sources, the investigators interviewed one Francisco Enrique Villalba, who was a member of the death squad that carried out the massacre and who had witnessed the prior coordination of the raid between the army and Castaño's lieutenants. The attack on El Aro was one of dozens of atrocities that Human Rights Watch alleges were assisted by the Fourth Brigade. Villalba testified that the brigade would "legalise" the killings his squad carried out. The paramilitaries would hand the corpses of the civilians they had murdered to the soldiers, and in return the soldiers would give them grenades and munitions.[4] The brigade would then dress the corpses in military uniforms and claim them as the bodies of rebels it had shot.

A separate investigation by the Colombian internal affairs agency documented hundreds of mobile phone and pager communications between the death squads and officers of the Fourth Brigade, among them Lieutenant-Colonel Ospina.[5] On Tuesday, Ospina fiercely denied the allegations, claiming that they were politically motivated and that "honest people around the world know that we are serving our people well".[6]

In the same press conference, however, he also revealed that this month the Colombian government will start to deploy a new kind of "self-defence force", composed of armed civilians backed by the army. Human rights groups allege that the government has simply legalised the death squads.

Official paramilitary forces of this kind were first mobilised by the current president, Alvaro Uribe, when he was governor of the state of Antioquia in the mid-1990s. The civilian forces he established there, like all the paramilitaries working with the army, carried out massacres, the assassination of peasant and trade union leaders, and what Colombians call "social cleansing": the killing of homeless people, drug addicts and petty criminals. They joined forces with the unofficial death squads and began to profit from drug trafficking.[7] They were banned after Uribe ceased to be governor. One of his first acts when he became president in August last year was to promote General Ospina and instruct him to develop similar networks throughout the contested regions of Colombia.

Uribe, a landowner with major business interests, was the US government's favoured candidate. After he was elected, but before he assumed the presidency, it granted Colombia a special package of military aid worth $80 million.[8] Its military funding, through programmes it calls Plan Colombia and the Andean Regional Initiative, now amounts to $2 billion over the past four years.[9] At the beginning of last month, US special forces arrived in Colombia to help train General Ospina's troops. One of the two brigades they are assisting – the Fifth – has also been named by Human Rights Watch for alleged involvement in paramilitary killings. It has been equipped with helicopters by the US army.[10]

The United States has been at war in Colombia for over 50 years. It has, however, hesitated to explain precisely whom it is fighting. Officially, it is now involved there in a "war on terror". Before September 2001, it was a "war on drugs"; before that, a "war on communism". In essence, however, US intervention in Colombia is unchanged: it remains a war on the poor.

There is little doubt that the FARC, the main left-wing rebel group, has been diverted from its original revolutionary purpose by power politics and the struggle for the control of drugs money. It finances itself partly through extortion and kidnap. Whether it could fairly be described as a terrorist network, though, is open to question. What is unequivocal is that the great majority of the country's political killings are committed not by FARC or the other rebels, but by the right-wing paramilitaries working with the army. Their task is to terrorise the population into acquiescence to the government's programmes.

The purpose of this unending war is to secure those parts of the country that are rich in natural resources for Colombian landowners and foreign multinationals. Colombia has one of the most unequal economies in the world – the top 10% of the population earns 60 times as much as the bottom 10%[11] – and there is no room in that country for both the aspirations of the poor and the aspirations of the super-rich. One faction has to be suppressed. The Colombian army is making the country safe for business. This is why, over the past 10 years, the paramilitaries it works with have killed some 15,000 trade unionists, peasant and indigenous leaders, human rights workers, land reform activists, left-wing politicians and their sympathisers. This is why it is the world's third largest recipient (after Israel and Egypt) of US military aid.[12]

The people funding this programme are Britain's allies in the war against terror. They are the people who have awarded themselves the power to arbitrate between good and evil. They are the people who will, within the next few weeks, attack Iraq on behalf of civilisation. "Throughout the twentieth century", Bush told the United States last week, "small groups of men seized control of great nations, built armies and arsenals, and set out to dominate the weak and intimidate the world. In each case, their ambitions of cruelty and murder had no limit."[13] America's continuing adventure in Colombia suggests that little has changed.

February 4 2003

Back to Front Coup

The relationship between governments and those who seek favours from them has changed. Not long ago, lobbyists would visit politicians and bribe or threaten them until they got what they wanted. Today, ministers lobby the lobbyists. Whenever a big business pressure group holds its annual conference or dinner, Tony Blair or Gordon Brown or another senior minister will come and beg it not to persecute the government. George Bush flies around the United States flattering the companies that might support his re-election, offering tax breaks and subsidies even before they ask.

But while we are slowly becoming aware of the corporate capture of our governments, we appear to have overlooked the growing power of another recipient of this back-to-front lobbying. In the United States, a sort of reverse military coup appears to be taking place. Both the president and the opposition seem to be offering the armed forces, though they do not appear to have requested it, an ever greater share of the business of government.

Every week, the State Department makes a list of Mr Bush's most important speeches and visits, to distribute to its embassies around the world. The embassy in London has a public archive dating from June last year. During this period, Bush has made 41 major speeches to live audiences. Of these, 14 – just over a third – were delivered to military personnel or veterans.[1]

Now Bush, of course, is commander-in-chief as well as president, and he has every right to address the troops. But this commander-in-chief goes far beyond the patriotic blandishments of previous leaders. He sometimes dresses up in the uniform of the troops he is meeting. He quotes their mottoes and songs, retells their internal jokes, mimics their slang. He informs the "dog-faced soldiers" that they are "the rock of Marne",[2] or asks naval cadets whether they give "the left-handed salute to Tecumseh, the God of 2.0".[3] The television audience is mystified, but the men love him for it. He is, or so his speeches suggest, one of them.

He starts by leading them in chants of "Hoo-ah! Hoo-ah!", then plasters them with praise, then reminds them that (unlike those of any other workers in America) their pay, healthcare and housing are being upgraded. After this, they will cheer everything he says. So he uses these occasions to attack his opponents and announce new and often controversial policies. The Marines were the first to be told about his interstate electricity grid;[4] he instructed the American Legion about the reform of the Medicare programme;[5] last week he explained his plans for the taxation of small businesses to the National Guard.[6] The troops may not have the faintest idea what he's talking about, but they cheer him to the rafters anyway. After that, implementing these policies looks like a patriotic duty.

This strikes me as an abuse of his position as commander-in-chief, rather like the use of Air Force One (the presidential aeroplane) for political fundraising tours. The war against terror is a feeble excuse. Indeed, all this began long before September 2001: between February and August of that year he gave eight major speeches to the military, some of which were stuffed with policy announcements.[7]

But there is a lot more at stake than merely casting the cloak of patriotism over his corporate welfare programmes. Appeasing the armed forces has become, for President Bush, a political necessity. He cannot win the next election without them. Unless he can destroy the resistance in Iraq, the resistance will destroy his political career. But crushing it requires the continuous presence of a vast professional army and tens of thousands of reservists. There is plenty of evidence to suggest that the troops do not want to be there, and that at least some of their generals regard the invasion as poorly planned. At the moment, Bush is using Donald Rumsfeld, the defence secretary, as his lightning conductor, just as Blair is using Geoff Hoon. But if he is to continue to deflect the anger of the troops, the president must give them everything they might want, whether or not they have asked for it.

This is one of the reasons for a military budget that is now entirely detached from any possible strategic reality. As the website www.wsws.org has pointed out, when you add together the $368bn for routine spending, the $19bn assigned to the Department of Energy for new nuclear weapons, the $79bn already passed by Congress to fund the war in Iraq, and the $87bn that Bush has just requested to sustain it, you find that the federal government is now spending as much on war as it is on education, public health, housing, employment, pensions, food aid and welfare put together[8] (though, of course, the federal government provides only some of the money for these items). This is the sort of allocation you would expect in a third world military dictatorship. But all this has come from the civilian leadership. It is not just Bush. Such is the success of his reordering of national priorities that not a single Democrat on the congressional appropriations panel dared to challenge the government's latest request.[9]

Bush's other big problem, which has quietly tracked him ever since he declared his candidacy, is that he is a draft-dodger who failed even to discharge his duties as a national guardsman,[10] while some of his most prominent political opponents are war heroes and generals. To win the Republican nomination, he had to beat John McCain, the fighter pilot and prisoner of war who won the Silver Star, Bronze Star, Purple Heart, Legion of Merit and Distinguished Flying Cross for his bravery in Vietnam. To go to war with Iraq, Bush had to overcome the resistance of his Secretary of State, Colin Powell, the general who was formerly chairman of the joint chiefs of staff. To win the next election, he may have to beat Wesley Clark, commander of Nato forces during the war in Yugoslavia and currently the Democrats' favoured candidate. Bush's reverse coup has meant that the Democrats must suck up to the armed forces as well, in order to be seen as a patriotic party. Wesley Clark's campaigning slogan is "a new American patriotism".[11]

The last general to have been appointed president, though as belligerent as any other, understood that there was a potential conflict between his two public roles. As a result, Dwight Eisenhower never wore a uniform while in office, or engaged in the hooting and chest-thumping with which George Bush greets his troops. His warning about the dangers of failing to contain "the military-industrial complex" has been forgotten.[12]

Tony Blair has also played the tin soldier, but with less success. He was the first western leader to arrive in Iraq after George Bush prematurely announced victory there. But when he addressed the troops, they remained silent. I am told by a good source that the generals are furious with him for sending them to war on false pretences.

But in America, the armed forces, whether they want it or not, are being dragged into the heart of political life. A mature democracy is in danger of turning itself into a military state.

October 14 2003

Peace Is for Wimps

It's described by a senior official at the Ministry of Defence as "a dead duck . . . expensive and obsolete".[1] The editor of World Defence Systems calls it "10 years out of date".[2] A former defence minister remarked that it is "essentially flawed and out of date".[3] So how on earth did BAe Systems manage to sell 72 Eurofighters to Saudi Arabia on Friday?

One answer is that it had some eminent salesmen. On July 2 2005, Tony Blair secretly landed in Riyadh to persuade the Saudi princes that this flying scrapheap was the must-have accessory every fashionable young despot would be buying.[4] Three weeks later the defence secretary, John Reid, turned up to deploy his subtle charms.[5] Somehow the deal survived, and last week his successor, Des Browne, signed the agreement. All of which raises a second question. Why are government ministers, even Blair himself, prepared to reduce themselves to hawkers on behalf of our arms merchants?

Readers of this column will know that British governments are not averse to helping big business, even when this conflicts with their stated policies. But the support they offer the defence industry goes far beyond the assistance they provide to anyone else.

Take the Defence Export Services Organisation (DESO), for example. This is a government agency founded 40 years ago to smooth out foreign deals for British arms companies. From its inception, this smoothing involved baksheesh. It was established as a channel for "financial aids and incentives" to corrupt officials in foreign governments.[6]

In 2003, after bribery of this kind became illegal in the United Kingdom, the Guardian found an internal DESO document explaining its guidelines for arms sales. "In certain parts of the world," it said, "it has become commonplace for special commissions to be required. This is a matter for DESO, to whom all requests for special commission should be referred. If DESO confirm that such payments can be made, contracts staff may need to provide the means for payment."[7] A "special commission" is civil service code for a bribe. The document suggests, in other words, that the British government is overseeing the payment of bribes to foreign officials.

BAe's previous deals with Saudi Arabia are surrounded by allegations of corruption. It is alleged to have run a £60 million "slush fund" to oil the Al Yamamah contracts brokered by Margaret Thatcher. The fund is said to have been used to provide cash, cars, yachts, hotel rooms and prostitutes to Saudi officials.[8] One of the alleged beneficiaries was Prince Turki bin Nasser, the Saudi minister for arms procurement.[9] The Serious Fraud Office was bounced by the Guardian's revelations into opening an investigation. But among the conditions the Saudi government laid down for the new deal is that the investigation be dropped.[10] Let's see what happens.*

With this exception, the big arms companies appear to have been granted immunity from inquiry or prosecution. Letters from the

---

* The investigation was indeed dropped, at the behest of the attorney general.

permanent secretary at the Ministry of Defence, Sir Kevin Tebbit, show that he prevented the ministry's fraud squad from investigating the allegations against BAe; that he failed to tell his minister about the investigation by the Serious Fraud Office; and that he tipped off the chairman of BAe about the contents of a confidential letter the Serious Fraud Office had sent him.[11] When the US government told him that BAe had allegedly engaged in corrupt practice in the Czech Republic, Sir Kevin failed to inform the police.[12]

For 14 years, the government has suppressed a report by the National Audit Office into the Al Yamamah deals. Earlier this summer the auditor general refused even to hand it over to the Serious Fraud Office.[13] A parliamentary committee on arms exports published a report this month that expresses its continuing frustration over the government's reluctance to assist its inquiries.[14]

It also shows that Mark Thomas, the stand-up comedian, has done more to expose illegal arms deals than the Ministry of Defence, the Export Control Organisation and HM Revenue and Customs put together, simply by searching the internet and the trade press and attending the arms fairs the British government hosts. In response, the government has investigated not the companies, but the comedian. A confidential email from a civil servant suggested that the trade minister, Richard Caborn, was seeking to gather "background/dirt on him in order to rubbish him".[15] Caborn claims he was misrepresented.

The only arms dealers to have been prosecuted since 2000 are five very small fish. All of them escaped with a small fine or a suspended sentence, including a man who made repeated attempts to export military parts to Iran.[16] Compare this with the treatment of those who upset the arms industry. Nine anti-war campaigners in Derry who occupied the offices of the arms company Raytheon have just been charged with aggravated burglary and unlawful assembly.[17] If convicted, they could be imprisoned for years.

Every government policy designed to protect our national interests or promote world peace is torn up at the arms companies' request.

They are not supposed to sell to dodgy regimes or countries in the midst of conflict. So let them first export their arms to the Channel Islands, from where they can be resold.[18] Weapons may not be exported to any country unless it shows "respect for human rights".[19] So get the Foreign Office to note "a small but significant improvement" in the Saudi government's performance, and carry on as before.[20]

Should we be surprised to find, as The Times revealed yesterday, that Israeli soldiers have found night-vision equipment made by a British company in Hizbullah bunkers?[21] Should we be surprised to discover that despite a government commitment to sell Israel "no weapons, equipment or components which could be deployed aggressively in the Occupied Territories",[22] British companies have been supplying parts for its Apache helicopters and F-16 bombers?[23] The government seems to see the escalating dangers in the Middle East as nothing but an opportunity for business.

Perhaps most damning is this. Blair claims that Britain's security comes first. Yet one of the means by which his government managed to secure this deal was to speed it up. How? The Sunday Times reports that "the first 24 planes for the Saudis will be those at present allotted to the Royal Air Force, with the RAF postponing its deliveries until later in the production run."[24] In other words, the Saudis" perceived need for fighter planes takes precedence over our own.

So why does Her Majesty's Government behave like a subsidiary of BAe? A report by the Campaign Against the Arms Trade (CAAT) shows that 39% of all the senior public servants who go to work for the private sector are employees of the Ministry of Defence moving into arms firms. In return, scores of arms dealers are seconded to the ministry.[25] The man who runs DESO, for example, previously worked for BAe, selling arms in the Middle East.[26]

CAAT lists the government committees stuffed with arms executives, the donations, the lobbyists, the Labour peers taking the corporate shilling, and I am sure all this plays an important role. But it seems to me that there is also something else at work. There appears to be a sense among some of those at the core of government that peace, human rights and democracy are for wimps, while the serious business, for real players, is war and the means by which it is enacted.

August 24 2006

Asserting Our Right to Kill and Maim Civilians

The central mystery of the modern state is this. The necessary resources, both economic and political, will always be found for the purpose of terminating life. The project of preserving it will always struggle. When did you last see a sponsored marathon raising money for nuclear weapons? But we must beg and cajole each other for funds whenever a hospital wants a new dialysis machine. If the money and determination expended on waging war with Iraq had been used to tackle climate change, our carbon emissions would already be in freefall. If as much money were spent on foreign aid as on fighter planes, no one would ever go hungry.

When the state was run by warrior kings, this was comprehensible: they owed their existence to overwhelming force. Now weapons budgets and foreign wars are, if anything, an electoral liability. But the pattern has never been broken.

In Geneva today, at the new review of the Conventional Weapons Treaty, the British government will be using the full force of its diplomacy to ensure that civilians continue to be killed, by blocking a ban on the use of cluster bombs. Sweden, supported by Austria, Mexico and New Zealand, has proposed a convention making their deployment illegal, like the Ottawa Treaty banning anti-personnel landmines. But the United Kingdom, working with the US, China and Russia, has spent the past month trying to prevent negotiations from being opened.[1] Perhaps this is unsurprising. Most of the cluster bombs dropped over the past 40 years have been delivered by its two principal allies in the "war on terror", the US and Israel. And the UK used hundreds of thousands of them during the two Gulf wars.

Cluster munitions are tiny bombs – generally about the size of a drinks can – packed inside bigger bombs or artillery shells. They scatter over several hectares, and they are meant to be used to destroy tanks and planes and to wipe out anti-aircraft positions. There are two problems.

The first is that the bombs, being widely dispersed, cannot be accurately targeted. The second is that many of them don't detonate when they hit the ground. Officially, cluster bombs have a failure rate of between 5 and 7%. In reality it's much higher. Between 20 and 25% of the cluster munitions NATO forces dropped during the Kosovo conflict failed to go off when they landed.[2] The failure rate of the bombs dropped by the US in Indochina was roughly 30%;[3] 40% of the cluster bombs Israel scattered over Lebanon did not detonate.[4]

The unexploded bombs then sit and wait to be defused – leg by human leg. They are as devastating to civilian populations as landmines – possibly worse, because far more of them have been dropped. Even 30 years or more after they land, as the people of Vietnam and Laos know, they can still be detonated by the slightest concussion.

A report published last week by Handicap International estimates that around 100,000 people have been killed or wounded by cluster bombs. Of the known casualties, 98% are civilians.[5] Most of them are hit when farming or walking or clearing the rubble where their homes used to be. Many of the victims are children, partly because the bombs look like toys. Handicap's report tells terrible and heartbreaking stories of children finding these munitions and playing catch with them, or using them as boules or marbles. Those who survive are often blinded, lose limbs and suffer horrible abdominal injuries.

Among the case histories in the report is that of a family in Kosovo who went to swim in a lake a few kilometres from their village. One of the children, a six-year-old called Adnan, found an odd metal can on the bank and showed it to his family. It exploded. His father and older brother were killed and he was gravely wounded. His sister later returned to the lake to collect the family's belongings, stepped on another NATO cluster bomb and was killed.

The economic effects of cluster bombs can also be deadly. Like landmines, they put many agricultural areas out of bounds, because of the risk of detonating one while ploughing or harvesting. In some parts of Lebanon the fields have remained unharvested this year. Cluster bombs dropped on to the rubble of Lebanese towns have made reconstruction slow and dangerous.

The numbers deployed are mind-boggling. The US air force released 19 million over Cambodia, 70 million in Vietnam, and 208 million in Laos.[6] Over much shorter periods, the US and the UK dropped some 54 million cluster bombs on Iraq during the first Gulf war, and around 2 million during the second Gulf war.[7] Israel scattered 4 million cluster bombs over Lebanon during its latest invasion, almost all of them during the final 72 hours.[8] It looked like revenge, or an attempt (like its deliberate bombing of the Jiyeh power plant, causing a massive oil spill which has wrecked the tourism industry) to cripple Lebanon's economy. Since the invasion, an average of 2.5 Lebanese civilians every day have been blown up by cluster bombs.

The only other nation that has used cluster bombs extensively since the Second World War is Russia, which dropped large quantities in Afghanistan, and which scatters them in Chechnya, sometimes deliberately bombing market places and other civilian targets. Apart from that, they've been deployed in small numbers by Sudan, Libya, Eritrea and Ethiopia, Nigeria, Serb forces, Hizbullah, and warring factions in Tajikistan. What good company we keep.

These weapons are arguably already illegal. Protocol 1 to the Geneva conventions prohibits attacks which "are of a nature to strike military objectives and civilians or civilian objects without distinction" and "which may be expected to cause incidental loss of civilian life, injury to civilians, damage to civilian objects, or a combination thereof, which would be excessive in relation to the concrete and direct military advantage anticipated".[9] I think 98% would be a fair definition of "excessive".

But their deployment will continue until there is a specific treaty banning them. It's clear that the US and UK governments know their use is wrong. Handicap International reports that the Coalition Provisional Authority (the US administration set up to govern Iraq in 2003) "strongly discouraged casualty data collection, especially in relation to cluster submunitions".[10] During a debate in the House of Lords last month, the Foreign Office minister Lord Triesman made a show of justifying their use so feeble that you can't help suspecting he was batting for the other side. The only argument he could devise to justify their use was that, unlike landmines, cluster bombs are not intended to lie around undetonated.[11] Even this is questionable. How else could you explain the fact that one of their official purposes is "area denial"?

Two days ago a letter sent to the defence minister by the international development secretary, Hilary Benn, was leaked to the press. He argued that "cluster munitions have a very serious humanitarian impact, pushing at the boundaries of international humanitarian law. It is difficult then to see how we can hold so prominent a position against land mines, yet somehow continue to advocate that use of cluster munitions is acceptable."[12]

But he appears to be alone. The Foreign Office maintains that "existing humanitarian law is sufficient for the conduct of military operations, including the use of cluster munitions, and no treaty is required."[13] The government seems unable to break its habit of killing.

November 7 2006

A War Dividend

No one noticed. Or if they did, no one complained. The government didn't even bother to issue a press release. Last week, the Ministry of Defence (MoD) quietly secured a £1.7bn increase in its budget.[1] The spending for 2006–7 was allocated months ago, which means that another fund must have been raided to find the extra money. It's the equivalent of half the annual budget for the Department for International Development.[2] But another billion or two doesn't make much difference when we are already sloshing out £32bn a year on a programme whose purpose is a mystery.[3]

On Friday, the National Audit Office published a report that appeared to congratulate the MoD for going only 11% over budget on 30 acquisitions, such as attack submarines, destroyers, Eurofighter aircraft and anti-tank weapons.[4] This overspending – a mere £3bn or so – is a heroic improvement on the ministry's usual efforts. The story was spoilt a little when we discovered that it would have looked much worse were it not for some creative manoeuvres by the 1st Armoured Accounts Division, confounding the enemy by shifting money between different parts of the budget.

But what the audit report failed to answer, or even to ask, was why we need attack submarines, destroyers, Eurofighter aircraft and anti-tank weapons in the first place. Are the Russians coming? Is Angela Merkel preparing to mobilise a few Panzer divisions? It is preposterous to suggest that we face the threat of invasion, now or in the foreseeable future.

Even the MoD acknowledges this. In the White Paper it published at the end of 2003, it admits that "there are currently no major conventional military threats to the UK or NATO . . . it is now clear that we no longer need to retain a capability against the re-emergence of a direct conventional strategic threat".[5]

NATO agrees. The leaked policy document it will discuss at its summit this week concedes that "large-scale conventional aggression against the alliance will be highly unlikely".[6] No country that is capable of attacking NATO countries is willing to do so. No country that is willing is capable. Submarines, destroyers, Eurofighters and anti-tank rounds are of precious little use against people who plant bombs on trains.

Instead, the MoD redefines the purpose of the armed forces as "meeting a wider range of expeditionary tasks, at greater range from the United Kingdom and with ever-increasing strategic, operational and tactical tempo".[7] It wants to be able to fight either three small foreign wars at the same time or one large one, which "could only conceivably be undertaken alongside the US".[8]

In other words, our "defence" capability is now retained for the purpose of offence. Our armed forces no longer exist to protect us. They exist to go abroad and cause trouble.

But even such wars of choice can no longer be fought. The disaster in Iraq destroyed every pretence of benign or necessary intervention. It is hard to see how any British government, however powerful its case appeared to be, could claim the moral authority to launch another adventure for at least a generation. Iraq disqualifies us from the role the ministry envisages as surely as Suez did. We can kiss goodbye to the idea of going into battle alongside the US as well.

This, then, grants us a marvellous opportunity: to pay ourselves a war dividend. If the war in Iraq means that the current era of invasion and intervention is over, there is no point in maintaining armed forces designed for this purpose. If we were to cut the military budget by 80 or 90%, we would do ourselves nothing but good.

But the danger and paradox of military spending is that the bigger the budget, the more powerful the defence lobby becomes. As the Guardian's revelations about the corrupt relationships they have culti-vated with Saudi princes show,[9] the civil servants in the MoD write their own rules. Much of the time they seem to be defending not the realm but the arms companies. So does the prime minister. In his book, Blair's Wars, John Kampfner records that "from his first day in office Blair was eager not to antagonise British arms companies, and BAe Systems in particular, which developed extremely close relationships with senior figures in Downing Street."[10] A Downing Street aide reported that whenever the head of BAe encountered a problem, "he'd be straight on the phone to Number 10 and it would get sorted".[11]

Having obtained its stupendous budget – the second-biggest defence allocation in the world[12] – our military-industrial complex must justify it. It does so by producing ever more paranoid assessments of the capabilities of terrorists. Bin Laden might possess no submarines, but we must retain our anti-submarine aircraft in case he, or someone like him, acquires some. We don't know what Blair's proposed new nuclear missiles are for, but after the money has been spent, a justification is bound to emerge. In the ministry's Defence Vision paper, I found this gobsmacking contradiction: "We face new challenges and unpredictable new conditions. Our strategy must evolve to reflect these new realities. For the future this means [among other positions] . . . holding fast, in the face of change, to our underpinning military traditions."[13] Was there ever a clearer sign that the tail is wagging the dog?

A report published by the Oxford Research Group this summer argues that our defence policies are self-defeating. They concentrate on the wrong threats and respond to them in a manner that is more likely to exacerbate than to defuse them. The real challenges to world peace, it contends, are presented by climate change, competition over resources, the marginalisation of the poor, and our own military deployments.[14]

By displacing people from their homes and exacerbating food shortages, climate change will cause social breakdown and mass migration. Competition for resources means that the regions that possess them, particularly the Middle East, will remain the focus of conflict. As improved education is not matched by better prospects for many of the world's poor, the resulting sense of marginalisation provides a more hospitable environment for insurrection. Aids leaves a generation of orphaned children vulnerable to recruitment by paramilitary groups and criminal gangs. The war on terror has created the threats it was supposed to defeat, by driving people to avenge the civilians it has killed. By developing new weapons of mass destruction, the rich nations challenge others to try to match them.

Military spending enhances all these threats. The jets and ships and tanks it buys make a large (though so far unquantified) contribution to climate change and the competition for resources. It diverts money from helping the poor; it generates a self-justifying momentum that stimulates conflict. The budget would contribute far more to our security, the report says, if it were spent on energy efficiency, foreign aid and arms control.

So what role remains for our armed forces? A small one. A shrunken army should concentrate on helping the civil authorities to catch terrorists and deal with epidemics, floods and power cuts; the navy should be deployed to protect fisheries and catch drug smugglers; the air force is largely redundant. Now that foreign adventures are no longer an option, it is time we turned our war spending into what it claims to be: a budget for our defence.

November 28 2006

The Darkest Corner of the Mind

After thousands of years of practice, you might have imagined that every possible means of inflicting pain had already been devised. But you should never underestimate the human capacity for invention. United States interrogators, we now discover, have found a new way of destroying a human being.

Last week, defence lawyers acting for Jose Padilla, a US citizen detained as an "enemy combatant", released a video showing a mission fraught with deadly risk – taking him to the prison dentist. A group of masked guards in riot gear shackled his legs and hands, blindfolded him with black-out goggles and shut off his hearing with headphones, then marched him down the prison corridor.[1]

Is Padilla really that dangerous? Far from it: his warders describe him as so docile and inactive that he could be mistaken for "a piece of furniture". The purpose of these measures appeared to be to sustain the regime under which he has lived for over three years: total sensory deprivation. He had been kept in a blacked-out cell, unable to see or hear anything beyond it. Most importantly, he had had no human contact, except for being bounced off the walls from time to time by his interrogators. As a result, he appears to have lost his mind. I don't mean this metaphorically. I mean that his mind is no longer there.

The forensic psychiatrist who examined him says that he "does not appreciate the nature and consequences of the proceedings against him, is unable to render assistance to counsel, and has impairments in reasoning as the result of a mental illness, i.e., post-traumatic stress disorder, complicated by the neuropsychiatric effects of prolonged isolation".[2] Jose Padilla appears to have been lobotomised: not medically, but socially.

If this was an attempt to extract information, it was ineffective; the authorities held him without charge for three-and-a-half years. Then, threatened by a Supreme Court ruling, they suddenly dropped their claims that he was trying to detonate a dirty bomb. They have now charged him with some vague and lesser offences to do with support for terrorism.

He is unlikely to be the only person subjected to this regime. Another "enemy combatant", Ali al-Marri, claims to have been subject to the same total isolation and sensory deprivation, in the same naval prison in South Carolina.[3] God knows what is being done to people who have disappeared into the CIA's foreign oubliettes.

That the US tortures, routinely and systematically, while prosecuting its "war on terror" can no longer be seriously disputed. The Detainee Abuse and Accountability Project (DAA), a coalition of academics and human rights groups, has documented the abuse or killing of 460 inmates of US military prisons in Afghanistan, Iraq and Guantanamo Bay.[4] This, it says, is necessarily a conservative figure; many cases will remain unrecorded. The prisoners were beaten, raped, forced to abuse themselves, forced to maintain "stress positions", and subjected to prolonged sleep deprivation and mock executions.

The New York Times reports that prisoners held by the US military at Bagram airbase in Afghanistan were made to stand for up to 13 days with their hands chained to the ceiling, naked, hooded and unable to sleep.[5] The Washington Post alleges that prisoners at the same airbase were "commonly blindfolded and thrown into walls, bound in painful positions, subjected to loud noises and deprived of sleep", while kept, like Jose Padilla and the arrivals at Guantanamo Bay, "in black hoods or spray-painted goggles".[6]

Alfred McCoy, professor of history at the University of Wisconsin-Madison, argues that the photographs released from the Abu Ghraib prison in Iraq reflect standard CIA torture techniques: "stress positions, sensory deprivation, and sexual humiliation".[7] The famous picture of the hooded man standing on a box, with wires attached to his fingers, shows two of these techniques being used at once. Unable to see, he has no idea how much time has passed or what might be coming next. He stands in a classic stress position; maintained for several hours, it causes excruciating pain. He appears to have been told that if he drops his arms he will be electrocuted. What went wrong at Abu Ghraib is that someone took photos. Everything else was done by the book.

Neither the military nor the civilian authorities have broken much sweat in investigating these crimes. A few very small fish have been imprisoned; a few others have been fined or reduced in rank. In most cases the authorities have either failed to investigate or failed to prosecute. The DAA points out that no officer has yet been held to account for torture practised by his subordinates.[8] US torturers appear to enjoy impunity, until they are stupid enough to take pictures of each other. But Padilla's treatment also reflects another glorious American tradition: solitary confinement. Some 25,000 US prisoners are currently held in isolation, a punishment only rarely used in other democracies. In some places, like the federal prison in Florence, Colorado, they are kept in soundproofed cells and might scarcely see another human being for years on end.[9] They may touch or be touched by no one. Some people have been kept in solitary confinement in the United States for more than 20 years.

At Pelican Bay, in California, where 1200 people are held in the isolation wing, inmates are confined to tiny cells for twenty-two-and-a-half hours a day, then released into an "exercise yard" for "recreation". The yard consists of a concrete well about 12 feet in length, with walls 20 feet high and a metal grille across the sky. The recreation consists of pacing back and forth, alone.[10]

The results are much as you would expect. As National Public Radio reveals, 10% of the isolation prisoners at Pelican Bay are now in the psychiatric wing, and there's a waiting list.[11] Prisoners in solitary confinement, according to Dr Henry Weinstein, a psychiatrist who studies them, suffer from "memory loss to severe anxiety to hallucinations to delusions ... under the severest cases of sensory deprivation, people go crazy".[12] People who went in bad and dangerous come out mad as well. The only two studies conducted so far, in Texas and Washington state, both show that the recidivism rates for prisoners held in solitary confinement are worse than for those allowed to mix with other prisoners.[13] If we were to judge the United States by its penal policies, we would perceive a strange beast: a Christian society that believes in neither forgiveness nor redemption.

From this delightful experiment, US interrogators appear to have extracted a useful lesson: if you want to erase a man's mind, deprive him of contact with the rest of the world. This has nothing to do with obtaining information: torture of all kinds, physical or mental, produces the result that people will say anything to make it end. It is about power, and the discovery that in the right conditions one man's power over another is unlimited. It is an indulgence that turns its perpetrators into everything they claim to be confronting.

President Bush maintains that he is fighting a war against threats to the "values of civilised nations": terror, cruelty, barbarism and extremism. He asked his nation's interrogators to discover where these evils are hidden. They should congratulate themselves. They appear to have succeeded.

December 12 2006

Arguments With Power

I'm With Wolfowitz

It's about as close to consensus as the left is ever likely to come. Everyone this side of Atilla the Hun and the Wall Street Journal agrees that Paul Wolfowitz's appointment as president of the World Bank is a catastrophe. Except me.

Under Wolfowitz, my fellow progressives lament, the World Bank will work for America. If only someone else were chosen it would work for the world's poor. Joseph Stiglitz, the Bank's renegade former chief economist, champions Ernesto Zedillo, the former president of Mexico.[1] A leading article in the Guardian suggested Colin Powell or, had he been allowed to stand, Bono.[2] But what all this hand-wringing and wishful thinking reveals is a profound misconception about the role and purpose of the body Wolfowitz will run.

The World Bank and the IMF were conceived by the US economist Harry Dexter White. Appointed by the US Treasury to lead the negotiations on post-war economic reconstruction, White spent most of 1943 banging the heads of the other allied nations together.[3] They were appalled by his proposals. He insisted that his institutions would place the burden of stabilising the world economy on the countries suffering from debt and trade deficits rather than on the creditors. He insisted that "the more money you put in, the more votes you have".[4] He decided, before the meeting at Bretton Woods in 1944, that "the US should have enough votes to block any decision".[5]

Both the undemocratic voting arrangement and the US veto remain to this day. The result is that the body, which works mostly in poor countries, is entirely controlled by rich ones. White demanded that national debts be redeemable for gold, that gold be convertible into dollars, and that all exchange rates be fixed against the dollar. The result was to lay the ground for what was to become the dollar's global hegemony. White also decided that both the Fund and the Bank would be sited in Washington.

No one was in any doubt at the time that these two bodies were designed as instruments of US economic policy. But somehow all this has been airbrushed from history. Even the admirable Joe Stiglitz believes that the World Bank was the brainchild of the British economist John Maynard Keynes (Keynes was, in fact, its most prominent opponent).[6] When the development writer Noreena Hertz claimed in the Guardian last month that "the Bush administration is a very long way from the Bank's espoused goals and mandate", she couldn't have been more wrong.[7]

From the perspective of the world's poor, there has never been a good president of the World Bank. In seeking contrasts with Wolfowitz, it has become fashionable to look back to the reign of that other Pentagon hawk, Robert McNamara. He is supposed to have become, in the words of an Observer leader, "one of the most admired and effective of World Bank presidents".[8] Admired in Washington perhaps. Robert McNamara was the man who concentrated almost all the Bank's lending on vast prestige projects – dams, highways, ports – while freezing out less glamorous causes such as health and education and sanitation. Most of the major projects he backed have, in economic or social terms or both, failed catastrophically.[9]

It was he who argued that the Bank should not fund land reform because it "would affect the power base of the traditional elite groups".[10] Instead, as Catherine Caufield shows in her book, Masters of Illusion, it should "open new land by cutting down forests, draining wetlands, and building roads to previously isolated areas".[11] He bankrolled Mobutu and Suharto, deforested Nepal,[12] trashed the Amazon,[13] and promoted genocide in Indonesia.[14] The countries in which he worked were left with unpayable debts, wrecked environments, grinding poverty and unshakeable pro-US dictators.

Except for the language in which US demands are articulated, little has changed at the Bank. In the meeting on Thursday at which Wolfowitz's nomination was confirmed, its executive directors also decided to approve the construction of the Nam Theun 2 hydroelectric dam in Laos. This will flood 6000 people out of their homes, damage the livelihoods of a further 120,000, destroy a critical ecosystem, and produce electricity not for the people of Laos but for their richer neighbours in Thailand.[15]

But it will also generate enormous construction contracts for western companies. The decision to build it was made not on Wolfowitz's watch but on that of the current president, James Wolfensohn. In practical terms, there will be little difference between the two wolves. The problem with the Bank is not the management, but the board, which is dominated by the US, the UK and the other rich nations.

The nationality of the Bank's president, which has been causing so much fuss, is of only symbolic importance. Yes, it seems grossly unfair that all its presidents are Americans, while all IMF presidents are Europeans. But it doesn't matter where the technocrat implementing the US Treasury's decisions comes from. What matters is that he's a technocrat implementing the US Treasury's decisions.

Wolfowitz's appointment is a good thing for three reasons. It highlights the profoundly unfair and undemocratic nature of decision-making at the Bank. His presidency will stand as a constant reminder that this institution, which calls on the nations it bullies to exercise "good governance and democratisation", is run like a medieval monarchy.

It also demolishes the hopeless reformism of men like George Soros and Joseph Stiglitz, who, blithely ignoring the fact that the US can veto any attempt to challenge its veto, keep waving their wands in the expectation that a body designed to project US power can magically be transformed into a body that works for the poor.[16] Had Stiglitz's attempt to tinker with the World Bank's presidency succeeded, it would simply have lent credibility to an illegitimate institution, thus enhancing its powers. With Wolfowitz in charge, its credibility plummets.

Best of all is the outside chance that the neocons might just be stupid enough to use the new wolf to blow the Bank down. The former British minister Clare Short laments that "it's as though they are trying to wreck our international systems".[17] Well, what a tragedy that would be. I would sob all the way to the party.

Martin Jacques argued convincingly in the Guardian last week that the US neocons are "reordering the world system to take account of their newly defined power and interests".[18] Wolfowitz's appointment is, he suggested, one of the "means of breaking the old order". But what this surely illustrates is the unacknowledged paradox in neocon thinking. They want to drag down the old, multilateral order and replace it with a new, American one. What they consistently fail to understand is that the "multilateral" system is in fact a projection of US unilateralism, cleverly packaged to grant the other nations just enough slack to prevent them from fighting it. Like their opponents, the neocons have failed to understand how well Roosevelt and Truman stitched up the international order in America's interests. They are seeking to replace a hegemonic system that is enduring and effective with one that is untested and (because the other nations must fight it) unstable. Anyone who believes in global justice should wish them luck.

April 5 2005

Still the Rich World's Viceroy

The glacier has begun to creak. In the world's most powerful dictator-ship, we detect the merest hint of a thaw. I am not talking about China, or Uzbekistan, Burma or North Korea. This state runs no torture cham-bers or labour camps. No one is executed, though plenty starve to death as a result of its policies. The unhurried perestroika is taking place in Washington, in the offices of the International Monetary Fund.

Like most concessions made by dictatorial regimes, the reforms seem designed not to catalyse further change, but to prevent it. By slightly increasing the shares (and therefore the voting powers) of China, South Korea, Mexico and Turkey, the regime hopes to buy off the most powerful rebel warlords, while keeping the mob at bay. It has even thrown a few coppers from the balcony for the great unwashed to scuffle over. But no one – except the leaders of the rich nations and the leader writers of just about every newspaper in the rich world – could regard this as an adequate response to its problems.

The Fund is a body with 184 members. It is run by seven of them – the US, Japan, Germany, the UK, France, Canada and Italy. These happen to be the seven countries that (with Russia) promised to save the world at the G8 meeting in 2005. The junta sustains its control by insisting that each dollar buys a vote. The bigger a country's financial quota, the more say it has over the running of the Fund. This means that the IMF is run by the countries that are least affected by its policies.

A major decision requires 85% of the vote, which ensures that the US, with 17%, has a veto over its substantial business.[1] The UK, Germany, France and Japan have 22% between them, and each has a permanent seat on the board. By a weird arrangement permitting rich nations to speak on behalf of the poor, Canada and Italy have effective control over a further 8%.[2] The other European countries are also remarkably powerful: Belgium, for example, has a direct entitlement to 2.1%, and indirect control over 5.1% of the vote: over twice the allocation of India or Brazil. Europe, Japan, Canada and the US wield a total of 63%. The 80 poorest countries, by contrast, have 10% between them.[3]

These quotas no longer even reflect real financial contributions to the running of the Fund: it now obtains much of its capital from loan repayments by its vassal states.[4] But the G7 nations still behave as if it belongs to them. They decide who runs it (the managing director is always a European and his deputy always an American) and how the money is spent. You begin to wonder why the developing countries bother to turn up.

In principle, this power is supposed to be balanced by something called the "basic vote" – 250 shares (entitling them to $25m worth of votes) are allocated to every member. But while the value of the rich countries' quotas has risen since the IMF was founded in 1944, the value of the basic votes has not. It has fallen from 11.3% of the total allocation to 2.1%.[5] The leaked paper passed to me by an excellent organisation called the Bretton Woods Project (everything we know about the IMF has to be leaked) shows that the Fund intends to democratise itself by "at least doubling" the basic vote.[6] That sorts it all out then: the 80 poorest countries will be able to claim, between them, another 0.9%. Even this pathetic concession was granted only after the African members took a political risk by publicly opposing the Fund's proposals.[7] Doubtless the US government is currently reviewing their trading status.

All this is compounded by an internal political process that looks as if it was contrived in Pyongyang, not Washington. There are no formal votes, just a "consensus process" controlled by the Dear Leaders of the G7. The decisions taken by each member state cannot be revealed to the public. Nor can the transcripts of the board's meetings, or the "working papers" on which it bases its internal reforms. Even reports by the Fund's ombudsman – the so-called "independent evaluation office" – are censored by the management, and their conclusions changed to shift the blame for the Fund's failures to its client states.[8] Needless to say, the IMF insists that the states it lends to must commit themselves to "good governance" and "transparency" if they are to receive its money.

None of this would matter so much if it had stuck to its original mandate of stabilising the international monetary system. But after the collapse of the Bretton Woods Agreement in 1971, the IMF more or less lost its mission to maintain exchange rates, and began to look for a new role. As a paper by the law professor Daniel Bradlow shows, when it amended its articles of association in 1978 they were so loosely drafted as to grant the IMF permission to interfere in almost any aspect of a country's governance.[9] It lost its influence over the economic policies of the G7 and became instead the rich world's viceroy, controlling the poorer nations at its behest. It began to micro-manage their economies without reference to the people or even their governments. Since then, no rich country has required its services, and few poor countries have been able to shake it off.

This casts an interesting light on the decision, to be endorsed at the IMF's meeting in Singapore next week, to enhance the quota for the four middle-income countries. After the Fund "helped" the struggling economies of east and south-east Asia in 1997, by laying waste to them on behalf of US hedge funds and investment companies,[10] the nations of that region decided that they would never allow themselves to fall prey to it again. They began indemnifying themselves against its tender loving care by building up their own reserves of capital. Now, just as China and South Korea have ensured that they will never again require the Fund's services, they have been granted more power to decide how it operates. In other words they are deemed fit to govern when, like the G7, they can exercise power without reaping the consequences. The smaller your stake in the outcome, the greater your vote.

None of this seems to cause any difficulties to the gatekeepers of mainstream opinion. On Saturday a leading article in the Washington Post observed that "to be legitimate, multilateral institutions must reflect the global distribution of power as it is now, not as it was when these institutions were set up more than half a century ago".[11] What a fascinating definition that is, and how wrong we must have been to imagine that legitimacy requires democracy. Hurrah for corporatism – it didn't die with Mussolini after all.

I am among those who believe that the IMF is and always will be the wrong body – inherently flawed and constitutionally unjust. But if its leaders and supporters are to persuade us that it might, one day, have a legitimate role in running the world's financial systems, they will have to do a hell of a lot better than this.

September 5 2006

On the Edge of Lunacy

Spare a thought this bleak new year for all those who rely on charity. Open your hearts, for example, to a group of people who, though they live in London, are in such desperate need of handouts that last year they received £7.6 million in foreign aid.[1] The Adam Smith Institute, the ultra-rightwing lobby group, now receives more money from Britain's Department for International Development (DfID) than Liberia or Somalia, two of the most desperate nations on earth.[2]

Are the members of the Adam Smith Institute starving? Hardly. They work in plush offices in Great Smith Street, just around the corner from the Houses of Parliament. They hold lavish receptions and bring in speakers from all over the world. Big business already contributes generously to this good cause.

It gets what it pays for. The Institute's purpose is to devise new means for corporations to grab the resources that belong to the public realm. Its president, Madsen Pirie, claims to have invented the word "privatisation".[3] His was the organisation that persuaded the Conservative government to sell off the railways, deregulate the buses, introduce the poll tax, cut the top rates of income tax, outsource local government services and start to part-privatise the National Health Service and the education system. "We propose things", Madsen Pirie once boasted, "which people regard as being on the edge of lunacy. The next thing you know, they're on the edge of policy."[4] In this spirit, his Institute now calls for the privatisation of social security, the dismantling of the NHS, and a shift from public to private education.[5] It opposes government spending on everything, in other words, except the Adam Smith Institute.

So what on earth is going on? Why are swivel-eyed ideologues in London a more deserving cause than starving refugees in Somalia? To understand what is happening, we must first revise our conception of what foreign aid is for.

Aid has always been an instrument of foreign policy. During the Cold War, it was used to buy the loyalties of states that might otherwise have crossed to the other side. Even today, the countries that receive the most money tend to be those that are of greatest strategic use to the donor nation, which is why the US gives more to Israel than it does to sub-Saharan Africa.

But foreign policy is also driven by commerce, and in particular by the needs of domestic exporters. Aid goes to countries that can buy our manufacturers' products. Sometimes it doesn't go to countries at all, but straight to the manufacturers. A US government website boasts that "the principal beneficiary of America's foreign assistance programs has always been the United States. Close to 80 percent of the U.S. Agency for International Development's contracts and grants go directly to American firms."[6]

A doctor working in Gondar hospital in Ethiopia wrote to me recently to spell out what this means. The hospital has none of the basic textbooks on tropical diseases it needs. But it does have 21 copies of an 800-page volume called Aesthetic Facial Surgery and 24 volumes of a book called Ophthalmic Pathology.[7] There is no ophthalmic pathologist in training in Ethiopia. The poorest nation on earth, unsurprisingly, has no aesthetic plastic surgeons. The US had spent $2m on medical textbooks that American publishers hadn't been able to sell at home, called them aid and dumped them in Ethiopia.

In Britain the Labour government claims to have abandoned such practices, partly because they infringe European rules on competition. But now it has found a far more effective means of helping the rich while pretending to help the poor. It is spending its money on projects that hand public goods to corporations.

It is now giving, for example, £342m to the Indian state of Andhra Pradesh.[8] This is a staggering amount of money, 15 times what it spent last year on the famine in Ethiopia. Why is Andhra Pradesh so lucky? Because its chief minister, or "chief executive" as he now likes to be known, is doing to his state what Pinochet did to Chile: handing everything that isn't nailed down, and quite a lot that is, to big business. Most of the money DfID is giving him is being used to "restructure" and "reform" the state and its utilities. His programme will dispossess 20 million people from the land,[9] and contribute massively to poverty. DfID's own report on the biggest of the schemes it is funding in the state reveals that it suffers from "major failings", has "negative consequences on food security", and does "nothing about providing alternative income for those displaced".[10] But it permits Andhra Pradesh to become a laboratory for the kind of mass privatisation the department is seeking to encourage all over the world.

In Zambia, DfID is spending just £700,000 on improving nutrition, but £56m on privatising the copper mines.[11] In Ghana, the department made its aid payments for upgrading the water system conditional on partial privatisation.[12] Foreign aid from Britain now means giving to the rich the resources that keep the poor alive.

So there are rich pickings for organisations like the Adam Smith Institute. It is being hired by DfID as a consultancy, telling countries like South Africa how to flog the family silver. It is hard to see how this helps the poor. The South African government's preparations for privatisation, according to a study by the Municipal Services Project, led to almost 10 million people having their water cut off, 10 million people having their electricity cut off, and over 2 million people being evicted from their homes for non-payment of bills.[13]

What we see here, in other words, is a revival of an ancient British charitable tradition. During the Irish potato famine, the British government made famine relief available to the starving, but only if they agreed to lose their tenancies on the land. The 1847 Poor Law Extension Act cleared Ireland for the landlords. Today, the British government is helping the corporations to seize not only the land from the poor, but also the water, the utilities, the mines, the schools, the health services and anything else they might find profitable. And you and I are paying for it.

All this was pioneered by the sainted Clare Short. Short's trick was to retain her radical credentials by publicly criticising the work of other departments, while retaining her job by pursuing in her own department policies that were far more vicious and destructive than those she attacked. Blair's trick was to keep her there, to assure Old Labour voters that they still had a voice in government, while ensuring that Short did what his corporate backers wanted.

I never thought I would hear myself say this, and I recognise that in doing so I may be handing ammunition to the right-wing lobby groups campaigning for a reduction in government spending, such as, for example, the Adam Smith Institute. But if this is what foreign aid amounts to, it seems to me that there is too much of it, rather than too little. Britain's Department for International Development is beginning to do more harm than good.

January 6 2004

This Is What We Paid for

Tony Blair has lost the election. It's true he wasn't standing, but we won't split hairs. His policies have just been put to the test by an electorate blessed with a viable opposition, and crushed. In throwing him out of their lives, the voters of the Indian state of Andhra Pradesh may have destroyed the world's most dangerous economic experiment.

Chandrababu Naidu, the state's chief minister, was the west's favourite Indian. Tony Blair and Bill Clinton both visited him in Hyderabad, the state capital. Time magazine named him South Asian of the Year; the governor of Illinois created a Naidu Day in his honour, and the British government and the World Bank flooded his state with money. They loved him because he did what he was told.

Naidu realised that to sustain power he must surrender it. He knew that as long as he gave the global powers what they wanted, he would receive the money and stature that count for so much in Indian politics. So, instead of devising his own programme, he handed the job to the US consultancy company McKinsey.

McKinsey's scheme, Vision 2020, is one of those documents whose summary says one thing and whose contents say another.[1] It begins, for example, by insisting that education and healthcare must be made available to everyone. Only later do you discover that the state's hospitals and universities are to be privatised and funded by "user charges".[2] It extols small businesses, but, way beyond the point at which most people will stop reading, reveals that it intends to "eliminate" the laws that defend them,[3] and replace small investors, who "lack motivation", with "large corporations".[4] It claims it will "generate employment" in the countryside, and goes on to insist that over 20 million people should be thrown off the land.[5]

Put all these – and the other proposals for privatisation, deregulation and the shrinking of the state – together, and you see that McKinsey has unwittingly developed a blueprint for mass starvation. You dispossess 20 million farmers from the land just as the state is reducing the number of its employees and foreign corporations are "rationalising" the rest of the workforce, and you end up with millions without work or state support. "The State's people", McKinsey warns, "will need to be enlightened about the benefits of change."[6]

McKinsey's vision was not confined to Naidu's government. Once he had implemented these policies, Andhra Pradesh "should seize opportunities to lead other states in such reform, becoming, in the process, the benchmark state".[7] Foreign donors would pay for the experiment, then seek to persuade other parts of the developing world to follow Naidu's example.

There is something familiar about all this, and McKinsey have been kind enough to jog our memories. Vision 2020 contains 11 glowing references to Chile's experiment in the 1980s. General Pinochet handed the economic management of his country to a group of neoliberal economists known as the Chicago Boys. They privatised social provision, tore up the laws protecting workers and the environment, and handed the economy to multinational companies. The result was a bonanza for big business, and a staggering growth in debt, unemployment, homelessness and malnutrition.[8] The plan was funded by the United States in the hope that it could be rolled out around the world.

Pinochet's understudy was bankrolled by Britain. In July 2001, Clare Short, then secretary of state for development, finally admitted to parliament that, despite numerous official denials, Britain was funding Vision 2020.[9] Blair's government has financed the state's economic reform programme, its privatisation of the power sector, and its "centre for good governance" (which means as little governance as possible).[10] Our taxes also fund the "implementation secretariat" for the state's privatisation programme. The secretariat is run, at Britain's insistence, by the far-right business lobby group the Adam Smith Institute.[11] The money for all this comes out of Britain's foreign aid budget.

It is not hard to see why Blair's government is doing this. As Stephen Byers revealed when he was secretary of state for trade and industry, "the UK Government has designated India as one of the UK's 15 campaign markets".[12] The campaign is to expand the opportunities for British capital. The people of Andhra Pradesh know what this means: they call it "the return of the East India Company".

This isn't the only aspect of British history that is being repeated in Andhra Pradesh. There's something uncanny about the way in which the scandals that surrounded Tony Blair during his first term in office are recurring there. Bernie Ecclestone, the formula one boss who gave

Labour £1m and later received an exemption from the ban on tobacco advertising, was negotiating with Naidu to bring his sport to Hyderabad. I have been shown the leaked minutes of a state cabinet meeting on January 10 this year.[13] McKinsey, they reveal, instructed the cabinet that Hyderabad should be a "world class futuristic city with Formula 1 as a core component". To make it viable, however, there would be a "state support requirement of Rs400–600 crs" (4–6bn rupees).[14] This means a state subsidy for formula one of £50–75m a year. It is worth noting that thousands of people in Andhra Pradesh now die of malnutrition-related diseases because Naidu previously cut the subsidy for food.

Then the minutes become even more interesting. Ecclestone's formula one, they note, should be exempted from the Indian ban on tobacco advertising. Mr Naidu had already "addressed the PM as well as the Health Minister in this regard", and was hoping to enact "state legislation creating an exemption to the Act".[15]

The Hinduja brothers, the businessmen facing criminal charges in India who were given British passports after Peter Mandelson intervened on their behalf, have also been sniffing round Vision 2020. Another set of leaked minutes I have obtained shows that in 1999 their representatives held a secret meeting in London with the Indian attorney general and the British government's export credit guarantee department, to help them obtain the backing required to build a power station under Naidu's privatisation programme.[16] When the attorney general began lobbying the Indian government on their behalf, this caused yet another Hinduja scandal.

The results of the programme we have been funding are plain to see. During the hungry season, hundreds of thousands of people in Andhra Pradesh are now kept alive on gruel supplied by charities.[17] Last year hundreds of children died in an encephalitis outbreak because of the shortage of state-run hospitals.[18] The state government's own figures suggest that 77% of the population has fallen below the poverty line.[19] The measurement criteria are not consistent, but this appears to be a massive rise. In 1993, there was one bus a week taking migrant workers from a depot in Andhra Pradesh to Mumbai. Today, there are 34.[20] The dispossessed must reduce themselves to the transplanted coolies of Blair's new empire.

Luckily, democracy still functions in India. In 1999, Naidu's party won 29 seats, leaving Congress with five. Last week, those results were precisely reversed. We can't yet vote Tony Blair out of office in Britain, but in Andhra Pradesh they have done the job on our behalf.

May 18 2004

Painted Haloes

An aura of sanctity is descending upon the world's most powerful men. On Saturday the finance ministers from seven of the G8 nations (Russia was not invited) promised to cancel the debts the poorest countries owe to the World Bank and the International Monetary Fund. The hand that holds the sword has been stayed by angels – angels with guitars rather than harps.

Who, apart from the leader writers of the Daily Telegraph,[1] could deny that debt relief is a good thing? Never mind that much of this debt – money lent by the World Bank and IMF to corrupt dictators – should never have been pursued in the first place. Never mind that, in terms of looted resources, stolen labour and now the damage caused by climate change, the rich owe the poor far more than the poor owe the rich. Some of the poorest countries have been paying more for debt than for health or education. Whatever the origins of the problem, that is obscene.

You are waiting for me to say "but", and I will not disappoint you. The "but" comes in paragraph two of the finance ministers' statement. To qualify for debt relief, developing countries must "tackle corruption, boost private sector development" and eliminate "impediments to private investment, both domestic and foreign".[2]

These are called "conditionalities". Conditionalities are the policies governments must follow before they receive aid and loans and debt relief. At first sight they look like a good idea. Corruption cripples poor nations, especially in Africa. The money that could have given everyone a reasonable standard of living has instead made a handful unbelievably rich. The powerful nations are justified in seeking to discourage it.

That's the theory. In truth, corruption has seldom been a barrier to foreign aid and loans: look at the money we have given, directly and through the World Bank and IMF, to Mobutu, Suharto, Marcos, Moi and every other premier-league crook. Robert Mugabe, the west's demon king, has deservedly been frozen out by the rich nations. But he has caused less suffering and is responsible for less corruption than Rwanda's Paul Kagame or Uganda's Yoweri Museveni, both of whom are repeatedly cited by the G8 countries as practitioners of "good governance". Their armies, as the UN has documented, are largely responsible for the meltdown in the eastern Democratic Republic of Congo (DRC), which has so far claimed 4 million lives, and have walked off with billions of dollars' worth of natural resources.[3] Yet the United Kingdom, which is hosting the G8 summit, remains their main bilateral funder. It has so far refused to make their withdrawal from the DRC a condition for foreign aid.

The difference, of course, is that Mugabe has not confined his attacks to black people; he has also dispossessed white farmers and confiscated foreign assets. Kagame, on the other hand, has eagerly supplied us with the materials we need for our mobile phones and computers – materials that his troops have stolen from the DRC. "Corrupt" is often used by our governments and newspapers to mean regimes that won't do what they're told.

Genuine corruption, on the other hand, is tolerated and even encouraged. Twenty-five countries have so far ratified the UN Convention Against Corruption, but none of them are members of the G8.[4] Why? Because our own corporations do very nicely out of it. In the UK companies can legally bribe the governments of Africa if they operate through our (profoundly corrupt) tax haven of Jersey.[5] Lord Falconer, the minister responsible for sorting this out, refuses to act. When you see the list of the island's clients, many of which sit in the FTSE-100 index, you begin to understand.

The idea swallowed by most commentators, that the conditions our governments impose help to prevent corruption, is laughable. To qualify for World Bank funding, our model client Uganda was forced to privatise most of its state-owned companies, before it had any means of regulating their sale. A sell-off that should have raised $500m for the Ugandan exchequer instead raised $2m.[6] The rest was nicked by government officials. Unchastened, the World Bank insisted that, to qualify for the debt relief programme the G8 has now extended, the Ugandan government sell off its water supplies, agricultural services and commercial bank, again with minimal regulation.[7]

And here we meet the real problem with the G8's conditionalities. They do not stop at pretending to prevent corruption, but intrude into every aspect of sovereign government. When the finance ministers say "good governance" and "eliminating impediments to private investment", what they mean is commercialisation, privatisation and the liberalisation of trade and capital flows. And what this means is new opportunities for western money.

Let's stick for a moment with Uganda. In the late 1980s, the IMF and World Bank forced it to impose "user fees" for basic healthcare and primary eduction. The purpose appears to have been to create new markets for private capital. School attendance, especially for girls, collapsed. So did health services, particularly for the rural poor. To stave off a possible revolution, Museveni reinstated free primary education in 1997 and free basic healthcare in 2001. Enrolment in primary school leapt from 2.5 million to 6 million, and the number of outpatients almost doubled. The World Bank and the IMF, which the G8 nations control, were furious.

At the donors' meeting in April 2001, the head of the Bank's delegation made it clear that, as a result of the change in policy, he now saw the health ministry as a "bad investment".[8]

There is an obvious conflict of interest in this relationship. The G8 governments claim they want to help poor countries to develop and compete successfully. But they have a powerful commercial incentive to ensure that they compete unsuccessfully, and that our companies can grab their public services and obtain their commodities at rock-bottom prices. The conditionalities we impose on the poor nations keep them on a short leash.

That's not the only conflict. The G8 finance ministers' statement insists that the World Bank and IMF will monitor the indebted countries' progress, and decide whether or not they are fit to be relieved of their burden.[9] The World Bank and IMF, of course, are the agencies that have the most to lose from this redemption. They have a vested interest in ensuring that debt relief takes place as slowly as possible.

Attaching conditions like these to aid is bad enough; it amounts to saying "we will give you a trickle of money if you give us the crown jewels." Attaching them to debt relief is in a different moral league: "we will stop punching you in the face if you give us the crown jewels." The G8's plan for saving Africa is little better than an extortion racket.

Do you still believe our newly sanctified leaders have earned their haloes? If so, you have swallowed a truckload of nonsense. Yes, they should cancel the debt. But they should cancel it unconditionally.

June 14 2005

The Corporate Continent

I began to realise how much trouble we were in when Hilary Benn, the secretary of state for international development, announced that he would be joining the Make Poverty History march on Saturday. What would he be chanting? I wondered. "Down with me and all I stand for"?

Benn is the man in charge of using British aid to persuade African countries to privatise their public services. Wasn't the march supposed to be a protest against policies like his? But its aims were either expressed or interpreted so loosely that anyone could join. This was its strength and its weakness. The Daily Mail ran pictures of Gordon Brown and Bob Geldof on its front page, with the headline "Let's Roll", showing that nothing either Live8 or Make Poverty History has done so far represents a threat to power. The G8 leaders and the business interests their summit promotes can absorb our demands for aid, debt, even slightly fairer terms of trade, and lose nothing. They can wear our colours, speak our language, claim to support our aims, and discover in our agitation not new constraints, but new opportunities for manufacturing consent. Justice, this consensus says, can be achieved without confronting power.

They invite our representatives to share their stage, we invite theirs to share ours. The economist Noreena Hertz offers, according to the commercial speakers' agency that hires her, "real solutions for businesses and individuals. Hertz teaches companies how to be smart and avoid the frictions which surface when corporate interests conflict with private life . . . the political right is not necessarily wrong."[1] Then she stands on the Make Poverty History stage and calls for poverty to be put at the top of the agenda. There is, as far as some of the MPH organisers are concerned, no contradiction; the new consensus denies that there's a conflict between ending poverty and business as usual.

The G8 leaders have seized this opportunity with both hands. Multinational corporations, they argue, are not the cause of Africa's problems, but the solution. From now on, they will be responsible for the relief of poverty.

In the United States, they have already been given control of the primary instrument of US policy towards Africa, the African Growth and Opportunity Act. The Act is a fascinating compound of professed philanthropy and raw self-interest. To become eligible for help, African countries must bring about "a market-based economy that protects private property rights", "the elimination of barriers to United States trade and investment", and a conducive environment for US "foreign policy interests".[2] In return they will be allowed "preferential treatment" for some of their products in US markets.

The important word is "some". Clothing factories in Africa will be allowed to sell their products to the US as long as they use "fabrics wholly formed and cut in the United States", or if they avoid direct competition with US products. The act, treading carefully around the toes of US manufacturing interests, is comically specific. Garments containing elastic strips, for example, are eligible only if the elastic is "less than 1 inch in width and used in the production of brassieres".[3] Even so, African countries' preferential treatment will be terminated if it results in "a surge in imports". It goes without saying that all this is classified as foreign aid. The act instructs the US Agency for International Development to develop "a receptive environment for trade and investment". What is more interesting is that its implementation has been outsourced to another agency, the Corporate Council on Africa.

The CCA is the lobby group representing the big US corporations with interests in Africa: Halliburton, Exxon Mobil, Coca-Cola, General Motors, Starbucks, Raytheon, Microsoft, Boeing, Cargill, Citigroup and others.[4] For the CCA, what is good for General Motors is good for Africa: "until African countries are able to earn greater income," it says, "their ability to buy U.S. products will be limited."[5] The US State Department has put it in charge of training African governments and businesses.[6] The CCA runs the US government's annual forum for African business, and hosts the Growth and Opportunity Act's steering committee.[7]

Now something very similar is being rolled out in the United Kingdom. Today, the Business Action for Africa summit will open in London with a message from Tony Blair. It is chaired by Sir Mark Moody Stuart, the head of Anglo American, and its speakers include executives from Shell, British American Tobacco, Standard Chartered Bank, De Beers and the Corporate Council on Africa.[8] One of its purposes is to inaugurate the Investment Climate Facility, a $550m fund that will be financed by the UK's foreign aid budget, the World Bank and the other G8 nations, but "driven and controlled by the private sector".[9] The fund will be launched by Niall Fitzgerald, currently head of Reuters, but formerly chief executive of Unilever, and before that Unilever's representative in apartheid South Africa.[10] He wants the facility, he says, to help create a "healthy investment climate" that will offer companies "attractive financial returns compared to competing destinations".[11] Anglo American and Barclays have already volunteered to help.[12]

Few would deny that one of the things Africa needs is investment. But investment by many of our multinationals has not enriched its people but impoverished them. The history of corporate involvement in Africa is a history of forced labour, evictions, murder, wars, the under-costing of resources, tax evasion and collusion with dictators. Nothing in either the Investment Climate Facility or the Growth and Opportunity Act imposes mandatory constraints on corporations. While their power and profits in Africa will be enhanced with the help of our foreign aid budgets, they will be bound only by voluntary commitments, of the kind that have been in place since 1976 and have proved useless.[13]

Just as Gordon Brown's "moral crusade" encourages us to forget the armed crusade he financed, so the state-sponsored rebranding of the companies working in Africa prompts us to forget what Shell has been doing in Nigeria, what Barclays and Anglo American and De Beers have done in South Africa, and what British American Tobacco has done just about everywhere. From now on, the G8 would like us to believe, these companies will be Africa's best friends. In the name of making poverty history, the G8 has given a new, multi-headed East India Company a mandate to govern the continent.

Without a critique of power, our campaign, so marvellously and so disastrously inclusive, will merely enhance this effort. Debt, unfair terms of trade and poverty are not causes of Africa's problems but symptoms. The cause is power: the ability of the G8 nations and their corporations to run other people's lives. Where, on the Live8 stages and at the rally in Edinburgh, was the campaign against the G8's control of the World Bank, the International Monetary Fund and the United

Nations? Where was the demand for binding global laws for multinational companies?

At the Make Poverty History march, the speakers insisted that we are dragging the G8 leaders kicking and screaming towards our demands. It seems to me that the G8 leaders are dragging us dancing and cheering towards theirs.

July 5 2005

The Flight to India

If you live in a rich nation in the English-speaking world, and most of your work involves a computer or a telephone, don't expect to have a job in five years' time. Almost every large company that relies upon remote transactions is starting to dump its workers and hire a cheaper labour force overseas. All those concerned about economic justice and the distribution of wealth at home should despair. All those concerned about global justice and the distribution of wealth around the world should rejoice. As we are, by and large, the same people, we have a problem.

Britain's industrialisation was secured by destroying the manufacturing capacity of India. In 1699 the British government banned the import of woollen cloth from Ireland, and in 1700 the import of cotton cloth (or calico) from India.[1] Both products were forbidden because they were superior to our own. As the industrial revolution was built on the textiles industry, we could not have achieved our global economic dominance if we had let them in. Throughout the eighteenth and nineteenth centuries, India was forced to supply raw materials to Britain's manufacturers, but forbidden to produce competing finished products.[2] We are rich because the Indians are poor.

Now the jobs we stole 300 years ago are returning to India. Last week the Guardian revealed that the National Rail Enquiries service is likely to move to Bangalore, in south-west India. Two days later, the

HSBC bank announced that it is cutting 4000 customer service jobs in Britain and shifting them to Asia. BT, British Airways, Lloyds TSB, Prudential, Standard Chartered, Norwich Union, BUPA, Reuters, Abbey National and Powergen have already begun to move their call centres to India. The British workers at the end of the line are approaching the end of the line.

There is a profound historical irony here. Indian workers can outcompete British workers today because Britain smashed their ability to compete in the past. Having destroyed India's own industries, the East India Company and the colonial authorities obliged its people to speak our language, adopt our working practices and surrender their labour to multinational corporations. Workers in call centres in Germany and Holland are less vulnerable than ours, as Germany and Holland were less successful colonists, with the result that fewer people in the poor world now speak their languages.

The impact on British workers will be devastating. Service jobs of the kind now being exported were supposed to make up for the loss of employment in the manufacturing industries that disappeared overseas in the 1980s and 1990s. The government handed out grants for cybersweatshops in places whose industrial workforce had been crushed by the closure of mines, shipyards and steelworks. But the companies running the call centres appear to have been testing their systems at government expense before exporting them to somewhere cheaper.

It is not hard to see why almost all of them have chosen India. The wages of workers in the service and technology industries there are roughly one-tenth of those of workers in the same sectors over here. Standards of education are high, and almost all educated Indians speak English. While British workers will take call centre jobs only when they have no choice, Indian workers see them as glamorous.[3] One technical support company in Bangalore recently advertised 800 jobs. It received 87,000 applications.[4] British call centres moving to India can choose the most charming, patient, biddable, intelligent workers the labour market has to offer.

There is nothing new about multinational corporations forcing workers in distant parts of the world to undercut each other. What is new is the extent to which the labour forces of the poor nations are also beginning to threaten the security of our middle classes. In August, the Evening Standard came across some leaked consultancy documents suggesting that at least 30,000 executive positions in Britain's finance and insurance industries are likely to be transferred to India over the next five years.[5] In the same month, the American consultants Forrester Research predicted that the US will lose 3.3 million white-collar jobs between now and 2015.[6] Most of them will go to India. Just over half of these are menial "back office" jobs, such as taking calls and typing up data. The rest belong to managers, accountants, underwriters, computer programmers, IT consultants, biotechnicians, architects, designers and corporate lawyers.[7] For the first time in history, the professional classes of Britain and America find themselves in direct competition with the professional classes of another nation. Over the next few years, we can expect to encounter a lot less enthusiasm for free trade and globalisation in the parties and the newspapers that represent them. Free trade is fine, as long as it affects someone else's job.

So a historical restitution appears to be taking place, as hundreds of thousands of jobs, many of them good ones, flee to the economy we ruined. Low as the wages for these positions are by comparison with our own, they are generally much higher than those offered by domestic employers. A new middle class is developing in cities previously dominated by caste. Its spending will stimulate the economy, which in turn may lead to higher wages and improved conditions of employment. The corporations, of course, will then flee to a cheaper country, but not before they have left some of their money behind. According to the consultants Nasscom and McKinsey, India, which is always short of foreign exchange, will be earning some $17bn a year from outsourced jobs by 2008.[8]

On the other hand, the most vulnerable communities in Britain are losing the jobs that were supposed to have rescued them. Almost two-thirds of call centre workers are women,[9] so the disadvantaged sex will slip still further behind. As jobs become less secure, multinational corporations will be able to demand ever harsher conditions of employment in an industry that is already one of the most exploitative in Britain. At the same time, extending the practices of their colonial predecessors, they will oblige their Indian workers to mimic not only our working methods, but also our accents, our tastes and our enthusiasms, in order to persuade customers in Britain that they are talking to someone down the road.[10] The most marketable skill in India today is the ability to abandon your identity and slip into someone else's.

So, is the flight to India a good thing or a bad thing? The only reasonable answer is both. The benefits do not cancel out the harm. They exist, and have to exist, side by side. This is the reality of the world order Britain established, and which is sustained by the heirs to the East India Company, the multinational corporations. The corporations operate only in their own interests. Sometimes these interests will coincide with those of one disadvantaged group, but only by disadvantaging another.

For centuries, we have permitted ourselves to ignore the extent to which our welfare is dependent on the denial of other people's. We begin to understand the implications of the system we have created only when it turns against us.

October 21 2003

How Britain Denies Its Holocausts

In reading the reports of the trial of the Turkish novelist Orhan Pamuk, you are struck by two things. The first, of course, is the anachronistic brutality of the country's laws. Mr Pamuk, like scores of other writers and journalists, is being prosecuted for "denigrating Turkishness", which means that he dared to mention the Armenian genocide in the First

World War and the killing of the Kurds in the past decade. The second is its staggering, blithering stupidity. If there is one course of action that could be calculated to turn these massacres into live issues, it is the trial of the country's foremost novelist for mentioning them.

As it prepares for accession, the Turkish government will discover that the other members of the European Union have found a more effective means of suppression. Without legal coercion, without the use of baying mobs to drive writers from their homes, we have developed an almost infinite capacity to forget our own atrocities.

Atrocities? Which atrocities? When a Turkish writer uses that word, everyone in Turkey knows what he is talking about, even if they deny it vehemently. But most British people will stare at you blankly. So let me give you two examples, both of which are as well documented as the Armenian genocide.

In his book Late Victorian Holocausts, published in 2001, Mike Davis tells the story of the famines that killed between 12 and 29 million Indians.[1] These people were, he demonstrates, murdered by British state policy.

When an El Niño drought destituted the farmers of the Deccan plateau in 1876 there was a net surplus of rice and wheat in India. But the viceroy, Lord Lytton, insisted that nothing should prevent its export to England. In 1877 and 1878, at the height of the famine, grain merchants exported a record 6.4 million hundredweight of wheat. As the peasants began to starve, government officials were ordered "to discourage relief works in every possible way".[2] The Anti-Charitable Contributions Act of 1877 prohibited "at the pain of imprisonment private relief donations that potentially interfered with the market fixing of grain prices". The only relief permitted in most districts was hard labour, from which anyone in an advanced state of starvation was turned away. Within the labour camps, the workers were given less food than the inmates of Buchenwald. In 1877, monthly mortality in the camps equated to an annual death rate of 94%.

As millions died, the imperial government launched "a militarised campaign to collect the tax arrears accumulated during the drought". The money, which ruined those who might otherwise have survived the famine, was used by Lytton to fund his war in Afghanistan. Even in places that had produced a crop surplus, the government's export policies, like Stalin's in the Ukraine, manufactured hunger. In the north-western provinces, Oud and the Punjab, which had brought in record harvests in the preceding three years, at least 1.25 million died.

Three recent books – Britain's Gulag by Caroline Elkins, Histories of the Hanged by David Anderson, and Web of Deceit by Mark Curtis – show how white settlers and British troops suppressed the Mau Mau revolt in Kenya in the 1950s. Thrown off their best land and deprived of political rights, the Kikuyu started to organise, some of them violently, against colonial rule. The British responded by driving up to 320,000 of them into concentration camps.[3] Most of the remainder – over a million – were held in "enclosed villages". Prisoners were questioned with the help of "slicing off ears, boring holes in eardrums, flogging until death, pouring paraffin over suspects who were then set alight, and burning eardrums with lit cigarettes".[4] British soldiers used a "metal castrating instrument" to cut off testicles and fingers. "By the time I cut his balls off," one settler boasted, "he had no ears, and his eyeball, the right one, I think, was hanging out of its socket."[5] The soldiers were told they could shoot anyone they liked, "provided they were black".[6] Elkins's evidence suggests that over 100,000 Kikuyu were either killed by the British or died of disease and starvation in the camps. David Anderson documents the hanging of 1090 suspected rebels – far more than the French executed in Algeria.[7] Thousands more were summarily executed by soldiers, who claimed they had "failed to halt" when challenged.

These are just two examples of at least 20 such atrocities overseen and organised by the British government or British colonial settlers. They include, for example, the Tasmanian genocide, the use of collective punishment in Malaya, the bombing of villages in Oman, the dirty war in North Yemen, the evacuation of Diego Garcia. Some of them might trigger a vague, brainstem memory in a few thousand readers, but most people would have no idea what I'm talking about. Max Hastings, on the next page, laments our "relative lack of interest in Stalin and Mao's crimes".[8] But at least we are aware that they happened.

In the Express we can read the historian Andrew Roberts arguing that for "the vast majority of its half millennium-long history, the British Empire was an exemplary force for good . . . the British gave up their Empire largely without bloodshed, after having tried to educate their successor governments in the ways of democracy and representative institutions" (presumably by locking up their future leaders).[9] In the Sunday Telegraph, he insists that "the British empire delivered astonishing growth rates, at least in those places fortunate enough to be coloured pink on the globe".[10] (Compare this to Mike Davis's central finding, that "there was no increase in India's per capita income from 1757 to 1947", or to Prasannan Parthasarathi's demonstration that "South Indian labourers had higher earnings than their British counterparts in the eighteenth century and lived lives of greater financial security".[11] In the Daily Telegraph, John Keegan asserts that "the empire became in its last years highly benevolent and moralistic". The Victorians "set out to bring civilisation and good government to their colonies and to leave when they were no longer welcome. In almost every country, once coloured red on the map, they stuck to their resolve."[12]

There is one, rightly sacred Holocaust in European history. All the others can be ignored, denied or belittled. As Mark Curtis points out, the dominant system of thought in Britain "promotes one key concept that underpins everything else – the idea of Britain's basic benevolence . . . Criticism of foreign policies is certainly possible, and normal, but within narrow limits which show 'exceptions' to, or 'mistakes' in, promoting the rule of basic benevolence."[13] This idea, I fear, is the true "sense of British cultural identity" whose alleged loss Max laments today. No judge or censor is required to enforce it. The men who own the papers simply commission the stories they want to read.

Turkey's accession to the European Union, now jeopardised by the trial of Orhan Pamuk, requires not that it comes to terms with its atrocities; only that it permits its writers to rage impotently against them. If the government wants the genocide of the Armenians to be forgotten, it should drop its censorship laws and let people say what they want. It needs only allow Richard Desmond and the Barclay brothers to buy up its newspapers, and the past will never trouble it again.

December 27 2005

A Bully in Ermine

I think I have discovered the clinching argument for closing the House of Lords. It is the presence in that chamber of a peer called Lady Tonge of Kew.

Last week, the baroness (formerly the Liberal Democrat MP Jenny Tonge) opened a debate about Botswana with an attack on the Gana and Gwi Bushmen of the Kalahari.[1] She suggested they were trying to "stay in the Stone Age", described their technology as "primitive", and accused them of "holding the government of Botswana to ransom" by resisting their eviction from their ancestral lands. How did she know? In 2002 she had spent half a day as part of a parliamentary delegation visiting one of the resettlement camps into which the Bushmen have been forced. Her guides were officials in the Botswanan government.

Lord Pearson of Rannoch, a man with whom I seldom find myself in sympathy, alleged that something was missing from her account: the trip, he claimed, including first class air travel, was funded by Debswana.[2] Debswana is the joint venture between De Beers and the government of Botswana, which owns the rights to mine diamonds in the Bushmen's land in the Kalahari.

"I took the precaution", Pearson reported, "of hiring my own interpreter, so I was able to hear exactly what some of the 200 Bushmen and their families who had recently been forcibly resettled in a camp at New Xade were saying. I heard them describe it as a place of death, where they had nothing to do but drink, take drugs and catch AIDS. Many of them felt that they had been evicted because Debswana wanted their land for its diamonds . . . I, for one, came home more convinced than ever that a great injustice was being done."[3]

He might have added that Debswana was being assisted by Hill and Knowlton, the public relations company famous for the unsavoury nature of its clients.[4] It advised the Chinese government in the wake of the Tiananmen massacre, set up lobby groups for tobacco companies, and coached the girl who told the false story about Kuwaiti babies being thrown out of incubators that helped to launch the first Gulf war.[5] Until recently, Hill and Knowlton provided "administrative services" to the parliamentary group of which Tonge and Pearson are members.[6] Now this task is discharged by the Botswanan High Commission,[7] whose line on the Bushmen is identical to Lady Tonge's. Its work on this issue is coordinated by Dawn Parr, a former employee of Hill and Knowlton's.[8] The PR company boasts on its website about how it "generated support" for Debswana among "UK parliamentarians".[9]

Tonge's timing was also unfortunate: she made this speech just six weeks after Survival International launched its campaign to try to discourage people from characterising indigenous people as primitive and living in the Stone Age.[10] It has its work cut out. Three days after Tonge gave her speech, I heard the BBC's Indonesia correspondent telling the World Service that the West Papuan's "way of life, until recently, had more in common with the Stone Age than the modern world".[11] He was probably not aware that John Kennedy approved the annexation of West Papua by the Indonesian government with the words: "those Papuans of yours are some seven hundred thousand and living in the Stone Age."[12] Stone-aged and primitive are what you call people when you want their land.

The animal theme comes up quite often too. "How can you have a Stone Age creature continue to exist in the age of computers?" asked the man who is now Botswana's president, Festus Mogae. "If the Bushmen want to survive, they must change, otherwise, like the dodo they will perish."[13] The minister for local government, Margaret Nasha, was more specific. "You know the issue of Basarwa [the Bushmen]?" she asked in 2002. "Sometimes I equate it to the elephants. We once had the same problem when we wanted to cull the elephants and people said no."[14]

When speaking to an international audience, the government takes a different line. Like Baroness Tonge, it insists that the Bushmen must be evicted from the Central Kalahari game reserve for their own good. "It has never been easy for Government to extend social services to the sparsely populated remote rural settlements. People have thus been encouraged to move into settlements with schools, health clinics and other training and vocational opportunities."[15]

"Encouraged" is an interesting word. Ten days ago a United Nations committee noted "persistent allegations that residents were forcibly removed, through, in particular, such measures as the termination of basic and essential services inside the Reserve, the dismantling of existing infrastructures, the confiscation of livestock, harassment and ill-treatment of some residents by police and wildlife officers, as well as the prohibition of hunting and restrictions on freedom of movement inside the Reserve".[16] People who have tried to remain in their lands have been tortured, beaten and starved.[17]

Since 2002, the Gana and Gwi have been seeking a court order allowing them to return to their lands. But the government, aware that eventually the Bushmen's supporters will run out of money, has been dragging out the case for as long as possible.[18] It has now repealed the section of the constitution to which they were appealing.

When, in the 1960s, the Innu of Canada were evicted from their lands by similar means and for similar purposes, they immediately fell prey to alcoholism, petrol-sniffing and suicide. Half the population now has diabetes; 35% of the Innu children in schools in Labrador have foetal alcohol syndrome. Suicide rates are around 12 times higher than the national average.[19] This will be a familiar story to anyone who has witnessed the forcible relocation of indigenous people. Though the Botswanan government refuses to keep separate statistics for the evicted Gana and Gwi, they appear to be succumbing to the same psychic and physical collapse with extraordinary speed.[20]

Lady Tonge later explained that she used the word primitive to mean belonging to "another age".[21] But the Gana and the Gwi, like indigenous people everywhere, exist today, and what they do belongs to the present as much as anything anyone else does. There is no scala natura of human validity which places them at the bottom and us at the top. Faced with a different set of ecological conditions and economic constraints to ours, the Bushmen trying to return to their lands see that their traditional practices and technologies, or some of them at any rate, are more likely to ensure their survival than sitting in a tin shed drinking moonshine. They can also understand the benefits of western healthcare and education, but they want to use them if and as they choose, not as the paternalists in Botswana or the House of Lords determine.

I would like to be able to say that Lady Tonge's characterisation of the Bushmen is itself primitive, meaning that it belongs to another age. But this would not be true. Not only are indigenous people still widely characterised as savages in order that their land can be seized; but there is still a House of Lords in which unelected people like Baroness Tonge talk like Victorian missionaries of the need to rescue people from their darkness. The incumbents of the House of Lords are just as much part of the modern world as the iPod and the Bushman hunting bow. Unlike the Bushmen, however, they do seem to merit eviction.

March 21 2006

Lady Tonge: An Apology

I now realise that I have misunderstood Baroness Tonge. When she stood up in the House of Lords last week and accused the Gana and Gwi Bushmen of trying to stay in the Stone Age and of holding the Botswanan government to ransom by resisting eviction from their lands, I thought she was a bully, using her unelected position to attack some of the most vulnerable people on earth.

When she appeared on the Today programme two days later and, having found herself in a hole, started digging a mineshaft, I thought she was a fool.

When I started reading her Response column in the Guardian today,[1] and saw her angry reply to allegations that had not been made – that she has been bribed and that her integrity is in question – I began to wonder whether there might be more to this story than I first supposed.

But when I reached the bottom of her column, and read that she, like me, wishes to see the closure of the House of Lords, all became clear. I owe Lady Tonge an apology. She is not a bully, a fool or a stooge. She is a brave and brilliant political campaigner. She is trying to abolish the upper house, and the method she has chosen is satire.

Her strategy works like this. First, she accepts a peerage, styles herself "Baroness Tonge of Kew in the London Borough of Richmond upon Thames", and adopts the airs and graces appropriate to that station. Then, she selects the traditional topic of conversation in the House of Lords – evicting impoverished people from their lands – and hams it up magnificently. Then, in perfect mimicry of the peers who for centuries have claimed from those benches that they know what is best for the poor, she hilariously pretends that a land-grabbing exercise is in fact a social welfare programme.

She plays all this with a perfectly straight face, until her listeners are gasping with rage and incredulity, and demanding that she and all the other barons and baronesses are flung out on their butts and replaced with elected representatives.

Greater love hath no baroness than this, that a baroness lay down her credibility for her subjects. Instead of attacking her, as I have done, we should offer our gratitude for this extraordinary act of self-sacrifice. She has shown us what we must do. We must call for that which she most desires: her expulsion from the legislature, along with all the other unelected halfwits in the House of Lords.

March 24 2006

Arguments With Money

Property Paranoia

A few days ago, after a furious argument, I was thrown out of a wood where I have walked for over 20 years. I must admit that I did not behave very well. As I walked away I did something I haven't done for a long time: I gave the gamekeeper a one-fingered salute. In my defence I would plead that I was overcome with unhappiness and anger.

The time I have spent in that wood must amount to months. Every autumn I would spend days there, watching the turning colours or grubbing for mushrooms and beechmast and knapped flints. In the summer I would look for warblers and redstarts. I saw a nightjar there once. It was one of the few peaceful and beautiful places in my part of the world that's within a couple of miles of a station: I could escape from the traffic without the help of a car. Part of me, I feel, belongs there. Or it did.

It is not that I wasn't trespassing before. Nor has the status of the land changed; it is still owned, as far as I know, by the same private estate. No one tried to stop me in those 20-odd years because no one was there. But now there is a blue plastic barrel every 50 yards, and the surrounding fields are planted with millet and maize. The wood has been turned into a pheasant run. Having scarcely figured in the landowner's books, it must now be making him a fortune. And I am perceived as a threat.

The words that rang in my ears as I stomped away were these. "You've got your bloody right to roam now – why do you need to come here?"

It struck me that this could be a perverse outcome of the legislation for which I spent years campaigning: that the right to walk in certain places is seen by landowners as consolidating their relations with the public. All that is not permitted will become forbidden.

But this, I suspect, is a secondary problem. The more important one is surely the surge of money foaming through the south-east of England. A thousand woods can be filled with pheasants and still there are not enough to serve the people who have the money required – the many hundreds of pounds a day – to shoot them. We were told that the rising tide would lift all boats. But I feel I am drowning in it.

Two weeks ago, writing in the Financial Times, the economist Andrew Oswald observed that "the hippies, the Greens, the road protesters, the downshifters, the slow-food movement – all are having their quiet revenge. Routinely derided, the ideas of these down-to-earth philosophers are being confirmed by new statistical work by psychologists and economists."[1] As I qualify on most counts, I will regard this as a vindication.

Oswald's point is that the industrialised countries have not become happier as they've become richer. Rates of depression and stress have risen, and people report no greater degree of satisfaction with their lives than their poorer ancestors did. In the United States, the sense of well-being has actually declined. One of the problems is that "humans are creatures of comparison . . . it is relative income that matters: when everyone in a society gets wealthier, average well-being stays the same."[2]

The same point has been made recently by the New Economics Foundation,[3] and by Professor Richard Layard, in his book Happiness.[4] New developments in both psychological testing and neurobiology allow happiness to be measured with greater confidence than before. Layard cites research that suggests that it peaked in the United Kingdom in 1975. Beyond a certain degree of wealth – an average GDP of around $20,000 per head – "additional income is not associated with extra happiness". Once a society's basic needs and comforts have been met, there is no point in becoming richer.

I am astonished by the astonishment with which their findings have been received. Compare, for example, these two statements:

"So one secret of happiness is to ignore comparisons with people who are more successful than you are: always compare downwards, not upwards." (Richard Layard, 2005)[5]

"It put me to reflecting, how little repining there would be among mankind, at any condition of life, if people would rather compare their condition with those that are worse, in order to be thankful, than be always comparing them with those which are better, to assist their murmurings and complainings." (Daniel Defoe, 1719)[6]

We have been led, by the thinking of people like the psychologist John B Watson and the economist Lionel Robbins, to forget what everyone once knew: that wealth and happiness are not the same thing.

Comparison is not the only reason the professors of happiness cite for our failure to feel better as we become richer. They point to the fact that we become habituated to wealth. Layard calls this "the hedonic treadmill". They blame the longer hours we work and our deteriorating relationships. But there is something I think they have missed: that wealth itself can become a source of deprivation.

Having money enhances your freedom. You can travel further and you can do more when you get there. But other people's money restricts your freedom. Where you once felt free, now you find fences. In fact, you must travel further to find somewhere in which you can be free.

As people become richer, and as they can extract more wealth from their property, other people become more threatening to them. We know that the fear of crime is a cause of unhappiness, but so is the sense of being seen as a potential criminal. The spikes and lights and cameras proclaim that society is not to be trusted, that we live in a world of Hobbesian relations. The story they tell becomes true, as property paranoia makes us hate each other. The harmless wanderer in the woods becomes a mortal enemy.

It is hard to see how that plague of pheasants could be deemed to have caused a net increase in happiness. A group of very wealthy people, who already have an endless choice of activities, have one more wood in which to shoot. The rest of us have one less wood in which to walk. The landowners tell us that by putting down birds they have an incentive to preserve the woods; this was one of the arguments the gamekeeper used as he was throwing me off. But what good does that do us if we are not allowed to walk there?

The Countryside and Rights of Way Act of 2000, which granted us the right to roam on mountains, moors, heath, downland and commons, has surely increased the sum of human happiness. But in those parts of the country that retain very little habitat of that kind (because it has been destroyed or enclosed by the landowners), the gains we made then might already have been cancelled out by the losses, as the landlords' new opportunities for making money reduce our opportunities for leaving money behind.

We need the full set of rights we were once promised, and which, in Scotland, have already been granted: access to the woods, the rivers and the coast, as well as the open country. But as these places are turned into money-making monocultures, the question changes. Will we still want to visit them?

January 31 2006

Britain's Most Selfish People

What greater source of injustice could there be, that while some people have no home, others have two? Yet the vampire trade in second homes keeps growing – by 3% a year – uninhibited by government or by the conscience of the buyers. Every purchase of a second house deprives someone else of a first one. But to speak out against it is to identify yourself as a killjoy and a prig.

If you travel to Worth Matravers, the chocolate-box village in Dorset in which 60% of the houses are owned by ghosts,[1] you will not find hordes of homeless people camping on the pavements in cardboard boxes. The market does not work like that. Young people from the village, unable to buy locally, have moved away and contributed to the housing pressure somewhere else. The impacts of the ghost market might be invisible to the purchasers, but this does not mean they aren't real. Second home owners are among the most selfish people in the United Kingdom.

In England and Wales there are 250,000 second homes.[2] In England there are 221,000 people classed as single homeless or living in hostels or temporary accomodation (these desperate cases comprise about 24% of those in need of social housing).[3] I am not arguing that if every underused house were turned back into a home the problem of acute homelessness would be solved. I am arguing that homelessness has been exacerbated by the government's failure to ensure that houses are used for living in.

This issue received some rare press coverage last week when the Affordable Rural Housing Commission published its report.[4] It suggested that second home owners might be taxed more heavily in some places, or that planning permission should be required to turn a home into a ghost house. Its ideas, though mild and tentative, were received with fury. "If the Government adopts these proposals," the Telegraph roared, "it will be in order further to punish middle-class voters and to benefit from a grievance culture stoked by envy."[5] In the Guardian, Simon Jenkins suggested that the commission's proposals would deny "existing homeowners the value of their property and thus mobility for themselves and their children. It is a crazy wealth tax on the rural poor . . . To imply that those bringing new money and, in many cases, new economic activity to rural Britain are a social evil is leftwing archaism."[6]

If caring about homelessness makes you a leftwing dinosaur, I raise my claw. It is true that clamping down on second homes would suppress house prices in the countryside, by a little. That is part of the point. But it is not as if rural homeowners are suffering from low values. The day before Simon's column was published, the Halifax produced figures showing that the average rural house costs £208,699 (or 6.7 times average annual earnings), while the average town house costs £176,115.[7] Jenkins seems to be asking us to care more about the profits of those who are already rich in capital than about the people who have nothing but a box to sleep in. It is also true that at weekends and during the holiday season, second home owners can bring new trade to local shops – especially the kind of picturesque boutiques that smoke their own fish and sell jam jars with paper hats on. But for the rest of the year, because the village is half empty, business dies.

The environmental impact must also be stupendous. It is hard enough to accommodate the houses we do need in the countryside, let alone the fake homes now being built for weekenders. Open the pages of any property supplement and you will find advertisements for new "holiday lodges" in Cornwall, Dorset, Pembrokeshire and Norfolk. Regional airports are springing up (or trying to spring up) wherever City brokers start pricing out the locals. (People with second homes abroad cause even more damage: one survey suggests they take an average of six return flights a year[8]). This is to say nothing of the environmental costs of maintaining two homes, and doubtless leaving the security lights on and the appliances on standby while you continue your life elsewhere.

For all these reasons, I believe the commission's proposals don't go far enough. It treats second home ownership as a local problem, confined to the most desirable parts of the countryside. It doesn't consider the wider contribution that owning them makes to home-lessness, or to the destruction of the environment. Nor does it make the point, almost always missed by the media, that the majority of second homes (155,000 of the 250,000) are in towns and cities, where middle-aged businessmen turn what might have been starter flats into pieds-à-terre. I accept that it's a rural housing commission, but I can't help wondering whether this acknowledgment might have caused some trouble for Elinor Goodman, the commission's chair, who has a second home in Westminster.[9]

I would like to see the ownership of second homes become prohibitively expensive, wherever they might be. It remains cheaper to own a second house than to own a first one. The government has reduced the rebate on council tax for ghost homes from 50% to 10%,[10] but it still seems outrageous that there should be a discount of any size. Worse, as a letter to the Guardian pointed out yesterday, people are buying up weekend homes as fake holiday lets and setting these "loss-making businesses" against tax.[11] Plainly this loophole needs to be closed. But why not a 500% council tax for all second homes, which local authorities would be obliged to hypothecate: to use, in other words, for new social housing? It wouldn't stop the richest people from buying extra houses, but at least the people at the bottom of the ladder would get something back.

We're often told that punitive taxes of this kind wouldn't work, because couples could register their homes separately. But this would surely be possible only for people who are neither married nor in a civil partnership. It doesn't stop the government from levying capital gains tax.

The real problem is that almost every MP with a constituency outside London has two homes or more, and there is scarcely a senior journalist who is not sucking the life out of a village somewhere, or a paper that does not depend on advertising by estate agents. Two weeks ago the Sunday Times revealed that the Labour MP Barbara Follett, who owns a £2m house in her constituency (in Stevenage), a flat in Soho and homes in Antigua and Cape Town, has claimed £76,357 in Commons expenses over the past four years for her London pad.[12] Perhaps it isn't hard to see why MPs aren't clamouring for something to be done. On Friday, Peter Mandelson – the man who says what Blair thinks – told a conference that Labour's primary challenge was to find solutions "to the angst of the hard-working middle-class . . . It's not old Labour territory we have forgotten and which is detaching itself but the New Labour territory we have occupied since 1997 which is at risk".[13]

In other words, the chances of getting the government to force the abandonment of second homes are approximately zero. But that should not stop us from pointing out that it is unacceptable to let the rich deprive the poor of their homes.

May 23 2006

Theft Is Property

For the past fortnight, the assorted voices of reason have been in uproar about the strange case of the owner-occupier squatters. In 1977, Jim Sykes and Sheila Fahy slipped into a derelict house in Islington. They lived, according to the Daily Mail, like ghosts, neither tending the front garden nor putting out rubbish, but they registered the property as their address. They acquired "possessory title" and, a few weeks ago, sold the house for £103,000.

The case has now been complicated by the discovery on the part of the Sunday Times of the original owner of the property, an old man who, like Tess of the D'Urbervilles, was probably perfectly happy until he was told he should have been entitled to greater things. He said he would be seeking legal advice to establish his rights. He does not seem to have much of a case. According to the 1980 Limitation Act, "No action shall be brought by any person to recover any land after the expiration of twelve years from the date on which the right of action accrued to him." Mr Rosamond let his chance slip by in 1989.

MPs are reported to be outraged, and are making "angry demands for a change in the law". They are on dangerous ground. The Palace of

Westminster is stuffed with landowners whose family fortunes were built on the statute of limitation. Many of the commoners, copyholders and small freeholders who were divested of their rights by enclosure had a solid legal case for retaining their land, but no practical means of fighting it. In the Scottish Highlands, thousands of cottars and runrig commoners were shoved off by the ancestors of some of our noble lords at the point of a pike, and forced on to ships bound for the Americas. The great-grandchildren of some of the dispossessed are still alive today.

All land ownership is in one way or another questionable. How many legal rights were thrust aside by William I's seizure of England? Or by the Belgae's dispossession of the former inhabitants of Kent? The notion of the absolute ownership of land and standing property is a comparatively novel one, even in many parts of Britain.

While the MPs clamouring for Mr Rosamond's rights might be quietly nudged by their more calculating colleagues, some of their constituents could stir up a lively fuss. The Advisory Service for Squatters reports that most enquiries about the use of the Limitation Act come from middle-class owner-occupiers who have surreptitiously extended their gardens on to derelict land or into a deceased neighbour's field.

The historical limitation of land claims is an explosive issue all over the world. Germany's reunification treaty allowed for the return of property seized by the Nazis up until 1945, and the communists from 1948 onwards, but not for the restitution of land expropriated by the Soviet occupation of 1945–8. Six years on, the former owners are still fighting furiously for recognition.

In South Africa, the Department of Land Affairs, which is handing back land seized by the apartheid government, has decided to consider only those claims arising since 1913. It has so far resisted several applications dating back to the seventeenth century. In the former Yugoslavia, just as much as on the West Bank, historical assertions and refutations of ownership are among the sources of enduring conflict.

The Helms-Burton law currently pitting the United States against its trading partners is all about old land claims: it imposes penalties on foreign companies owning property in Cuba that was seized from US companies or citizens during the revolution in 1959. The legislation begs the question of how the plaintiffs got their land in the first place. Expropriation and fraud were, of course, the means by which all white land ownership in the Americas and Caribbean was established.

All over the world, statutes of limitation were devised to support landowners' claims against those of the dispossessed. But as most of the major land-grabbing in Britain was completed long ago, the progressive way to change the law may be to reduce, rather than extend, the period of limitation. Jim Paton of the Advisory Service for Squatters suggests six years, which would bring land law into line with laws governing other forms of property. This might encourage the socially beneficial functions of squatting, pulling empty and derelict houses back into circulation.

But if MPs really do want to go ahead and repeal the Limitation Act, then let them, and we'll all have fun scouring our family trees for evidence of peasant proprietorship in the eleventh century. But we should not expect the owner-occupiers on whose behalf they have been huffing to thank them for it.

July 18 1996

Expose the Tax Cheats

Behind every great fortune there are two crimes: the crime required to obtain it, and the crime required to maintain it. Well, that isn't quite true. There may be no moral difference between evading tax and avoiding it, but there is a legal one. If a rich man is well advised, he can lawfully keep every penny to himself.

Until this has been sorted out, there is precious little point in proposing, as both the Liberal Democrats and a group of rebel Labour MPs did last week, that income tax be increased to 50% for people earning more than £100,000 a year.[1] It is just, it is necessary, but it simply raises the incentive for the very rich to find new means of staying that way.

Tax avoidance in the United Kingdom, according to the Tax Justice Network, deprives the Exchequer of between £25bn and £85bn a year.[2] It's hard to get your head round these figures, until you see that the low one more or less equates to the projected public sector deficit for this financial year.[3] The high figure represents 74% of the income tax the Exchequer receives.[4] It is more than we spend on the National Health Service.[5] The super-rich are fleecing us.

Gordon Brown keeps promising to deal with them, and keeps ensuring that he does no such thing. In his budget speech this year, he made bold claims about closing existing loopholes, before rejecting the only measure that could guarantee that new ones don't open up: a "general anti-avoidance rule". This rule would have made all tax avoidance measures illegal, whether they were devised before or after it was introduced.

A few minutes after his brave assault on tax cheats, Brown announced "an overall reduction of 40,500 staff" at the Inland Revenue and Customs and Excise. No one made the connection. Two years ago Nick Davies completed an exhaustive investigation of the Revenue for the Guardian. He discovered that the government's efforts to catch tax avoiders had already "collapsed in a heap of mismanagement and staff cuts". "All the specialist offices are struggling with too few experienced staff" as a result of massive cuts during the 1990s.[6]

In his speech in Brighton yesterday, Brown mentioned tax policy just once, when he scoffed at one of the means – European tax harmonisation – that would have made it harder for the rich to shift their money overseas.

The problem is that there is almost no public pressure for a real war on tax avoidance. Last week the Tax Justice Network opened an office in London to try to focus attention on the issue. But it's not likely to feature much in the corporate press. Patience Wheatcroft, the business editor of the Times, attacks the Treasury for regarding tax avoidance as "tantamount to extreme wickedness".[7] Coincidentally, her employer, Rupert Murdoch, is the most successful tax avoider of all. When the Daily Telegraph was owned by Lord Black, it argued that people have "a legal and moral right to work out how to pay as little tax as possible, a right which it is in the interest of all citizens to uphold".[8] It's not very likely to change its position: its new owners, the Barclay brothers, live in tax exile in Monaco. The tabloids slaughter the welfare cheats, and spare the tax cheats.

Understaffed, underfunded, detested, the Inland Revenue has found that the easiest way of dealing with its crisis is to appease the avoiders. In 2002 Nick Davies reported that it was covering for the corporations and the super-rich by refusing to release its figures on enforcement.[9]

My own, more limited, experience suggests that nothing has changed. I sent the Inland Revenue a list of questions last week. Is it true, I asked, that (as the Liberal Democrats have claimed) "the poorest fifth of the population pay a higher percentage of their income in tax than the richest fifth"? Has the contribution from the richest fifth been rising or declining? Is it true that there has been a shift of income tax receipts from the rich to the poor and middling over the past 10 years? What proportion of total public revenue does income tax provide? Has this been rising or falling?

The Revenue's press officer rang me back. "These questions", he told me, "are blatantly political."[10] Eventually he promised to send me an email. When it came through, the answer to all of them was: "No such analysis is published by the Inland Revenue."[11] I asked him whether the Revenue has produced an estimate of the amount of money lost through tax avoidance. It hasn't.

This is mind-blowing. The Inland Revenue claims that it has made no attempt to discover whether or not its policies are working, and whether or not the results are fair.

So, if the super-rich won't pay, because no one's interested in making them pay, what on earth can be done? How can the public's interest in fair taxation be revived? How could the government find the courage to stop the tax cheats?

I have a cruel and unusual proposal: everyone's tax returns should be published. If the teachers and dustmen of this country could see that certain multimillionaires are paying less tax than they are, they'd be so angry that the government would surely be obliged to act.

We had a taste of this four years ago, when the Sunday Times obtained a copy of the tax returns submitted by Lord Levy, the multi-millionaire Labour fundraiser. In the year 1998–9, he paid only £5000. Every lowly taxpayer in the country was scandalised. Levy denounced the newspaper for using details that had been obtained illegally. He claimed that he had been working for charity, and had started a new business that wasn't yet paying for itself. This might be true, but unless someone steals his subsequent tax returns, we have no way of knowing. Why shouldn't public funds be a matter of public record?

I put this to the Inland Revenue. "Taxpayer confidentiality is of paramount importance," it told me.[12] I tried out the same proposal with the human rights group Liberty, and this time I was surprised. "I think our position would be that we're in favour of transparency, so we wouldn't object to it," their spokesman told me. "There would be privacy implications, but we wouldn't be desperately hostile."[13]

Of course, this public information is also private information. But we already have access to a far more private set of data: wages. By looking through the job adverts, we can work out more or less what every employee in the country is paid. The trade unions bargain collectively and publicly over every term and condition. The salaries of the directors of public companies are not only made public, they are splashed all over the papers. Does anyone complain that his civil liberties are being infringed? If we can see how much people earn, it is hard to understand why we shouldn't see how much they pay.

The rich, of course, would go beserk. But as their newspapers are always reminding us, if people have nothing to hide, they have nothing to fear. We know where our money goes. Why can't we see where it comes from?

September 28 2004

Bleeding Us Dry

I have in my hands the epitaph for the first New Labour government. It consists of just two lines, contained in a table faxed to me by the Department of Health. The first line reads: Available beds in England, 1996–1997: 198,848. The second line reads: Available beds in England, 1999–2000: 186,290.[1] In these figures lies the real endowment that our radical government has bequeathed to the nation.

Labour's manifesto maintains that the NHS has "grown by a third" since 1997, and boasts that the government has overseen "the biggest sustained increase" in spending in the history of the health service. We know that its investment figures commonly turn out to be less impressive than they first appear. But there's no question that it has poured many billions of pounds into the NHS, partly to meet its promise of a sustained reduction in waiting times – a promise that can be met only by increasing the number of available beds. So when we discover that bed numbers have fallen by 12,500 in England (and some 5000 in Scotland), we can see that something is seriously wrong. Our money has evaporated. I think I have just found out where it's gone.

As readers of this column will, by now, be aware, the private finance initiative (under which much of the country's new infrastructure is being built) is a pernicious scam. The public hospitals, roads, schools and prisons constructed with private money generally cost more than their public equivalents, while delivering worse services. As private companies, unlike the government, seek to make a healthy profit on their investment, this should scarcely be surprising. But what I have discovered now suggests that the problem is far graver than anyone had guessed. Our money is being siphoned out of the NHS before the privately financed hospitals receive a single patient.

The Norfolk and Norwich university hospital is one of the biggest PFI schemes in Britain. It was bitterly opposed by local people. The old city-centre buildings will be shut and the land they occupy sold for executive housing. The new hospital is being built on greenfield land five miles from the centre of Norwich. But what upsets the people of Norfolk most is that, though its cost has risen from an initial estimate of £90m to the current £229m, the new hospital will provide only 953 beds, in comparison with the 1207 in the existing buildings. If the new complex costs so much, why is it so small? I think I have stumbled across part of the answer.

I have found definitive evidence that Octagon Healthcare, the private consortium building the hospital, will soon be in a position to suck £70m out of the project, over and above the profits it is due to make.[2] It can extract this money from the hospital scheme by means of a clever, complex but entirely legal process called "refinancing".

When a consortium has been chosen by the government to build a privately financed hospital, it borrows money from the banks. The interest rates the banks charge depend partly on how risky they believe the project to be. Once the hospital has been built, however, most of the risk disappears. And PFI schemes now turn out to be considerably less risky than the banks first assumed, not least because the government has guaranteed the private companies that their profits come first. If the NHS is faced with a choice of leaving patients to die in hospital corridors or paying the money it owes to the consortia, it is now legally and contractually bound to honour its financial commitments.

This means that when the corporations complete their hospital, they can borrow against their future earnings at a lower rate than before, and extend the period over which they must repay the money. So they re-borrow the same money more cheaply, pay off their original creditors, and then pocket the difference. The potential gains are enormous. Octagon Healthcare's five shareholders – Barclays Bank, the construction company John Laing, the financiers Innisfree and 3i, and the service providers Serco – invested some £30m of their own money. The figures I have seen show that they could walk away with £70m even before they start charging the NHS for their services.

All this might sound very boring and technical. But that £70m is money that would have stayed within the NHS had the hospital been publicly financed. It represents 1% of the government's entire 14-year hospital building programme. It is enough, by itself, to build a medium-sized hospital. And what is happening in Norwich is happening all over the country: scores of PFI projects are being refinanced by their shareholders, draining billions of pounds from our essential infrastructure.[3]

This refinancing represents just part of the difference between the terms on which the government can borrow and the terms on which private companies can borrow. Governments are regarded by lenders as a safer bet than corporations. PFI will always offer worse value for money than public funding because the debt required to support it costs more.

When I spoke to Octagon Healthcare's general manager, he stressed that the refinancing deal hasn't happened yet, and that financial conditions may change between now and the hospital's completion in the autumn.[4] But he agreed that £70m is a figure he has heard. He insisted that the hospital remains good value for money. Every PFI proposal, he pointed out, is tested by the NHS and the Treasury; if it isn't cheaper than its public equivalent, it won't be commissioned.

In principle, he's right. In practice, value for money has nothing to do with it. In July 1997, Alan Milburn, the health secretary, announced that new hospitals would not be built with public money: "it's PFI or bust."[5] He inherited this policy from the Tories, who commissioned the Norfolk and Norwich scheme. They made it clear to the NHS that whatever the financial case looked like there was no point in applying to the government for funding.

In previous columns and in my book Captive State I've shown how PFI projects are manipulated. I've seen how hospital refurbishment schemes are rejected because they are too cheap, and replaced with more lucrative demolition and rebuilding projects, which allow the companies to charge higher rents and sell valuable city-centre land.[6] But what these new findings show is that the private finance initiative will always deliver bad value for money, however it is conducted. It is a gift to big business and a disaster for everyone else.

Suddenly the decline in bed numbers makes sense. However much the government pours into the NHS, the service will continue to shrink, as our money is drained into the shareholders' accounts.

I can't blame the companies involved in PFI for taking everything they can get: their directors have, after all, a legal duty to maximise the value of their shares. But a government that lets them do it at public expense is a government unfit for office. Tony Blair has been asking us to "put schools and hospitals first" when we go to the polls on Thursday.[7] If you were to do as he suggests, you would vote for a change of government.

June 5 2001

Five years later, the refinancing story finally received widespread attention. This is how it evolved. As you will see, the deal turned out to be even bigger than I predicted.

An Easter Egg Hunt

Whenever a new scandal about the private finance initiative emerges, the government and its friends in the financial press blame it on "teething problems". When the first contracts permitting private companies to build and run our public services were signed, the argument goes, our civil servants didn't understand that they were being fleeced.

If only they had known then what they know today, they would have obtained better value for public money.

This, for example, was the argument made by the Financial Times last week, in response to the latest revelations about the "refinancing" of the Norfolk and Norwich university hospital, which allowed a group of private companies to carry off a windfall of £95m. "Acquiring wisdom can be an expensive business," its leader sighed. "Public sector and private companies now know much more about the private finance initiative than they did when it began."[1] The "hard lessons" they learnt will ensure that such mistakes will not happen again.

This story, though endlessly repeated, is nonsense. The bonus the corporations found in the hospital contract was not a mistake. It had been left there deliberately. It was a sweetener, hidden from the public, that was designed to make the private finance initiative attractive to private capital.

The new report on the hospital's refinancing, published last week by the House of Commons public accounts committee, explains how the Octagon consortium – a collaboration by Barclays, Serco, John Laing, 3i and Innisfree – managed to treble its rate of return on the hospital scheme, from 19% to 60%.[2] In 2003, five years after signing the contract, the corporations renegotiated the loans they used to build the hospital, obtaining lower rates of interest while increasing the payback time. This enabled them to extract their money, to great financial advantage, at the beginning of the project, rather than taking it gradually all the way through. In doing so, they managed greatly to reduce their own financial risk, while increasing the risk to which the hospital trust is exposed.

The trust, understandably, felt it was entitled to a share of the new money. But because there was no provision in the contract granting it any rights to a refinancing windfall, it had to make the most extraordinary concessions to obtain the miserly portion, £34m, it eventually extracted. It agreed to pay up to £257m more than it would otherwise have done if it ends the contract early. To help the investors extract more money, it agreed to extend the length of the contract from 34 years to 39. As it is impossible to predict clinical needs so far in advance, this increases the risk that the NHS will end up paying for services it cannot use. Unlike the companies, which took their share of the new money immediately, the hospital trust will receive its portion over 35 years. The chair of the public accounts committee – a Conservative who seldom loses sleep over excessive corporate profits – described the deal as "the unacceptable face of capitalism".[3]

All this appears to position the Norfolk and Norwich NHS trust, which negotiated the contract, somewhere on the spectrum between naive and raving mad. But it was nothing of the kind. It knew that the original deal offered terrible value for public money. But it had no choice. It was instructed to accept the corporations' terms by the Department of Health. Because this information was not included in the committee's summary, it was ignored by the press. But it is a theme to which the rest of the report keeps returning.

"Although the Department was aware of the potential for refinancing when entering this contract," the MPs reveal, "there was no contractual arrangement to share in refinancing gains."[4] Once the renegotiation began, the hospital was unable to demand more than 29% of the new money because "the Department . . . considered that it would have been inappropriate for the Trust to seek a larger share". The trust decided to take its money over 35 years, rather than immediately, "under guidance from the Department". As one of the Labour members of the committee, Ian Davidson, pointed out to the man from the health department: "it seems to me that you were tying hand and foot the trust in terms of what the limits of their expectation ought to be."[5]

Last week a spokesman for the hospital trust told me that it was "very much alive to the prospects of refinancing and wanted to include it in the contract. The advice centrally was to drop that issue. The Department was not keen to frighten the horses."[6]

After the report was published, another of the committee's members, the Conservative MP Richard Bacon, spelt it out still more clearly on his website. "The Department of Health would not allow the hospital to include a refinancing clause in the original contract. This meant the hospital had no right to receive any proceeds from the refinancing at all, let alone the 29% share it eventually secured. And that right was only obtained by taking on huge extra potential liabilities."[7]

"The Treasury had guidance specifically saying there should be no refinancing clauses," he told me. "It was a lure to get the private sector involved . . . Ultimately it all stems from Treasury guidance. It was the Treasury prohibiting refinancing clauses."[8]

The deal, in other words, was an Easter egg hunt. In order to persuade the corporations to participate, the government left an extra £95m in the contract for them to find. This money represents the difference between the financial risk the government claimed they would carry and the far smaller financial risk (attracting lower rates of interest) to which they were actually exposed. While the drafting of the contract began under the Tories, it was completed, by Labour, in 1998. By forcing the trust to strike a bad deal, the government appears to have been negotiating on behalf of the corporations and against the public interest.

The Treasury's press office wouldn't answer my questions on the grounds that it was "a Department of Health issue".[9] The Department of Health told me that the government had not demanded a refinancing share in its early PFI contracts because that would not have offered "value for money".[10] If the department believes that letting private companies walk off with £95m of free money represents good value, it's not surprising that the NHS is in crisis.

If it is true that this handout was a deliberate government policy and that the Treasury was ultimately responsible, this surely provides more evidence that those who see Gordon Brown as the radical alternative to Tony Blair are deceiving themselves as much as those who believed that Blair was the radical alternative to John Major. Brown did not invent the private finance initiative, but he keeps it alive, however many scandals it produces. His record on this issue suggests that he has established his reputation for prudence by two means: by loading future generations with debt in order to balance the books today, and by filling the coffers of the corporations to win himself friends in the financial press.

While I will join the dancing in the streets when Tony Blair goes, I am mystified by the left's enthusiasm for his successor. Why should we welcome the appointment of a man who treats public services as a pension fund for fat cats?

May 9 2006

A Vehicle for Equality

"Company directors who take big risks and achieve big success deserve big rewards."[1] That's what Patricia Hewitt, the trade and industry secretary, said at the British Motor Show last year, and I think you can guess who she was talking about. The directors of Rover certainly got their big rewards. We all now know about their big success. But big risks? It was as obvious then as it is today that the only people in the business who were subject to no risk at all were the ones being rewarded for risk-taking. They would walk off with millions, whatever happened to the company. An inability to distinguish between the risks to which people expose themselves and the risks to which they expose others appears to be the defining disease of modern capitalism.

I don't often find myself standing up for the car industry, but it's hard not to share the general outrage about what has happened at Rover. The four directors, who bought the company for £10, are reported to have siphoned, quite legally, £40m out of the fuel tank. The taxpayer has had to throw exactly the same amount at Rover's suppliers to prevent them from following it round the U-bend.[2] And the money that could have funded generous redundancy payments and filled the hole in the pension fund has been frittered away.

The problem here is easily identified: there was a conflict between the interests of the men who ran the business and the interests of the people who worked for them. As long as the directors could escape with their huge pay packets, they had little incentive to ensure that their employees escaped with anything at all.

Rover, we are told, was a special case. In companies in which the principal shareholders and the executives are different people, problems like this should not occur. The shareholders will reward the managers for looking after their capital in a responsible fashion. But in truth, because of the opportunity costs of capital, shareholders and executives have a common interest in securing jam today rather than jam tomorrow. The owners reward the executives for profit rather than investment, so the managers sacrifice the future to the present. It's arguable that the staggering returns the high-street banks made this year should not have been treated as profits at all, but as money that might have protected them, and us, against bad loans when the next recession arrives.

Is this really, as the proponents of the model always claim, the best way of running a business? Would the Rover workers not have been better off had they, rather than their bosses, bought the plant for a tenner in 2000?

For a country widely credited with inventing the idea, the United Kingdom is remarkably hostile to workers' cooperatives. In one form or another, they have existed since the division of labour began. But it was our own enlightened capitalist, Robert Owen, who formalised the idea. The workers' communities he founded in the early 19th century soon collapsed. We still have one very large workers' co-op (the John Lewis Partnership), and hundreds, or, if you count professional partnerships, thousands of smaller ones. But the manufacturing co-ops Owen envisaged are few and tiny. The reason, we are always told, is that they are simply not as competitive as hierarchical capitalism. Given that there is no law against forming them, why, if they are such a good idea, have they not out-competed the standard business model?

There is, I think, an interesting answer to this question. If the principle on which workers' co-ops are organised (ownership of the company by its employees) is uncompetitive, why are so many big companies now mimicking it, by turning their executives into shareholders? Their incentive schemes recognise, like the co-ops, that people who own part of the business will make sure it works. Of course, the schemes are mostly confined to the executives, who tend to be more mobile than the rest of the workforce. Being pegged to profits, they do little to encourage the executives to invest. So they don't address the conflict of interest. But the central idea of the co-op is now a standard feature of corporate capitalism.

In several other countries, workers' co-ops, in which all the workers have a stake in the business and a voice in its decision-making processes, have flourished. After the Argentinian economy collapsed in 2001, about 160 businesses were taken over by co-ops.[3] Some of them have done so well that the owners, who had been unable to make them pay, are now suing the workers in the hope of taking the factories back. One of the reasons for their success, according to the Washington Post, is that they have dropped their "higher-paid managers from the payroll".[4] (How often do you read that in the Post?) The money that would have been snaffled by the executives has instead been reinvested.

Dutch and Danish farmers have survived the invasion of the superstores because, unlike British farmers, they process and market much of their produce cooperatively, and so can bargain collectively. They can also achieve economies of scale, which is why British people eat Danish butter and Danish bacon. The Mondragon co-op is now the biggest industrial group in Euskadi (the Basque country) and the seventh biggest in Spain, with 71,000 workers.[5] Altogether, workers' co-ops around the world employ about 100 million people.[6]

There are problems with the model, however. The Harvard economist Michael Kremer has used some elegant maths to show how dividends are, in effect, transferred from the more productive to the less productive workers, and how worker democracy can militate against innovation and efficiency.[7] The greater the capital investment, he shows, the greater the potential inefficiency, which could explain the scarcity of manufacturing co-ops. Co-ops, in other words, like hierarchical firms, suffer from conflicts of interest. There are other constraints too: the lack of access to capital (keeping the business in the hands of the workers means keeping absentee owners, and their money, out); and the lack of opportunities for capital (you can't move it around as freely as other shareholders can). The Mondragon co-op appears to have overcome both these problems, by establishing its own bank, which circulates money among its 200 affiliated businesses, and by encouraging diversification.

It is also clear that cooperatives can be as predatory as firms owned by absentee capital. As a solution to exploitation, they present the same problem as anarchism: internal democracy can be accompanied by external oppression. But while a company run by its workers has just as great an incentive to nail us to the wall as a company run by absentee capital, at least within the firm wealth is widely distributed. An economy dominated by cooperatives would be a more equal one than an economy like ours.

As far as Rover is concerned, it is hard to see how a workers' co-op could have made a bigger cock-up of the business than its bosses did. Next time a company is sold for the price of four pints of beer, the workers should pick up the bill.

April 12 2005

Too Soft On Crime

It would be a lot for you or me. For Balfour Beatty plc £150,000 is nothing. Its turnover, in the first six months of this year, was nearly £2bn. But this, on Friday, was the price of a human life. Michael Mungovan was a student trying to make a bit of money. He was told to switch off a live rail on a train line in south London. He wasn't qualified to do it, and his partner wasn't authorised to supervise him. But they were sent out at midnight on to the Vauxhall viaduct, one of the most dangerous sections of track in the United Kingdom. Michael was walking down the line when he was hit from behind by an empty train.[1]

It was a staggering example of corporate neglect. The fine was supposed to "reflect the seriousness of the offence". But penalties like this are levied in proportion to the turnover of the business that employs the workers, rather than the turnover of the parent company. Balfour Beatty Rail Infrastructure Services is a mere spore from the gills of the Balfour Beatty mushroom. It's in the interests of any company whose workers are exposed to danger to ensure that they are hired by a subsidiary.

But the real issue is that, though the coroner's inquest reached a verdict of "unlawful killing", the company was prosecuted not for corporate manslaughter, but for the lesser offence of exposing its workers to risk.[2] If you drop a brick from a tower block and it lands on the pavement, you can expect to be prosecuted for endangering the public. If you drop a brick from a tower block and it lands on someone's head, you can expect to be prosecuted for manslaughter. In Friday's case, the fact that someone was killed did not change the nature of the offence. Michael's death was legally irrelevant.

The government's Health and Safety Executive (HSE) knew that there was no point in prosecuting the firm for killing Michael Mungovan. To make this charge stick, you must prove that one of the directors of the company was personally responsible for the death. The bigger the company, the harder this is. The result is that the only corporations that have been convicted of manslaughter are one-horse outfits in which the director himself was supervising the dangerous work.

This is why the Hatfield case collapsed last month. The train crash in October 2000, in which four people died and 120 were injured, was the result of a broken rail which Railtrack and its contractors had failed to fix. But the prosecutors were unable to prove that the directors had "consented or connived" in the failure to mend the track. A board can avoid prosecution by demonstrating that it hadn't the faintest idea what its company was doing. Neglect can thus be used as a defence against the charge of neglect.

It would be easier to prosecute directors if they had a legal duty to ensure that their company was complying with health and safety laws. But, bizarrely, they do not. As the Centre for Corporate Accountability (CCA) points out, it is the directors who make all the key decisions governing safety at work. They decide how much money is spent on safety training and equipment; whether or not anything is done when a dangerous practice has been identified; how the conflicting objectives of safety and profit are balanced.[3] The HSE's studies suggest that 70% of the deaths and major injuries in the workplace are the result of management failure.[4] But as the directors have no legal duty, they can't be charged with neglecting it.

For seven years the British government has been promising to do something about this. In 1997, soon after the Southall rail crash, the Home Secretary, Jack Straw, announced that he would introduce "laws which provide for conviction of directors of companies where it's claimed that as a result of dreadful negligence by the company as a whole, people have lost their lives".[5] Nothing happened until 2000. Then the Home Office produced a report proposing a law to permit directors, in extreme cases, to be charged with gross carelessness or reckless killing.[6]

Labour's manifesto in 2001 promised "law reform . . . to make provisions against corporate manslaughter". Nothing has happened. In May last year, the Home Office published a press release announcing "a draft Bill on corporate manslaughter", with "a timetable for legislation".[7] It promised to release the details in autumn 2003. Autumn came and went. Nothing was announced.

The Home Office promised the CCA that the bill would be published "by the end of the year".[8] It wasn't. The Home Office then announced that it would publish "proposals" at the beginning of 2004.[9] It didn't.

It then said they would be produced "in the spring".[10] They weren't. Last month Tony Blair told the TUC conference, "we will publish proposals on corporate manslaughter in the current parliamentary session."[11] It's not clear why we should believe him, or why we should assume that if they do materialise, they will ever be turned into law.

But even if they are, it is now clear that there will be no legal penalties for directors. In 2002, the Home Office, without announcing to the public that there had been a change of policy, sent a letter to British corporations. It assured them that "individual directors etc will not be held liable".[12]

The government has been nobbled. Since Straw first promised to change the law, big business has used its lobbying power to stop this from happening. The minutes of a meeting of the Health and Safety Commission (which oversees the HSE) in 2003 reveal that it decided to drop its demand for a new law after "a note from the CBI [the Confederation of British Industry] . . . was circulated".[13]

Now the HSE has adopted the corporate line: that the best way of dealing with the problem is to rely on voluntary compliance. There is no evidence that this works, and plenty that it doesn't. In 1996, the Conservatives, using the same argument, cut health and safety enforcement by 25%. The following year, for the first time in decades, the number of deaths at work rose, by 20%.[14] Even the directors accept that prosecution is the most effective way of holding them to account: when 120 of them were questioned about it in 2000, two thirds agreed that "an increase in the possibility of inspection and prosecution, especially of individuals, would provide the best prompt for employers to improve their approach."[15]

And why shouldn't it? There are criminal sanctions for every other kind of manslaughter, because the authorities understand that fear of the law is what stops us from doing other people in. But somehow, according to everyone from the CBI to a prominent Guardian columnist,[16] this doesn't apply to company directors. Perhaps they belong to a different species.

The health and safety enforcers now have no choice but to rely on corporate goodwill: their funding has been slashed by the government. They no longer have the resources to enforce the existing laws, let alone any new ones. Enforcement of the safety laws is being dismantled, life by bloody life.

October 5 2004

Media Fairyland

On Thursday, the king of fairyland will be re-crowned. He was elected on a platform suspended in mid-air by the power of imagination. He is the leader of a band of men who walk through ghostly realms unvisited by reality. And he remains the most powerful person on earth.

How did this happen? How did a fantasy president from a world of make-believe come to govern a country whose power was built on hard-headed materialism? To find out, take a look at two squalid little stories that have concluded over the past ten days.

The first involves the broadcaster CBS. In September, its 60 Minutes programme ran an investigation into how George Bush avoided the Vietnam draft. It produced memos that appeared to show that his squadron commander in the Texas National Guard had been persuaded to "sugarcoat" his service record. The programme's allegations were immediately and convincingly refuted; Republicans were able to point to evidence suggesting the memos had been faked. Last week, following an inquiry into the programme, the producer was sacked, and three CBS executives were forced to resign.

The incident couldn't have been more helpful to Bush. Though there is no question that he managed to avoid serving in Vietnam, the collapse of CBS's story suggested that all the allegations made about his war record were false, and the issue dropped out of the news. CBS was furiously denounced by the rightwing pundits, with the result that between then and the election hardly any broadcaster dared to criticise George Bush. Mary Mapes, the producer whom CBS fired, was the network's most effective investigative journalist; she was the person who helped bring the Abu Ghraib photos to public attention. If the memos were faked, the forger was either a moron or a very smart operator.

It's true, of course, that CBS should have taken more care. But I think it is safe to assume that if the network had instead broadcast unsustainable allegations about John Kerry, none of its executives would now be looking for work. How many people have lost their jobs, at CBS or anywhere else, for repeating bogus stories released by the Swift Boat Veterans for Truth about Kerry's record in Vietnam? How many were sacked for misreporting the Jessica Lynch affair? Or for claiming that Saddam Hussein had an active nuclear weapons programme in 2003? Or that he was buying uranium from Niger, or using mobile biological weapons labs, or had a hand in 9/11? How many people were sacked during Clinton's presidency for broadcasting outright lies about the Whitewater affair? The answer, in all cases, is none.

You can say what you like in the US media, as long as it helps a Republican president. But slip up once while questioning him, and you will be torn to shreds. Even the most grovelling affirmations of loyalty won't help. The presenter of 60 Minutes, Dan Rather, is the man who once told his audience, "George Bush is the President, he makes the decisions and, you know, as just one American, he wants me to line up, just tell me where."[1] CBS is owned by the conglomerate Viacom, whose chairman told reporters, "we believe the election of a Republican administration is better for our company."[2] But for Fox News and the shock jocks syndicated by ClearChannel, Rather's faltering attempt at investigative journalism is further evidence of "a liberal media conspiracy".

This is not the first time something like this has happened. In 1998, CNN made a programme that claimed that, during the Vietnam war, US special forces dropped sarin gas on defectors who had fled to Laos.[3]

In this case, there was plenty of evidence to support the story. But after four weeks of furious denunciations, the network's owner, Ted Turner, publicly apologised in terms you would expect to hear during a show trial in North Korea: "I'll take my shirt off and beat myself bloody on the back." CNN had erred, he said, by broadcasting the allegations when "we didn't have evidence beyond a reasonable doubt".[4] As the website wsws.org has pointed out, it's hard to think of a single investigative story – Watergate, the My Lai massacre, Britain's arms to Iraq scandal – that could have been proved at the time by journalists "beyond a reasonable doubt".[5] But Turner did what was demanded of him, with the result that, in media fairyland, the atrocity is now deemed not to have happened.

The other squalid little story broke three days before the CBS people were sacked. A US newspaper discovered that Armstrong Williams, a television presenter who (among other jobs) had a weekly slot on a syndicated TV show called America's Black Forum, had secretly signed a $240,000 contract with the US Department of Education.[6] The contract required him "to regularly comment" on George Bush's education bill "during the course of his broadcasts" and to ensure that "Secretary Paige [the Education Secretary] and other department officials shall have the option of appearing from time to time as studio guests".[7]

It's hard to see why the administration bothered to pay him. Williams has described as his "mentors" Lee Atwater, the man who, under Reagan's presidency, brought a new viciousness to Republican campaigning, and the segregationist senator Strom Thurmond.[8] His broadcasting career has been dedicated to promoting extreme Republican causes and attacking civil rights campaigns.

What makes this story interesting is that the show he worked on was founded, in 1977, by the radical black activists Glen Ford and Peter Gamble, to "allow Black reporters to hold politicians and activists of all persuasions accountable to Black people".[9] They sold their shares in 1980 and the programme was later bought by the Uniworld Group. With Williams's help, the new owners have reversed its politics and turned it into a recruitment vehicle for the Republican party. Williams appears to have been taking money for doing what he was doing anyway.

These stories, in other words, are illustrations of the ways in which the US media is disciplined by corporate America. In the first case, the other corporate broadcasters joined forces to punish a dissenter in their ranks. In the second case, a corporation captured what was once a dissenting programme and turned it into another means of engineering conformity.

The role of the media corporations in the United States is similar to that of repressive state regimes elsewhere: they decide what the public will and won't be allowed to hear, and either punish or recruit the social deviants who insist on telling a different story. The journalists they employ do what almost all journalists working under repressive regimes do: they internalise the demands of the censor and understand, before anyone has told them, what is permissible and what is not.

So, when they are faced with a choice between a fable that helps the Republicans and a reality that hurts them, they choose the fable. As their fantasies accumulate, the story they tell about the world veers further and further from reality. Anyone who tries to bring the people back down to earth is denounced as a traitor and a fantasist. And anyone who seeks to become president must first learn to live in fairyland.

January 18 2005

The Net Censors

"Several of this cursed brood, getting hold of the branches behind, leaped up into the tree, whence they began to discharge their excrements on my head."[1] Thus Gulliver describes his first encounter with the Yahoos. Something similar seems to have happened to democracy.

In April, Shi Tao, a journalist working for a Chinese newspaper, was sentenced to 10 years in prison for "providing state secrets to foreign entities". He had passed details of a censorship order to the Asia Democracy Forum and the website Democracy News.[2]

The pressure group Reporters Without Borders (RSF) was mystified by the ease with which Mr Tao had been caught. He had sent the message through an anonymous Yahoo! account. But the police had gone straight to his offices and picked him up. How did they know who he was?

Last week, RSF obtained a translation of the verdict, and there it found the answer. Mr Tao's account information was "furnished by Yahoo Holdings". Yahoo!, the document says, gave the government his telephone number and the address of his office.[3]

So much for the promise that the internet would liberate the oppressed. This theory was most clearly formulated in 1999, by the New York Times columnist Thomas Friedman. In his book The Lexus and the Olive Tree, Friedman argues that two great democratising forces, global communications and global finance, would sweep away any regime that was not open, transparent and democratic.

"Thanks to satellite dishes, the internet and television," he asserts, "we can now see through, hear through and look through almost every conceivable wall . . . no one owns the internet, it is totally decentralised, no one can turn it off . . . China's going to have a free press . . . Oh, China's leaders don't know it yet, but they are being pushed straight in that direction." The same thing, he claims, is happening all over the world. In Iran, he saw people ogling Baywatch on illegal satellite dishes. As a result, he claims, "within a few years, every citizen of the world will be able to comparison shop between his own . . . government and the one next door."[4]

He is partly right. The internet at least has helped to promote revolutions, of varying degrees of authenticity, in Serbia, Ukraine, Georgia, Kyrgyzstan, Lebanon, Argentina and Bolivia. But the flaw in Friedman's theory is that he forgets the intermediaries. The technology that runs the internet did not sprout from the ground. It is provided by people with a commercial interest in its development. Their interest will favour freedom in some places and control in others. And they can and do turn it off. In 2002, Yahoo! signed the Chinese government's pledge of "self-regulation"; it promised not to allow "pernicious information that may jeopardise state security" to be posted.[5] Last year Google published a statement admitting that it would not be showing links to material banned by the authorities on computers stationed in China.[6] If Chinese users of Microsoft's internet service MSN try to send a message containing the words "democracy", "liberty" or "human rights", they are warned that "This message includes forbidden language. Please delete the prohibited expression."[7]

A study earlier this year by a group of scholars called the OpenNet Initiative revealed what no one had thought possible: that the Chinese government is succeeding in censoring the net.[8] Its most powerful tool is its control of the routers, the devices through which data is moved from one place to another. With the right filtering systems, these routers can block messages containing forbidden words. Human rights groups allege that western corporations, in particular Cisco Systems, have provided the technology and the expertise.[9] Cisco is repeatedly cited by Thomas Friedman as one of the facilitators of his global revolution.

"We had the dream that the internet would free the world, that all the dictatorships would collapse," says Julien Pain of Reporters Without Borders. "We see it was just a dream."[10] Friedman was not the first person to promote these dreams. In 1993 Rupert Murdoch boasted that satellite television was "an unambiguous threat to totalitarian regimes everywhere".[11] The Economist had already made the same claim on its cover: "Dictators beware!" The Chinese went berserk, and Murdoch, in response, ensured that the threat did not materialise.

In 1994 he dropped BBC world news from his Star satellite feeds after it broadcast an unflattering portrait of Mao Zedong. In 1997 he ordered his publishing house HarperCollins to ditch a book by Chris Patten, the former governor of Hong Kong. He slagged off the Dalai Lama,[12] and his son James attacked the dissident cult Falun Gong.[13]

His grovelling paid off, and in 2002 he was able to start broad-casting into Guangdong. "We won't do programmes that are offensive in China," Murdoch's spokesman Wang Yukui admitted. "If you call this self-censorship then of course we're doing a kind of self-censorship."[14]

I think, if they were as honest as Mr Wang, everyone who works for Rupert Murdoch, or for the corporate media anywhere in the world, would recognise these restraints. To own a national newspaper or a television or radio station, you need to be a multimillionaire. What multimillionaires want is what everybody wants: a better world for people like themselves. The job of their journalists is to make it happen. As Piers Morgan, former editor of the Mirror, confessed, "I've made it a strict rule in life to ingratiate myself with billionaires."[15] They will stay in their jobs for as long as they continue to interpret the inter-ests of the proprietorial class correctly.

What the owners don't enforce, the advertisers do. Over the past few months, AdAge.com reveals, both Morgan Stanley and BP have instructed newspapers and magazines that they must remove their adverts from any edition containing "objectionable editorial coverage".[16] Car, airline and tobacco companies have been doing the same thing.[17] Most publications can't afford to lose these accounts; they lose the offending articles instead. Why are the papers full of glowing profiles of the advertising boss Martin Sorrell? Because they're terrified of him.

So instead of democracy, we get Baywatch. They are not the same thing. Aspirational TV might stimulate an appetite for more money, or more plastic surgery, and this in turn might encourage people to look, for better or worse, to the political systems that deliver them, but it is just as likely to be counter-democratic. As a result of pressure from both ratings and advertisers, for example, between 1993 and 2003 environmental programmes were cleared from the schedules of BBC TV, ITV and Channel 4. Though three or four documentaries have slipped out since then, the ban has not yet been wholly lifted. To those of us who have been banging our heads against this wall, it feels like censor-ship.

Indispensable as the internet has become, political debate is still dominated by the mainstream media; a story on the net changes nothing until it finds its way into the newspapers or on to television. What this means is that while the better networking Friedman celebrates can assist a democratic transition, the democracy it leaves us with is filtered and controlled. Someone else owns the routers.

September 13 2005

Arguments With Culture

The Antisocial Bastards in Our Midst

The road rage lobby couldn't have been more wrong. Organisations like the Association of British Drivers and "Safe Speed" – the boy racers' club masquerading as a road safety campaign – have spent years claiming that speeding doesn't cause accidents. Safe Speed, with the help of some of the most convoluted arguments I've ever read, even seeks to prove that speed cameras "make our roads more dangerous".[1] Other groups, such as Motorists Against Detection (officially known as MAD) have been toppling, burning and blowing up the hated cameras.[2] Speed limits, speed traps and the government's "war on the motorist", these and about a thousand such campaigns maintain, are shakedown operations, whose sole purpose is to extract as much money as possible from the poor oppressed driver.

Well, last week the Department for Transport published the results of the study it had commissioned into the efficacy of its speed cameras.[3] It found that the number of drivers speeding down the roads where fixed cameras had been installed fell by 70%, and the number exceeding the speed limit by more than 15mph dropped by 91%. As a result, 42% fewer people were killed or seriously injured in those places than were killed or injured on the same stretches before the cameras were erected. The number of deaths fell by over 100 a year. The people blowing up speed cameras have blood on their hands.

But this is not, or not really, an article about speed, or cameras, or even cars. It is about the rise of the antisocial bastards who believe they should be allowed to do what they want, whenever they want, regardless of the consequences. I believe that while there are many reasons for the growth of individualism in the UK, the extreme libertarianism now beginning to take hold here begins on the road. When you drive, society becomes an obstacle. Pedestrians, bicycles, traffic calming, speed limits, the law: all become a nuisance to be wished away. The more you drive, the more bloody-minded and individualistic you become. The car is slowly turning us, like the Americans and the Australians, into a nation that recognises only the freedom to act, and not the freedom from the consequences of other people's actions. We drive on the left in Britain, but we are being driven to the right.

It is not just because of his celebration of everything brash and flash that Jeremy Clarkson has become the Britsh boy racer's hero. He articulates, with a certain wit and with less equivocation than any other writer in this country, the doctrine that he should be permitted to swing his fist, whoever's nose is in the way. For years he has championed the unrestrained freedom of the road. He takes it so far that from time to time he appears to incite his disciples to vandalise and even kill. "If the only way of getting their [the government's] attention", he told the readers of the Sun in 2002, "is to destroy the tools that pay for their junkets and their new wallpaper, then so be it. I wish the people from MAD all the very best."[4] In February this year, he suggested that speed cameras might be "filled . . . with insulating foam that sets rock hard".[5] After the London bombings in July, he observed that "many commuters are now switching to bicycles . . . can I offer five handy hints to those setting out on a bike for the first time. 1. Do not cruise through red lights. Because if I'm coming the other way, I will run you down, for fun. 2. Do not pull up at junctions in front of a line of traffic. Because if I'm behind you, I will set off at normal speed and you will be crushed under my wheels . . ."[6] Clarkson wants society out of his way when he's driving, and he isn't too particular about how it's done. One day, one of his fans will take him seriously.

But, doubtless cheered by the response of his readers, he has expanded his journalism from attacks on "the Lycra-Nazi sandalistas of Islington" (cyclists) to polemics against every kind of government intervention. He now rails against "nannying bureaucrats sticking their index linked snouts into the trough" (he means health and safety inspectors);[7] complains that he has to tell the police why he wants to keep a gun;[8] appears to champion the right of householders to shoot burglars in the back;[9] and ponders the use of landmines to deter ramblers.[10]

His acolytes are also venturing on to new ground. The website of the Association of British Drivers carries the usual links to campaigns against humps in the road (yes, people really are that sad), speed cameras and the congestion charge.[11] But it also directs its readers to about 50 sites claiming that global warming is a fraud and a lie, several tirades against the evils of the nanny state, and an article by John Redwood calling for lower taxes. Libertarianism has left the road and is now driving down the pavement.

Of course, these politics are possible only while we have a state capable of picking up the pieces. If there were not a massive hidden subsidy for private transport, those who decry the nannying bureaucrats couldn't afford to leave their drives. Speed cameras, according to the government's study, now save the country £258m in annual medical bills, a fraction of the billions in health costs inflicted by Mr Clarkson's chums. Just as the leftwing movements of the 1970s, in David Harvey's words, "failed to recognize or confront . . . the inherent tension between the quest for individual freedoms and social justice",[12] the new libertarians fail to recognise the extent to which their freedoms depend on an enabling state. They hate the institution that allows them to believe that they can live without institutions.

It is strange to see how the car has been overlooked as an agent of political change. We know that the breaking of the unions, the dismantling of the welfare state and the sale of council houses that Margaret Thatcher pioneered made us more individualistic. But the way in which

the transition from individualism to the next phase of neoliberalism
– libertarianism – was assisted by her transport policies has been largely
ignored. She knew what she was doing. She spoke of "the great car-
owning democracy", and asserted that "a man who, beyond the age of
26, finds himself on a bus can count himself as a failure".[13] Her road-
building programme was an exercise in both civil and social engineering. "Economics are the method," she told us, "the object is to
change the soul."[14] The slowly shifting consciousness of the millions
who spend much of their day sitting in traffic makes interventionist
government ever harder. The difference between the age of Herbert
Morrison and the age of Peter Mandelson can be, in part, accounted
for by the motorcar.

It shouldn't be hard to see how politically foolish are the current
government's transport policies. The £11.4bn it is spending on road
building[15] is an £11.4 billion subsidy to the Conservative party.
However much Blair seeks to accommodate the new libertarianism,
he cannot consistently position himself to the right of the opposition. The longer he sustains Thatcher's social engineering programme,
the more trouble he stores up for his successors. Every branch line
that's closed, every bus that is taken off the road, every new lane
added to a motorway hastens the day when the Tories get back behind
the wheel.

December 20 2005

Driven Out of Eden

It is surely one of the most brazen evasions of reality ever painted.
John Constable's The Cornfield, completed in 1826, and now hanging
ιɯ the National Gallery's new exhibition, Paradise, evokes, at the very
height of the enclosure movement, a flawless rural harmony. Just as
the commoners were being dragged from their land, their crops

destroyed, their houses razed, the dissenters transported or hanged, Constable conjures the definitive English Arcadia. A dog walks a herd of sheep into the deep shade of an August day. A ruddy farm boy drinks from a glittering stream, his donkeys browsing quietly behind him. In the background, framed by great elms, men in hats and neckerchiefs work a field of wheat. Beyond them a river shimmers through water meadows. A church emerges from the trees to bless the happy natives and their other Eden.

In the midst of the rural hell, Constable invents his heaven. It is a glittering lie, and we should not be surprised to read in the gallery's brochure that this is "one of the nation's favourite paintings, reproduced countless times and in thousands of homes".[1] For what Constable has done is what human beings have always done. Confronted by atrocities, we invoke a prelapsarian wonder. We construct our Gardens of Eden, real or imagined, out of other people's hells.

The timing of the exhibition is good, as it is in this season that we leave our homes in search of paradise. In doing so, we immiserate other people. It is not just the noise with which we fill their lives while pursuing our own tranquillity. In order to create an Eden in which we may disport ourselves in innocence and nakedness, we must first commission others to clear its inhabitants out of the way. Like Constable, we are adept at hiding this truth from ourselves.

The Yosemite Valley in California was set aside by Abraham Lincoln as the world's first public wilderness. As the historian Simon Schama records, "the brilliant meadow floor which suggested to its first eulogists a pristine Eden was in fact the result of regular fire-clearances by its Ahwahneechee Indian occupants".[2] The first whites to enter the valley were the soldiers sent to kill them.[3] Eden, in an inversion of the biblical story, was thus created by man's expulsion. The colonists redefined the Ahwahneechee's managed habitat as wilderness in order to assert both a temporal and spiritual dominion over it.

America's Garden of Eden, in other words, is in fact its Canaan, the

land of milk and honey whose indigenous people had first to be elim-
inated before the invaders could claim it as their birthright. The Mosaic
doctrine of *terra nullius* (the inhabitants possess no legal rights to their
land), which permitted the Lord's appointed to "smite the corners of
Moab, and destroy all the children of Sheth",[4] has become the founding
creed of the usurper all over the world. It continues to inform the land
seizures in modern Israel, seeking now to turn itself into a walled
garden; it continues to guide the expropriations upon which much of
the global tourism industry is based.

In the second half of the twentieth century, as the cost of international transport fell, governments discovered a powerful financial incentive to create, from the lands of the poor, a paradise for the rich. All
over east and southern Africa, the most fertile lands of the nomads
and hunter-gatherers were declared "primordial wilderness".[5] The inhabitants were shut out; only those who could afford to pay were permitted
to enter heaven. You can read about the Maasai Mara reserve on the
Kenya Tourist Board's website, under the heading "Wilderness". It
informs you that the indigenous people, the Maasai, "regard themselves ... as much a part of the life of the land as the land is part of
their lives. Traditionally, the Maasai rarely hunt and living alongside
wildlife in harmony is an important part of their beliefs."[6] What it does
not tell you is that the Maasai have been expelled from the "wilderness" in which they lived in harmony with wildlife, because the tourists
did not expect to see them there.

The government of Botswana has just completed its expulsion of
the Gana and Gwi Bushmen from the Central Kalahari game reserve,
on the grounds that their hunting and gathering has become "obsolete" and their presence is no longer compatible with "preserving
wildlife resources".[7] To get rid of them, as Survival International has
shown, it cut off their water supplies, taxed, fined, beat and tortured
them.[8] Bushmen have lived there for some 20,000 years; the wildlife
is not threatened by them, but the freedom of the diamond mining
and tourism industries might be. Having expelled the Bushmen from

their ancestral lands, the government now invites tourists to visit what its website calls "the Last Eden".[9]

The precursors of these game reserves were the deer parks and other earthly paradises the aristocracy built for itself in Britain. In Stowe gardens in Buckinghamshire, landscaped by Capability Brown in the 1740s on behalf of the Whig politician Lord Cobham, is a valley called the "Elysian Fields", the paradise of the ancient Greeks. Hidden in the trees in the heart of paradise is a church: the only remaining evidence of one of the villages cleared to make way for the estate. You can scour the National Trust's literature for any reference to the people who lived there, or in the other places that were turned into the grand estates it preserves, but you will be wasting your time.[10] Britain's biggest NGO recounts the history of heaven, but shields its eyes from hell.

We deceive ourselves by precisely the same means in building our virtual Edens. Paul Gauguin sought his garden of innocence in the South Pacific, but found instead a society ravaged by French colonisation and venereal disease. Like Constable, he painted paradise anyway; the tableau displayed in the National Gallery was largely copied from a frieze in a Javanese temple, into whose implausible Eden Gauguin inserted his ethereal Tahitians.[11] Perhaps the most disturbing painting in the exhibition is François Boucher's Landscape with a Watermill. In the French countryside in 1755, the peasants were living on husks, grass and acorns, but Boucher has plump maids in white linen sauntering through their tasks, while boys lounge in bucolic splendour on the riverbank. The painting appears to have been produced for the walls of a landowner's home. Today, we find such lies repeated on our television screens, in the travel and wildlife programmes that seek to persuade us that all is well in the white man's playground. The BBC's only recent series on the Congo, filmed in the midst of the massacres there, informed us that "the Congo may once have been known as the "heart of darkness" – today it seems more like a bright, beautiful wilderness."[12] It ignored the killings altogether.

Paradise is the founding myth of the colonist. Unable to contemplate the truth of what we do, we extract from our fathomless collective guilt a story of primordial innocence.

August 8 2003

Breeding Reptiles in the Mind

Had The X-Creatures come to any other conclusion, there would have been a television-shaped hole in my living-room window. I had guessed that the BBC series, in common with almost all the other treatments of the Loch Ness mystery, would aver that the existence of the monster hadn't yet been proved, but couldn't be discounted. But, to his credit, the presenter explained what anyone with a shred of common sense should surely be able to work out for themselves: that there isn't, and can't possibly be, a Loch Ness monster.[1]

You don't need a PhD in ecology to be able to see that one member of any species isn't going to get very far. After a while – within 70 years for most large vertebrates – the thing will keel over and die. So any creature that wanted its genes to survive from the Jurassic to the present day would have to be in the company of other members of its species. For a breeding population to remain viable across even the most fleeting of geological epochs, it would, as the programme pointed out, have to contain at least 5000 animals.

The monster is said to be a reptile of some kind, in which case it must breathe air. It must, in other words, come to the surface not once every few years, or even once every few days, but, more probably, once every few hours. It would spend a good part of its life either on the water's surface, breathing, looking around and basking in the sun, or hauled out on the side of the loch.

Now take a far smaller air-breathing vertebrate, the harbour porpoise. It's a mere four feet long, and lives in a much bigger and rougher place than Loch Ness – the sea. While it generally stays close to the shore, it can travel scores of miles to good feeding grounds. Yet visit the sparsely habited coast of the Highlands and Islands and ask whether the harbour porpoises are around, and the people who work on the sea will be able to tell you straight away. Skittering around on the surface, blowing noisily, making great bow waves as they chase their prey, the little monsters couldn't hide from us, however hard they tried. Biologists have no trouble keeping track of them and recording the minutest details of their behaviour. Quite aside from the fact that Loch Ness is too cold and too devoid of life to support a population of plesiosaurs, were there a school of 5000 monsters, there couldn't be a mystery: you could watch them from the banks whenever you wanted.

Yet there's one mystery the programme didn't clear up: namely why, on every day of the tourist season, coach after coach arrives in the laybys beside the loch, a piper hurriedly stuffs his cigarettes into his sporran and starts playing his pipes, and a bunch of eager people, some of whom, presumably, hold down responsible jobs, scan the placid waters of the loch in the hope of seeing a dinosaur.

The piper, of course, is just as much a part of the mythology of the Highlands as the monster. The coach will move from Loch Ness to Ben Nevis, will stop for a few minutes in Glencoe, where the passengers can buy shortbread and prints of The Monarch of the Glen, pause in a car park on the bonny banks of Loch Lomond, then, without stopping in Glasgow, trundle back to royal Edinburgh. There might be a gory painting of the Glencoe massacre on the shortbread tins, but that is as close as the occupants will get to the Scotland of reality rather than the Scotland of their dreams.

It's the same story the world over. Pulling up at a fishing village on a bank of the Amazon, I was once greeted by a group of peasants covered in paint and feathers, with trembling bows and arrows in their hands, grunting and whooping. I asked them what on earth they were doing. "Oh, sorry," one of the men said, "we thought it was the tourist boat." They went into their houses and put their T-shirts back on. Amerindian cultures on the banks of the Amazon collapsed three centuries ago.

You might object that these fantasies are harmless, that local myths simply provide a bit of fun for the tourists and a bit of money for the hosts. But it's the exoticisation of the other, the apprehension that the rest of the world conforms to different laws, that surely lies at the root of our age-old failure to understand the impacts – economic, political and ecological – that our activities exert upon other places. The more we extol the exotic and deny the real, the more we breed reptiles in the mind.

October 10 1998

Willy Loman Syndrome

If this were Iraq, or Somalia or Chechnya, the trend would not be difficult to understand. But this is Britain, during the longest period of domestic peace and prosperity in modern history. After 54 successive quarters of growth and low inflation, with high employment and a low chance of being murdered in your bed, we should be the happiest, calmest, least fearful people who have ever lived. But something has gone wrong.

A report published last week by the British Medical Association suggests that there has been a steady increase in mental health disorders among children between five and 16 years old.[1] Today, 9.6% of them – very nearly one in 10 – suffer from psychological problems that are "persistent, severe and affect functioning on a day-to-day basis". Roughly "1.1 million children under the age of 18 . . . would benefit from specialist services." I don't think it would be an exaggeration to describe this as a social catastrophe.

What is going on? The BMA isn't sure. It suggests that diet may be a factor, in particular a possible deficiency of omega-3 fatty acids. It notes that while there has been no increase in the number of 11- to 15-year-olds who drink alcohol, consumption among those who do has doubled in 14 years. It found that children living in poverty were much more likely to develop disorders than those with richer parents. But as child poverty is falling, you would expect this to mean that psychological problems were declining.

The BMA also points to changing family lives. But another report on the same issue, published by the Nuffield Foundation in 2004, found that "marked changes in family type . . . were not the main reason for rising trends in behaviour problems".[2]

The same study contains one of the most arresting statements I have ever read: "Rises in mental health problems seem to be associated with improvements in economic conditions." As our GDP increases, we become more disturbed. Among other possible causes, it blames rising pressures at school, changing relationships with other children, and a decline in the limits and rules set by parents. But all these, it admits, are "untested hypotheses". As anyone's guess is as good as anyone else's, I feel justified in hazarding one of my own. I accept that this is a complex problem, and that there are doubtless many causes. But I propose that one of them is Willy Loman syndrome.

Willy Loman is the hero of Arthur Miller's play Death of a Salesman. He is torn apart by the gulf between his expectations – the promise held out to everyone of fame and fortune – and reality. Even as his modest powers decline and his career falls apart, he believes that he can still be number one. This used to be called the American dream. Now it is everyone's nightmare.

A survey published in April by the economist Tom Hertz showed that the United States has one of the lowest levels of intergenerational mobility in the rich world.[3] A child born into a poor family has a 1% chance of growing up to become one of the richest 5%, while a child born into a wealthy family has a 22% chance. Another study, published by Business Week, found that in 1978 23% of adult men whose fathers were in the bottom quartile made it into the top quartile. In 2004 the figure was 10%.[4] But reality and public perceptions are travelling in opposite directions. A poll for the New York Times published in 2005 showed that 80% of respondents thought it was possible for poor people to become wealthy by working hard. In 1983 the figure was only 60%.[5]

Hertz noted that "among high-income countries for which comparable estimates are available, only the United Kingdom had a lower rate of mobility than the United States." In April, the Joseph Rowntree Foundation published a study showing that UK citizens in their 30s today are twice as likely to be stuck in the same economic class as their parents than people born 10 years earlier.[6]

Here too, declining mobility is accompanied by rising expectations. In January the Learning and Skills Council found that 16% of the teenagers it interviewed believed they would become famous, probably by appearing on a show like Big Brother.[7] Many of them saw this as a better prospect than obtaining qualifications; 11% of them, it found, were "sitting around waiting to be discovered". The council claimed that the probability of being chosen by Big Brother and of becoming rich and famous as a result is 30 million to one. But the promise held out to us is that it can happen to anyone. The teenagers seemed to believe it can happen to everyone.

And this is surely how much of our economy now works. A vast industry is devoted to selling people images of themselves that bear no relation to reality. The most obvious of these (this is hardly an original point) is the celebration of extreme thinness, just as childhood obesity becomes an epidemic.

The headline on the cover of this month's edition of the girls' magazine Sugar is "Get this Bikini Body with no effort". Most pages are devoted to either bodies or celebrities. A feature on Theo Walcott's partner, Melanie Slade, shows how she is about to exchange her modest life for mansions, sports cars, health spas and shopping in Bond Street. Sugar's drawing of a typical "celeb wedding" contains an enclosure for "ugly relatives". A fat woman is being hosed with fake tan by a makeup artist, who is "trying to make the uglies photogenic".

A couple of readers seek to rebel against these impossible dreams, but they are slapped down. "After reading 'How to be sexy by Christina Aguilera'", one girl writes, "I realised: how can a girl say she's individual, but look plastic?" The letters editor replies: "She has an individual approach to fashion, image and attitude – which is why we think she's fab." Another letter asks: "Why is a celeb always on the cover of *Sugar*? People who aren't celebrities are people, too, and readers would respond better to seeing their mate's older sister than a star who they wish they were!" She's told: "We've done our research and most of you'd prefer to see a celeb on the cover."

One of the conditions that is growing fastest, the British Medical Association says, is self-harm: cutting or burning yourself, pulling out your hair, swallowing poisons. It is commoner in girls than in boys: one survey found that 11.2% of girls had committed an act of this kind.[8] If girls are attacking or seeking to erase their bodies, it is surely because they have been taught to hate them.

The gulf between what we are told we should be and what we are is growing. As children's expectations lose contact with reality, they are torn between their inner lives of fame and fortune and the humdrum reality their minds no longer inhabit. Advertising (and the businesses supported by it) is not the clattering of the stick in the swill bucket that Orwell perceived so much as the carrot that keeps the donkey moving. You are never allowed to come close enough to eat, however hard you pull. An economy driven by dissatisfaction could scarcely fail to cultivate mental illness.

June 27 2006

The New Chauvinism

Out of the bombings a national consensus has emerged: what we need in Britain is a renewed sense of patriotism. The rightwing papers have been making their usual noises about old maids and warm beer, but in the past 10 days they've been joined by Jonathan Freedland in the Guardian, Tristram Hunt in the New Statesman, the New Statesman itself, and just about everyone who has opened his mouth on the subject of terrorism and national identity. Emboldened by this consensus, the Sun now insists that anyone who isn't loyal to this country should leave it.[1] The way things are going, it can't be long before I'm deported.

The argument runs as follows: patriotic people don't turn on each other. If there are codes of citizenship and a general belief in Britain's virtues, acts of domestic terrorism are unlikely to happen. As Jonathan Freedland points out, the United States, in which "loyalty is instilled constantly" has never "had a brush with home-grown Islamist terrorism".[2]

This may be true (though there have been plenty of attacks by non-Muslim terrorists in the US – think of the lynchings following emancipation). But while patriotism might make citizens less inclined to attack each other, it makes the state more inclined to attack other countries, for it knows it is likely to command the support of its people. If patriotism were not such a powerful force in the US, could Bush have invaded Iraq?

To argue that national allegiance reduces human suffering, you must assert that acts of domestic terrorism cause more grievous harm than all the territorial and colonial wars, ethnic cleansing and holocausts pursued in the name of national interest. To believe this, you need be not just a patriot, but a chauvinist.

Freedland and Hunt and the leader writers of the New Statesman, of course, are nothing of the kind. Hunt argues that Britishness should be about "values rather than institutions"; Britain has "a superb record of political liberalism and intellectual inquiry, giving us a public sphere open to ideas, religions and philosophy from across the world".[3] This is true, but these values are not peculiar to Britain, and it is hard to see why we have to become patriots in order to invoke them. Britain also has an appalling record of imperialism and pig-headed jingoism, and when you wave the flag no one can be sure which record you are celebrating. If you want to defend liberalism, then defend it, but why conflate your love for certain values with love for a certain country?

And what, exactly, would a liberal patriotism look like? When confronted with a conflict between the interests of your country and those of another, patriotism, by definition, demands that you should choose those of your own. Internationalism, by contrast, means choosing the option that delivers most good or least harm to people, regardless of where they live. It tells us that someone living in Kinshasa is of no less worth than someone living in Kensington, and that a policy that favours the interests of 100 British people at the expense of 101 Congolese is one we should not pursue. Patriotism, if it means anything, tells us we should favour the interests of the 100 British people. How do you reconcile this choice with liberalism? How, for that matter, do you distinguish it from racism?

This is the point at which every right-thinking person in Britain scrambles for his Orwell. Did not the sage assert that "patriotism has nothing to do with conservatism",[4] and complain that "England is perhaps the only great country whose intellectuals are ashamed of their own nationality"?[5] He did. But he wrote this during the Second World War. There was no question that we had a duty to fight Hitler and, in so doing, to take sides. And the sides were organised along national lines. If you failed to support Britain, you were assisting the enemy. But today the people trying to kill us are British citizens. They are divided from most of those who live here by ideology, not nationality. To the extent that it was the invasion of Iraq that motivated the terrorists, and to the extent that it was patriotism that made Britain's participation in the invasion possible, it was patriotism that got us into this mess.

The allegiance that most enthusiasts ask us to demonstrate is a selective one. The rightwing press, owned by the grandson of a Nazi sympathiser, a pair of tax exiles and an Australian with American citizenship, is fiercely nationalistic when defending our institutions from Europe, but seeks to surrender the lot of us to the US. It loves the Cotswolds and hates Wales. It loves gaunt, aristocratic women and second homes, and hates oiks, gypsies, council estates and caravan parks.

Two weeks ago, the Telegraph published a list of "ten core values of the British identity" the adoption of which, it argued, would help to prevent another terrorist attack.[6] These were not values we might choose to embrace, but "non-negotiable components of our identity". Among them were "the sovereignty of the Crown in Parliament" ("the Lords, the Commons and the monarch constitute the supreme authority in the land"), "private property", "the family", "history" ("British children inherit . . . a stupendous series of national achievements"), and "the English-speaking world" ("the atrocities of September 11, 2001, were not simply an attack on a foreign nation; they were an attack on the anglosphere"). These non-negotiable demands are not so different from those of the terrorists. Instead of an eternal caliphate, an eternal monarchy. Instead of an Islamic vision of history, a Etonian one. Instead of the ummah, the anglosphere.

If there is one thing that could make me hate this country, it is the Telegraph and its "non-negotiable components". If there is one thing that could make me hate America, it was the sight of the crowds at the Republican convention standing up and shouting "USA, USA", while Zell Miller informed them that "nothing makes this Marine madder than someone calling American troops occupiers rather than liberators."[7] As usual, we are being asked to do the job of the terrorists, by making this country ugly on their behalf.

I don't hate Britain, and I am not ashamed of my nationality, but I have no idea why I should love this country more than any other.

There are some things I like about it and some things I don't, and the same goes for everywhere else I've visited. To become a patriot is to lie to yourself, to tell yourself that whatever good you might perceive abroad, your own country is, on balance, better than the others. It is impossible to reconcile this with either the evidence of your own eyes or a belief in the equality of humankind. Patriotism of the kind Orwell demanded in 1940 is necessary only to confront the patriotism of other people. The Second World War, which demanded that the British close ranks, could not have happened if Hitler hadn't exploited the national allegiance of the Germans. The world will be a happier and safer place when we stop putting our own countries first.

August 9 2005

Notes

Introduction

1 John Lloyd Jones, 3 April 2007, at the launch of Transition Town Lampeter.
2 Martin Parry et al., "Millions at Risk: Defining Critical Climate Change Threats and Targets", *Global Environmental Change*, 11 (2001), 181–3.
3 Eleanor J. Burke, Simon J. Brown and Nikolaos Christidis, "Modelling the Recent Evolution of Global Drought and Projections for the Twenty-first Century with the Hadley Centre Climate Model", *Journal of Hydrometeorology*, 7 (2006), 1113–25.
4 Clive Hamilton, "Building on Kyoto", *New Left Review*, May–June 2007 <http://newleftreview.org/?page=article&view=2671>.
5 *Detroit News*, 4 June 2003, cited by Want to Know, 11 July 2005, Car Mileage: 1908 Ford Model T – 25MPG, 2004 EPA Average All Cars – 21 MPG <http://www.wanttoknow.info/050711carmileageaveragempg>.
6 US Environmental Protection Agency, July 2006, Light-Duty Automotive Technology and Fuel Economy Trends: 1975 Through 2006 <http://www.epa.gov/otaq/cert/mpg/fetrends/420s06003.htm>.

Arguments With God

Bring On the Apocalypse

1 <http://www.harriscountygop.com/sections/sdconv/sdconv.asp>.
2 Committee on Resolutions, Harris County Republican Party, 27 March 2004, Final Report of Senatorial District 17 Convention <http://www.harriscountygop.com/sections/sdconv/sdconv.asp>.
3 Ibid.
4 The preachers were Edward Irving and John Nelson Darby.

5 Paul Vallely, "The Eve of Destruction", *Independent on Sunday*, 7 September 2003.

6 <http://www.raptureready.us>.

7 <http://www.raptureready.com/rap16.html>. (Note: the references in notes 6 and 7 are to rival sites.)

8 Megan K. Stack, "House's DeLay Bonds with Israeli Hawks", *Los Angeles Times*, 31 July 2003; Matthew Engel, "Meet the New Zionists", *Guardian*, 28 October 2002; Vallely, op. cit.

9 Donald E. Wagner, "Marching to Zion: The Evangelical-Jewish Alliance", *Christian Century*, 28 June 2003.

10 Leader, "DeLay's Foreign Meddling", *Los Angeles Times*, 1 August 2003.

11 Jane Lampman, "The End of the World", *Christian Science Monitor*, 18 February 2004.

The Virgin Soldiers

1 The Silver Ring Thing, April 2004 <http://www.silverringthing.com/newsletter.html>.

2 Nadeeja Koralage, "American Virgins", *British Medical Journal*, 328 (31 January 2004), 292.

3 George W. Bush, 20 January 2004, State of the Union Address.

4 Unicef, A League Table of Teenage Births in Rich Nations, Innocenti Report Card No. 3, UNICEF Innocenti Research Centre, Florence, July 2001.

5 Ibid.

6 Ann Widdecombe, "The Libertarian Experiment Has Failed; Abstinence Is the Way Forward", *Independent on Sunday*, 9 May 2004.

7 Denny Pattyn, cited in Natalie Clarke, "The New Sexual Revolution", *Sunday Mail* (Queensland, Australia), 9 November 2003.

8 Figures from the UNFPA's State of World Population Report, 2003, for births per 1000 women between 15 and 19 years of age; presented in graph and graphic form at <http://globalis.gvu.unu.edu/indicator.cfm?IndicatorID=127&country=GB#rowGB>.

9 Ibid.

10 Unicef, op. cit.

11 Ibid.

12 Ibid.

13 Ibid.

14 P. S. Bearman and H. Bruckner, "Promising the Future: Virginity Pledges and the Transition to First Intercourse", *American Journal of Sociology*, 106(4) (2001), 859–912. This paper is reproduced at <http://www.sociology.columbia.edu/downloads/other/psb17/virginity.pdf>.

15 Alba DiCenso et al., "Interventions to Reduce Unintended Pregnancies Among Adolescents: Systematic Review of Randomised Controlled Trials", *British Medical Journal*, 324 (15 June 2002), 1426.
16 Olga Craig, "No Sex Please . . . They're American, and Their Teenage Pregnancy Rates Are at a 10-Year Low. In Stark Contrast, the UK's Record Is the Worst in Western Europe", *Sunday Telegraph*, 11 January 2004.
17 Union of Concerned Scientists, Scientific Integrity in Policymaking: An Investigation into the Bush Administration's Misuse of Science, February 2004.
18 Ibid.
19 Advocates for Youth, Science or Politics? George W. Bush and the Future of Sexuality Education in the United States, [no date] <http://www.advocatesforyouth.org/publications/factsheet/fsbush.pdf>.

Is the Pope Gay?

1 Bertrand Russell, *Proposed Roads to Freedom: Socialism, Anarchism and Syndicalism* (New York: Cornwall Press, 1918).
2 BBC Online, 9 July 2000, Pope Condemns Gay Rights March <http://news.bbc.co.uk/1/hi/world/europe/825852.stm>.
3 See Demanded by the CDF: Gramick–Nugent Profession of Faith, San Francisco Bay Catholic <http://sfbayc.org/magazine/html/ngpof.htm>.
4 Cited by Peter Tatchell, Papal Prejudice: Catholic Homophobia Exposed. An edited version of this article was published in the *Independent*, 31 May 1994.
5 B. A. Robinson, Roman Catholic Church and Homosexuality, 8 March 2000 <http://www.religioustolerance.org/hom_rom.htm>.
6 Bruce Bagemihl, *Biological Exuberance: Animal Homosexuality and Natural Diversity* (New York: St Martin's Press, 1999).
7 Gail Vines, "Queer Creatures", *New Scientist*, 7 August 1999.

A Life With No Purpose

1 Debora Mackenzie, "A Battle for Science's Soul", *New Scientist*, 9 July 2005.
2 See <http://www.moeh.org/main/index.htm>.
3 Lisa Anderson, "Museum Exhibits a Creationist Viewpoint", *Chicago Tribune*, 7 August 2005.
4 Christoph Schönborn, "Finding Design in Nature", *New York Times*, 7 July 2005.
5 Michael McCarthy, "Evolution Dispute Now Set to Split Roman Catholic Hierarchy", *Independent*, 5 August 2005.
6 David Wroe, "Intelligent Design an Option: Nelson", *The Age*, 11 August 2005.

7 Tania Branigan, "Creationist Row Blamed on Support for Faith Schools", *Guardian*, 19 March 2002.

8 Thomas Dawson, "Intelligent Design and Evolution", *American Chronicle*, 10 August 2005.

9 See Marcus Chown, "Did the Big Bang Really Happen?", *New Scientist*, 2 July 2005.

10 Anderson, op. cit.

11 Joseph Campbell, *The Hero with a Thousand Faces* (1949; London: Paladin, 1988).

12 Daniel L. Everett, "Cultural Constraints on Grammar and Cognition in Piraha", *Current Anthropology*, 46 (4) (August–October 2005).

13 Bede, *A History of the English Church and People* (AD731): "Another of the king's chief men . . . went on to say: 'Your majesty, when we compare the present life of man with that time of which we have no knowledge, it seems to me like the swift flight of a lone sparrow through the banqueting-hall where you sit in the winter months to dine with your thanes and counsellors. Inside there is a comforting fire to warm the room; outside, the wintry storms of snow and rain are raging. This sparrow flies swiftly in through one door of the hall, and out through another. While he is inside, he is safe from the winter storms; but after a few moments of comfort, he vanishes from sight into the darkness whence he came. Similarly, man appears on earth for a little while, but we know nothing of what went before this life, and what follows.'"

14 W. H. Auden and Christopher Isherwood, *The Dog Beneath the Skin* (London: Faber and Faber, 1935).

America the Religion

1 Lieutenant General Ricardo Sanchez, Commander, Coalition Ground Forces, 23 July 2003, Briefing on the Confirmation of the Deaths of Uday and Qusay Hussein <http://www.defenselink.mil/news/Jul2003/g030723-D-6570C.html>.

2 President George W. Bush, 1 May 2003, Address to Troops on the USS *Abraham Lincoln*.

3 Clifford Longley, *Chosen People: The Big Idea That Shapes England and America* (London: Hodder and Stoughton, 2002).

4 Thomas Jefferson, cited in ibid.

5 George Washington, cited in ibid.

6 George W. Bush, 21 May 2003, Remarks to the United States Coast Guard Academy, New London, Connecticut.

7 Ronald Reagan, cited in Longley, op. cit.

8 Rudy Giuliani, cited in ibid.

9 Ibid.

10 George W. Bush, State of the Union Address, 28 January 2003.

11 Kita Ikki, cited in Piers Brendon, *The Dark Valley: A Panorama of the 1930s*
    (London: Pimlico, 2000).

Arguments With Nature

Junk Science

1 David Bellamy, "Glaciers Are Cool", *New Scientist*, 16 April 2005.

2 Conversation with Nigel Wonnacott, press officer at the Society of
   Motor Manufacturers and Traders, 2 July 2004. This part of the conversation
   is reproduced at <http://www.monbiot.com/archives/2004/08/19/
   correspondence-with-david-bellamy/>.

3 Conversation with Dr Frank Paul, WGMS, 5 May 2005.

4 Email from Dr Frank Paul. WGMS, 5 May 2005.

5 Bellamy cited Frank Paul et al., "Rapid Disintegration of Alpine Glaciers
   Observed with Satellite Data", *Geophysical Research Letters*, 31, L21402
   (12 November 2004); and WGMS, Fluctuations of Glaciers 1990–1995,
   Vol. VII (1998) <http://www.wgms.ch/fog/fog7.pdf>. A fuller list of recent
   publications on glacial movements and mass balance is available at
   <http://www.wgms.ch/literature.html>.

6 <http://www.coasttocoastam.com/guests/225.html>.

7 <http://www.iceagenow.com/Growing_Glaciers.htm>.

8 Terry Kirby, "The Cult and the Candidate", *Independent*, 21 July 2004, Chip
   Bertlet, 20 December 1990 <http://www.skepticfiles.org/socialis/woo_left.htm>.

9 Roger Boyes, "Blame the Jews", *The Times*, 7 November 2003; David Bamford,
   "Turkish Officials Carpeted", *Guardian*, 30 July 1987; Michael White, "Will the
   Democrats Wear this Whig?", *Guardian*, 3 May 1986.

10 Francis Wheen, "Branded: Lord Rees-Mogg, International Terrorist",
    Guardian, 21 August 1996.

11 Extract from Chip Berlet and Matthew N. Lyons, *Right-Wing Populism in
    America: Too Close for Comfort* (New York: Guilford Press, 2000), online at
    <http://www.publiceye.org/larouche/synthesis.html>.

12 This is the constant theme of *21st Century Science and Technology*.

13 <http://www.21stcenturysciencetech.com/ Articles%202004/Spring2004/
    ScienceYo uth.pdf>.

14 <http://www.junkscience.com/nov98/moore.htm>

<http://www.globalwarming.org/article.php?uid=296>
<http://www.nationalcenter.org/NPA218.html>.

15 John K. Carlise, "Global Warming: Watch the Glaciers", *Washington Post*, 17 November 1998.

16 <http://www.sepp.org/controv/glaciers.html>.

17 Email from David Bellamy, 5 May 2005.

18 Conversation with Mike Holderness, deputy letters editor, 5 May 2005.

Mocking Our Dreams

1 Song of Solomon, 2: 11, 12.

2 George Monbiot, "America's War With Itself", *Guardian*, 21 December 2004; also available at <http://www.monbiot.com/archives/2004/12/21/americas-war-with-itself-/>.

3 *New Scientist*, 3 February 2005, reports a study by Malte Meinshausen from the Swiss Federal Institute of Technology in Zurich, that suggests that global carbon emissions must fall by between 30% and 50% of 1990 levels by 2050 in order to stabilise CO_2 in the atmosphere at 450 parts per million. This would introduce "a 50–50 chance that the world's average temperature rise will not exceed 2°C by 2050". The committee report from the Exeter conference (see note 6 below) warns that "limiting warming to a 2°C increase with a relatively high certainty requires the equivalent concentration of CO_2 to stay below 400 ppm". But even 2°C is way above the level at which grave impacts will be felt by hundreds of millions of people.

4 Meteorological Office, Avoiding Dangerous Climate Change, Table 2a, Impacts on Human Systems Due to Temperature Rise, Precipitation Change and Increases in Extreme Events, 1–3 February 2005 <http://www.stabilisation2005.com/impacts/impacts_human.pdf>.

5 See, for example, "Meet the Sceptics", *New Scientist*, 12 February 2005; and <www.exxonsecrets.org>.

6 Meteorological Office, International Symposium on the Stabilisation of Greenhouse Gases: Report of the Steering Committee, Hadley Centre, Met Office, Exeter, UK, 3 February 2005 <http://www.stabilisation2005.com/Steering_Commitee_Report.pdf>.

Preparing for Take-Off

1 Martin Broughton, Speech to the Aviation Club, 6 December 2006 <http://www.flightglobal.com/Articles/2006/12/07/Navigation/179/210975/Transcript+ BA+chairman+calls+for+ICAO+to+establish+global+emissions+trading+scheme+as+UK+ doubles.html>.

2 Ruth Kelly, Shaping a Low Carbon Future – Our Environmental Vision, 13 December 2006 <http://www.communities.gov.uk/index.asp?id=1505202>.

3 Department for Transport, The Future of Air Transport Progress Report, 14 December 2006 <http://www.dft.gov.uk/stellent/groups/dft_aviation/documents/pdf/dft_aviation_pdf_6 13840.pdf>.

4 This assumes that current annual emissions from aviation are 8 million tonnes of carbon (MtC). B. Owen and D. Lee, Allocation of International Aviation Emissions from Scheduled Air Traffic – Future Cases, 2005–2050 (Report 3), Manchester Metropolitan University Centre for Air Transport and the Environment, Final report to DEFRA Global Atmosphere Division, Plus Data Appendix, March 2006; cited in Sally Cairns and Carey Newson, Predict and Decide: Aviation, Climate Change and UK Policy, Environmental Change Institute, University of Oxford, September 2006 <http://www.eci.ox.ac.uk/research/energy/downloads/predictanddecide.pdf>

5 House of Commons Environmental Audit Committee, Reducing Carbon Emissions from Transport, 7 August 2006 <http://www.publications.parliament.uk/pa/cm200506/cmselect/cmenvaud/981/981-i.pdf>.

6 Alice Bows, Paul Upham and Kevin Anderson, Growth Scenarios for EU & UK Aviation: Contradictions with Climate Policy, Report for Friends of the Earth Trust Ltd, Tyndall Centre for Climate Change, 16 April 2005 <http://www.foe.co.uk/resource/reports/aviation_tyndall_research.pdf>.

7 Owen and Lee, op. cit.; cited in Cairns and Newson, op. cit.

8 Intergovernmental Panel on Climate Change, Aviation and the Global Atmosphere: Executive Summary, 2001 <http://www.grida.no/climate/ipcc/aviation/064.htm>.

9 Jonathan Leake, "Exposed: Britain's Dirty Secret", New Statesman, 18 December 2006.

10 Broughton, op. cit.

11 HM Treasury, Pre-Budget Report 2006, Chapter 7, 6 December 2006 <http://www.hm-treasury.gov.uk/media/571/CF/pbr06_chapter7.pdf>.

12 Department for Transport, White Paper: The Future of Air Transport, December 2003, p. 150 <http://www.dft.gov.uk/stellent/groups/dft_aviation/ documents/page/dft_aviation_031516. pdf>.

13 Ibid, p. 154.

14 Department for Transport, The Future of Air Transport Progress Report, p. 33.

15 Climate Action Network Europe and European Federation for Transport and Environment, Clearing the Air: The Myth and Reality of Aviation and

Climate Change, 4 July 2006 <http://www.transportenvironment.org/ docs/ Publications/2006/2006-06_aviation_clearing_the_air_ myths_reality.pdf>.

16 Owen Bowcott, "Ruling to Reveal Local Council's Secret Deal to Lure Ryanair", *Guardian*, 13 December 2006.

17 Department for Transport, The Future of Air Transport Progress Report.

18 See the graph at <http://www.carbonpositive.net/>.

19 Department for Transport, The Future of Air Transport Progress Report, Table C1, Annex C <http://www.dft.gov.uk/stellent/groups/dft_aviation/ documents/page/dft_aviation_6138 41.pdf>.

A Lethal Solution

1 HM Treasury, Budget 2007, Chapter 7, March 2007.

2 Department for Transport, Renewable Transport Fuel Obligation (RTFO) Feasibility Report, Executive Summary, 21 December 2005 <http://www.dft.gov.uk/pgr/roads/environment/rtfo/secrtfoprogdocs/ renewabletranspor tfuelobliga3849?page=1>.

3 George W. Bush, State of the Union Address, 23 January 2007 <http://www.whitehouse.gov/news/releases/2007/01/20070123-2.html>.

4 The US Energy Information Administration gives US gasoline consumption for October 2006 (the latest available date) at 287,857,000 barrels. If this month is typical, annual consumption amounts to 3.45 billion barrels, or 145 billion gallons <http://tonto.eia.doe.gov/dnav/pet/ pet_cons_psup_dc_nus_mbbl_m.htm>. In the State of the Union Address, Bush proposed a mandatory annual target of 35 billion gallons.

5 George Monbiot, "Feeding Cars, Not People", *Guardian*, 23 November 2004 <http://www.monbiot.com/archives/2004/11/23/feeding-cars-not-people/>.

6 Nils Blythe, Biofuel Demand Makes Food Expensive, BBC Online, 23 March 2007 <http://news.bbc.co.uk/1/low/business/6481029.stm>.

7 Eoin Callan and Kevin Morrison, "Food Prices to Rise as Biofuel Demand Keeps Grains Costly", *Financial Times*, 5 March 2007.

8 Keith Collins, Chief Economist, US Department of Agriculture, quoted by Callan and Morrison, op. cit.

9 Food and Agriculture Organisation, Food Outlook 2, December 2006 <http://www.fao.org/docrep/009/j8126e/j8126e01a.htm>.

10 UNEP and UNESCO, The Last Stand of the Orangutan: State of Emergency: Illegal Logging, Fire and Palm Oil in Indonesia's National Parks, February 2007 <http://www.unep-wcmc.org/resources/PDFs/LastStand/ full_orangutanreport.pdf>.

11 Wetlands International, Bio-fuel Less Sustainable than Realised, 8 December 2006 <http://www.wetlands.org/news.aspx?ID=804eddfb-4492-4749-85a9-5db67c2f1bb8>.

12 <http://www.biofuelwatch.org.uk/resources.php#2007Jan31>.

13 David Miliband, Malaysian Diary, 14 July 2006 <http://www.davidmiliband.defra.gov.uk/blogs/ministerial_blog/archive/2006/07/14/1 497.aspx>.

14 Commission of the European Communities, Results of the Review of the Community Strategy to Reduce CO_2 Emissions from Passenger Cars and Light-Commercial Vehicles, COM(2007) 19 Final, 7 February 2007 <http://ec.europa.eu/environment/co2/pdf/com_2007_19_en.pdf>.

15 HM Treasury, op.cit.

16 E4Tech, ECCM and Imperial College, London, Feasibility Study on Certification for a Renewable Transport Fuel Obligation. Final Report, June 2005.

17 Robert F. Service et al., "Cellulosic Ethanol: Biofuel Researchers Prepare to Reap a New Harvest", *Science*, 315 (2007), 1488 (DOI: 10.1126/science.315.5818.1488).

Giving Up On Two Degrees

1 Intergovernmental Panel on Climate Change, Climate Change 2007: The Physical Science Basis, Summary for Policymakers, February 2007 <http://www.ipcc.ch/WG1_SPM_17Apr07.pdf>.

2 Rachel Warren, "Impacts of Global Climate Change at Different Annual Mean Global Temperature Increases", in Hans Joachim Schellnhuber (ed.-in-chief), *Avoiding Dangerous Climate Change* (Cambridge: Cambridge University Press, 2006).

3 F. R. Rijsberman and R. J. Swart (eds), Targets and Indicators of Climate Change: Report of Working Group II of the Advisory Group on Greenhouse Gases, Stockholm Environment Institute, 1990.

4 Council of the European Union, Information Note 7242/05, 11 March 2005 <http://register.consilium.europa.eu/pdf/en/05/st07/st07242.en05.pdf>.

5 Malte Meinshausen, "What Does a 2°C Target Mean for Greenhouse Gas Concentrations? A Brief Analysis Based on Multi-Gas Emission Pathways and Several Climate Sensitivity Uncertainty Estimates", in Schellnhuber, op. cit.

6 Intergovernmental Panel on Climate Change, Mitigation of Climate Change, Unpublished Draft Report, Version 3.0, Table SPM 1, 2007. The IPCC uses the words "Unlikely" and "Very Unlikely". These have precise definitions in the IPCC process: a 33% likelihood and a 10% likelihood. For the full set of definitions, see Intergovernmental Panel on Climate Change, Climate Change

2007.

7 The figures the IPCC uses in Table SPM 1 suggest that the other greenhouse gases account for 21% of the climate change due to carbon dioxide alone. This is a high estimate; other authors (eg Sir Nicholas Stern for the UK environment department), suggest 10 or 15%.

8 Again, I use the IPCC's formula here. Other estimates would produce a slightly lower figure.

9 Sir Nicholas Stern, The Economics of Climate Change. HM Treasury, Part 3, October 2006, p. 194 <http://www.hm-treasury.gov.uk/independent_reviews/ stern_review_economics_climate_change/stern_rev iew_report.cfm>.

10 DEFRA, The Scientific Case for Setting a Long-Term Emission Reduction Target, 2003 <http://www.defra.gov.uk/environment/climatechange/ pubs/pdf/ewp_targetscience.pdf>.

11 HM Government, Climate Change: The UK Programme 2006, March 2006 <http://www.defra.gov.uk/environment/climatechange/uk/ukccp/pdf/ ukccp06-all.pdf>.

12 Council of the European Union, op. cit.

13 Nick Hurd MP and Clare Kerr, Don't Give Up on 2°C, Conservative Party's Quality of Life Commission, April 2007 <http://www.qualityoflifechallenge. com/documents/TwoDegreesApril2007.pdf>.

14 This is on the basis of a metric developed by Colin Forrest. He is not a professional climate scientist but his calculations can be replicated by any numerate person. For details, see chapter one of Heat.

15 Nathan Rive et al., To What Extent Can a Long-Term Temperature Target Guide Near-Term Climate Change Commitments? Table 1, Climatic Change 82:373–91 (DOI: 10.1007/s10584-006-9193-4), 10 March 2007.

16 John Vidal, "China Could Overtake US as Biggest Emissions Culprit by November", Guardian, 25 April 2007.

Crying Sheep

1 Energy Intelligence, High Oil Prices: Causes and Consequences, 2005 <http://www.energyintel.com/datahomepage.asp?publication_id=65>.

2 Matthew Simmons, Twilight in the Desert: The Coming Saudi Oil Shock and the World Economy (Hoboken: Wiley, 2005); quoted by Peter Maass, "The Breaking Point", New York Times, 21 August 2005.

3 Adam Porter, How Much Oil Do We Really Have?, 15 July 2005 <http://news.bbc.co.uk/1/hi/business/4681935.stm>.

4 Jean Laherrere, Is USGS 2000 Assessment Reliable?, 2 May 2000 <http://energyresource2000.com>.

5 Porter, op. cit.

6 J. W. Schmoker and T. S. Dyman, US Geological Survey, World Petroleum Assessment 2000, Chapter RV, 2000 <http://energy.cr.usgs.gov/WEcont/chaps/RV.pdf>.

7 US Geological Survey, World Petroleum Assessment 2000, Executive Summary, 2000 <http://pubs.usgs.gov/dds/dds-060/>.

8 Cited in Aaron Naparstek, "The Coming Energy Crunch", *New York Press*, 17, issue 22, 2–8 June 2004.

9 Laherrere, op. cit.

10 Chris Vernon, OPEC Reveal Global Light Sweet Crude Peaked, 26 August 2005 <http://www.vitaltrivia.co.uk/2005/08/26>.

11 George W. Bush, Press Conference, 16 March 2005 <http://www.whitehouse.gov/news/releases/2005/03/20050316-3.html>.

12 Robert L. Hirsch, Roger Bezdek and Robert Wendling, for US Department of Energy, Peaking of World Oil Production: Impacts, Mitigation, & Risk Management, February 2005; this is now available at <http://www.hubbertpeak.com/us/NETL/OilPeaking.pdf>.

13 Richard Heinberg, Where Is the Hirsch Report?, 30 July 2005. <www.counterpunch.com>.

14 Hirsch, Bezdek and Wendling, op. cit.

15 Bjorn Lomborg, *The Skeptical Environmentalist* (Cambridge: Cambridge University Press, 2001).

16 "No Safety Net", *Economist*, 10 September 2005.

17 Philip Verleger, Institute for International Economics.

18 Hirsch, Bezdek and Wendling, op. cit.

19 Hirsch et al. are citing Cambridge Energy Research Associates, The Worst Is Yet to Come: Diverging Fundamentals Challenge the North American Gas Market, Spring 2004. In 2001 they said "The rebound in North American gas supply has begun and is expected to be maintained at least through 2005. In total, we expect a combination of US lower-48 activity, growth in Canadian supply, and growth in LNG imports to add 8.95 Bcf per day of production by 2005." (R. Esser et al., Natural Gas Productive Capacity Outlook in North America – How Fast Can It Grow? Cambridge Energy Research Associates, 2001.)

Feeding Frenzy

1 Ransom A. Myers et al., "Cascading Effects of the Loss of Apex Predatory Sharks from a Coastal Ocean", *Science*, 315 (2007), pp. 1846–50 (DOI: 10.1126/science.1138657).

2 Ransom A. Myers and Boris Worm, "Rapid Worldwide Depletion of Predatory Fish Communities", *Nature*, 423 (2003), 280–83 (DOI: 10.1038/

nature01610).

3 Shelley C. Clarke et al., "Global Estimates of Shark Catches Using Trade Records from Commercial Markets", *Ecology Letters*, 9 (10) (2006), 1115–26.

4 Myers et al., op. cit.

5 Francesca Colombo, Dangerous Waters – Even for Sharks, Inter Press Service News Agency, 12 March 2007 <http://ipsnews.net/news.asp?idnews=36885>.

6 Oceana, Conservationists Rally MEPs to Make, Not Break EU Ban on Shark Finning, Press Release, 24 September 2006.

7 Oceana, Oceana Requests Explanations from the Spanish Socialist and Popular Parties Regarding Their Efforts to Increase Shark Captures, Press Release, 5 December 2006.

8 Oceana, Conservationist Rally MEPs.

9 Oceana, Sharks Threatened by European Parliament Finning Report, Press Release, 23 August 2006.

10 Peter Popham, "Sharks Hunted to Extinction in the Mediterranean", *Independent*, 9 March 2007.

11 <http://www.cites.org/eng/disc/species.shtml>.

12 Oceana, Oceana Investigators Uncover Scandalous Fishing Practices: A Large Fleet of Illegal Driftnetters Are Fishing out of Sicilian and Calabrian Ports, Press Release, 29 June 2006; Oceana, Investigates French Ports in the Mediterranean to Uncover an Illegal Fleet of Driftnetters, Press Release, 4 August 2006; Oceana Presents Evidence in an International Meeting of Mediterranean Countries That Italy and France Are Using Illegal Driftnets, Press Release, 8 November 2006.

13 Council of the European Union, 2739th Council Meeting: Agriculture and Fisheries, 19 June 2006 <http://www.consilium.europa.eu/ueDocs/cms_Data/docs/pressData/en/agricult/90146.pdf>.

14 Boris Worm, "Impacts of Biodiversity Loss on Ocean Ecosystem Services", *Science*, 314 (2006), 787–90 (DOI: 10.1126/science.1132294).

15 Christopher P. Lynam, "Jellyfish Overtake Fish in a Heavily Fished Ecosystem", *Current Biology*, 16(13) (2006), 492–3.

Natural Aesthetes

1 Genesis 11:21.

2 Chris D. Thomas et al., January 2004. "Extinction Risk from Climate Change", *Nature*, 427 (2004).

3 See, for example, Raymond Bonner, *At the Hand of Man: Peril and Hope for Africa's Wildlife* (New York: Knopf, 1993); George Monbiot, *No Man's Land: An Investigative Journey Through Kenya and Tanzania* (London: Macmillan, 1994; reprinted Totnes: Green Books, 2003).

Bring Them Back

1 Gillian Harris, "Wolves Would Boost Tourism Says Landowner", *The Times*, 26 June 2002.

2 J. D. C. Linnell et al., The Fear of Wolves: A Review of Wolf Attacks on Humans, Norsk Institutt for Naturforskning, Trondheim, January 2002.

3 Ibid.

4 Ibid.

5 M. J. Goulding, Current Status and Potential Impact of Wild Boar (*Sus scrofa*) in the English Countryside: A Risk Assessment, Report to Conservation Management Division C, Ministry of Agriculture, Fisheries and Food, March 1998 <http://www.defra.gov.uk/wildlife-countryside/vertebrates/reports/Wild%20Boar%20Risk%20Assessment%201998.pdf>.

6 D. H. Lawrence, "Mountain Lion", from *Selected Poems* (London: Penguin, 1972).

7 These figures are explained at <www.bearsmart.com>.

Seeds of Distraction

1 Professor Derek Burke and others, Open Letter to the Right Honourable Tony Blair MP, 30 October 2003.

2 Biotechnology and Biological Sciences Research Council, Current Grants Awarded by Agri-Food Committee <http:www.bbsrc.ac.uk/science/areas/af.html_grants>.

3 Dick Taverne, "The Huge Benefits of GM Are Being Blocked by Blind Opposition", *Guardian*, 3 March 2004.

4 "Monsanto's Showcase Project in Africa Fails", *New Scientist*, 7 February 2004.

5 Alex Kirby, "Mirage" of GM's Golden Promise, BBC News Online, 24 September 2003 <http://news.bbc.co.uk/1/hi/sci/tech/3122923.stm>.

Arguments With War

Thwart Mode

1 George Bush, Iraqi Regime Danger to America is "Grave and Growing", Radio Address, 5 October 2002 <http://www.whitehouse.gov/news/releases/2002/10/20021005.html>.

2 Thom Shanker and David E. Sanger, "U.S. Blueprint to Topple Hussein Envisions Big Invasion Next Year", *New York Times*, 28 April 2002.

3 Patrick E. Tyler, "US is Dismissing Russia's Criticism of Strikes in Iraq", *New York Times*, 1 October 2002.

4 Eli J. Lake and Rick Tomkins, US Against UN Iraq Arms Inspection for Now, United Press International, 1 October 2002.

5 Draft of Resolution 1441.

6 Milan Rai, *War Plan Iraq: Ten Reasons Against War with Iraq* (New York: W. W. Norton, 2002).

7 Richard Butler, Letter to the Secretary General, 15 December 1998 <http://www.un.org/Depts/unscom/s98-1172.htm>.

8 See George Monbiot, "Diplomatic Impunity", *Guardian*, 23 April 2002. This can be read at <http://www.monbiot.com/archives/2002/04/23/diplomatic-impunity/>.

9 Todd S. Purdum and David Firestone, "Chief U.N. Weapons Inspector Backs Stiff U.S. Demand on Iraq", *New York Times*, 5 October 2002.

One Rule for Us

1 Donald Rumsfeld, United States Department of Defense, Transcript of CBS Face the Nation, 23 March 2003 <http://www.defenselink.mil/news/Mar2003/t03232003_t0323sdcbsface.html>.

2 Convention (III), relative to the Treatment of Prisoners of War, Geneva, 12 August 1949.

3 These were the conditions in Camp X-Ray. In Camp Delta, to which the prisoners have been moved, most of these omissions still appear to apply, and their confinement has become still stricter, though they are now permitted to exercise for two 15-minute sessions per week (Katty Kaye, No Fast Track at Guantanamo Bay, 11 January 2003 <http://news.bbc.co.uk/1/low/world/americas/2648547.stm>). The convention suggests that they should be able to exercise freely.

4 Duncan Campbell, "US Interrogators Turn to 'Torture Lite'", *Guardian*, 25 January 2003.

5 Frank Gardner, US Bides Its Time in Guantanamo, 24 August 2002 <http://news.bbc.co.uk/1/low/world/from_our_own_correspondent/2212874.stm>.

6 Convention (III), op. cit.

7 Afghan Massacre – Convoy of Death, now available on video from ACFTV, Studio 241, 24–28 St Leonards Road, Windsor, SL4 3BB, UK. All published details checked on 24 March 2003 with Jamie Doran.

8 Ibid.

9 Ibid.

10 Ibid.

11 Ibid.

12 Giuliana Sgrena and Ulrich Ladurner, Masar-i-Scharif Während des Afghanistan-Feldzugs gab es in Masar-i-Scharif ein Massaker. Zeugen sagen, US-Soldaten hätten daran mitgewirkt. Ein Beweis ist das noch nicht. Eine Spurensuche, *Die Zeit*, no date given. The cited text appeared, in translation, in Peter Schwarz, Further Evidence of a Massacre of Taliban Prisoners, 29 June 2002 <http://www.wsws.org/articles/2002/jun2002/afgh-j29.shtml>.

13 Physicians for Human Rights, Preliminary Assessment of Alleged Mass Gravesites in the Area of Mazar-I-Sharif, Afghanistan, January 16–21 and February 7–14, 2002.

14 Bill Vann, Film Exposing Pentagon War Crimes Premieres in US, 12 February 2003 <http://www.wsws.org/articles/2003/feb2003/afgh-f12.shtml>.

15 Jamie Doran, personal communication, 24 March 2003.

Dreamers and Idiots

1 David Aaronovitch, "Stop Trying to Stop the War. Start Trying to Win the Peace", *Independent*, 16 November 2001.

2 Throughout the bombing campaign in Afghanistan, the *Telegraph* ran a column on its leader page entitled "Useful Idiots", dedicated to attacking campaigners for peace.

3 George W. Bush, National Press Conference in the White House, 6 March 2003 <http://www.whitehouse.gov/news/releases/2003/03/20030306-8.html>.

4 James Risen, "Iraq Said to Have Tried to Reach Last-Minute Deal to Avert War", *New York Times*, 6 November 2003; Bill Vann, Washington Rejected Sweeping Iraqi Concessions on Eve of War, 7 November 2003 <http://www.wsws.org/articles/2003/nov2003/iraq-n07.shtml>; *Newsweek* Web Exclusive, Lost Opportunity? On the Eve of the Invasion of Iraq, Defense Officials Were Offered a Secret, Back-Channel Opportunity to Talk Peace With Saddam, 5 November 2003 <http://www.msnbc.com/news/989704.asp>; Julian Borger, Brian Whitaker and Vikram Dodd, "Saddam's Desperate Offers to Stave Off War", *Guardian*, 7 November 2003.

5 Borger, Whitaker and Dodd, op. cit.

6 Ibid.

7 Ibid.

8 *Newsweek* Web Exclusive, op. cit.

9 Risen, op. cit.

10 Bush, op. cit.

11 Tony Blair, Press Conference with George Bush and José María Aznar, Azores, 16 March 2003.

12 George W. Bush, Address to the Nation, 17 March 2003.

13 Luke Harding and Rory McCarthy, "Bush Rejects Bin Laden deal", *Guardian*, 21 September 2001.

14 Julian Borger, "White House Rejects Call for Proof; Taliban 'Ready to Negotiate'", *Guardian*, 3 October 2001.

15 Ibid.

16 Tony Blair, Speech to the Labour Party Conference, Brighton, 2 October 2001.

17 Article 33, Charter of the United Nations. The full text of this article reads: "1. The parties to any dispute, the continuance of which is likely to endanger the maintenance of international peace and security, shall, first of all, seek a solution by negotiation, enquiry, mediation, conciliation, arbitration, judicial settlement, resort to regional agencies or arrangements, or other peaceful means of their own choice. 2. The Security Council shall, when it deems necessary, call upon the parties to settle their dispute by such means."

The Moral Myth

1 Tony Blair, Prime Minister's Questions, *Hansard*, 19 November 2003, column 774.

2 David Aaronovitch, "Why I Say Welcome", *Observer*, 16 November 2003.

3 Arthur Koestler, *Darkness at Noon* (London: Penguin, 1940), p. 153.

4 Ibid., p. 124.

5 Paul Wolfowitz, Interview with Sam Tannenhaus for *Vanity Fair*, 9 May 2003; viewed on the Pentagon site <http://www.defenselink.mil/transcripts/2003/tr20030509-depsecdef0223.html>.

6 Ibid.

The Lies of the Press

1 Julian Borger, Richard Norton-Taylor, Ewen MacAskill and Brian Whitaker, "Iraq: The Myth and the Reality", *Guardian*, 15 March 2002.

2 George Monbiot, "Chemical Coup d'Etat", *Guardian*, 16 April 2002. This article can be read at <http://www.monbiot.com/archives/2002/04/16/a-war-against-the-peacemaker/>.

3 Chris Alden, "Defector Reveals Extent of Iraqi Weapons Programme", *Observer*, 4 April 2002.

4 David Rose and Ed Vulliamy, "US Hawks Accuse Iraq Over Anthrax",

Observer, 14 October 2001; David Rose, "The Iraqi Connection", *Observer*, 11 November 2001; David Rose, "The Case for Tough Action Against Iraq", *Observer*, 2 December 2001; David Rose, "A Blind Spot Called Iraq", *Observer*, 13 January 2002; David Rose, "Spain Links Suspect in 9/11 Plot to Baghdad", *Observer*, 16 March 2003.

5 Rose, "A Blind Spot Called Iraq".

6 Ibid.

7 Rose and Vulliamy, op. cit.; Rose, "The Iraqi Connection".

8 Kamal Ahmed, Ed Vulliamy and Peter Beaumont, "Blair and Bush: Iraq Poses Nuclear Threat", *Observer*, 8 September 2002.

9 Leading article, "Saddam Must Obey the UN, and Blair Must Rein in Bush", *Observer*, 10 November 2002.

10 David Rose, "Iraqi Defectors Tricked Us with WMD Lies, But We Must Not Be Fooled Again", *Observer*, 30 May 2004.

11 Leading article, "The *Times* and Iraq", *New York Times*, 26 May 2004.

12 Jessica Berry, Philip Sherwell and David Wastell, "Army Alert by Saddam Points to Iraqi Role", *Sunday Telegraph*, 23 September 2001.

13 Jessica Berry, "The West at War: Saddam Moves Chemical Weapons Factories Into No-Go Zone", *Sunday Telegraph*, 21 October 2001.

14 David Wastell, Philip Sherwell and Julian Coman, "Former Weapons Inspectors Are Certain that Iraq Is Prepared to Use a Deadly Array of Chemical and Biological Agents", *Sunday Telegraph*, 8 September 2002.

15 Julian Coman, "Evidence Shows Military Strike Is Only Way to Halt Baghdad's War Machine", *Sunday Telegraph*, 8 September 2002.

16 Philip Sherwell and David Wastell, "Iraq's Air Force Has Advanced Poison Bombs", *Sunday Telegraph*, 23 February 2003.

War Without Rules

1 You can watch the film at <http://www.rainews24.rai.it/ran24/inchiesta/video.asp>.

2 Captain James T. Cobb, First Lieutenant Christopher A. LaCour and Sergeant First Class William H. Hight, "TF 2–2 in FSE AAR: Indirect Fires in the Battle of Fallujah", *Field Artillery*, March–April 2005.

3 Darrin Mortenson, "Violence Subsides for Marines in Fallujah", *North County Times*, 10 April 2004 <http://www.nctimes.com/articles/2004/04/11/military/iraq/19_30_504_10_04.txt>.

4 Organisation for the Prohibition of Chemical Weapons, Convention on the Prohibition of the Development, Production, Stockpiling and Use of Chemical Weapons and on Their Destruction, Article 2.9(c).

5 Ibid., Article 2.2.

6 <http://www.globalsecurity.org/military/systems/munitions/wp.htm>.
7 Mallinckrodt Baker, Inc., Material Safety Data Sheet: Phosphorus
  Pentoxide, 2 November 2001 <http://164.107.52.42/MSDS/P/
  phosphorous%20pentoxide.pdf>.
8 US State Department, Did the U.S. Use "Illegal" Weapons in Fallujah?, viewed
  9 November 2005 <http://usinfo.state.gov/media/Archive_Index/
  Illegal_Weapons_in_Fallujah.html>.
9 Ibid., viewed 14 November 2005.
10 Adam Ingram, Written Answer, Hansard, 6 December 2004, column 339W,
   201991 <http://www.publications.parliament.uk/pa/cm200405/
   cmhansrd/cm041206/text/41206 w19.htm>.
11 Colonel Randolph Alles, quoted by James W. Crawley, "Officials
   Confirm Dropping Firebombs on Iraqi Troops", San Diego Union-Tribune,
   5 August 2003 <http://www.signonsandiego.com/news/military/
   20030805-9999_1n5bomb.html>.
12 Martin Savidge, Protecting Iraq's Oil Supply, CNN, 22 March 2003
   <http://edition.cnn.com/2003/WORLD/meast/03/21/otsc.irq.savidge/>.
13 Crawley, op. cit.
14 Adam Ingram, Written Answer, Hansard, 11 January 2005, column 374W, 207246
   <http://www.publications.parliament.uk/pa/cm200405/cmhansrd/
   cm050111/text/50111wo htm#50111w01.html_sbhd3>.
15 Colin Brown, "US Lied to Britain Over Use of Napalm in Iraq War",
   Independent, 17 June 2005.
16 Ann Clwyd, Letter, Guardian, 2 May 2005.

A War of Terror

1 George Bush, State of the Union Address, 28 January 2003
  <http://www.whitehouse.gov/news/releases/2003/01/20030128-19.html>.
2 Human Rights Watch, The Ties That Bind: Colombia and Military-
  Paramilitary Links, February 2000, Vol. 12 (1) (B).
3 Ibid.
4 Ibid.
5 Office of Special Investigations-Antioquia Region, Report, 21 September
  1998; cited by Human Rights Watch, loc. cit.
6 Matt Kelley, Colombia General Denies Rights Violation, Associated Press,
  28 January 2003.
7 Liz Atherton, Alvaro Uribe Velez: The Firm Hand of Fascism, Colombia Peace
  Association, September 2002.
8 Liz Atherton, US Imperialism in Colombia, Colombia Peace Association,
  November 2002.
9 Bill Vann, Rightist Death Squads Hail Colombia's New President, 29 May

2002 <http://www.wsws.org/articles/2002/may2002/colo-m29.shtml>.

10 Andrew Selsky, U.S. Will Train Colombians to Fight Insurgents, Associated Press, 29 September 2002.

11 Atherton, Alvaro Uribe Velez.

12. International Institute of Strategic Studies, "Colombia's War on Drugs: Disputing the Plan", *Strategic Comments*, 7(1) (2001).

13 Bush, op. cit.

Back to Front Coup

1 <http://www.usembassy.org.uk/bush.html>.

2 George W. Bush, Remarks by the President to the Troops of Fort Stewart Cottrell Field, Fort Stewart, Georgia, 12 February 2001 <http://www.whitehouse.gov/news/releases/20010212.html>.

3 George W. Bush, Remarks by the President at US Naval Academy Commencement, US Naval Academy Stadium, Annapolis, Maryland, 25 May 2001 <http://www.whitehouse.gov/news/releases/2001/05/20010525-1.html>.

4 George W. Bush, Remarks by the President at Camp Pendleton, California, 29 May 2001 <http://www.whitehouse.gov/news/releases/2001/05/20010529-6.html>.

5 George W. Bush, Remarks by the President at the American Legion's 83 Annual Convention, San Antonio Convention Center, 29 August 2001 <http://www.whitehouse.gov/news/releases/2001/08/20010829-2.html>.

6 George W. Bush, Remarks by the President to New Hampshire Air National Guard, Army National Guard, Reservists and Families, Pease Air National Guard Base, Portsmouth, New Hampshire, 9 October 2003 <http://www.whitehouse.gov/news/releases/2003/10/20031009-9.html>.

7 <http://www.whitehouse.gov/news/>.

8 Bill Vann, US Congress Passes $368 billion for Pentagon War Machine, 26 September 2003 <http://www.wsws.org/articles/2003/sep2003/pent-s26.shtml>.

9 Ibid.

10 Paul Krugman, "Man on Horseback", *New York Times*, 6 May 2003.

11 See <http://www.clark04.com/>.

12 Dwight D. Eisenhower, Farewell Radio and Television Address to the American People, 17 January 1961; read at <http://www.jfklink.com/speeches/dde/1960_61/dde421_60.html>.

Peace Is for Wimps

1 "RAF's New Eurofighter Force to Be Slashed by a Third in Defence Cuts",

Daily Telegraph, 9 November 2003 <http://www.telegraph.co.uk/news/main.jhtml?xml=%2Fnews%2F2003%2F11%2F09%2Fnmod09.xml&secure Refresh=true&_requestid=55495>.

2 Ibid.

3 Alan Clark MP, In the House of Commons, *Hansard*, 9 July 1997, column 855 <http://www.publications.parliament.uk/pa/cm199798/cmhansrd/vo970709 /debtext/70 709–02.htm>.

4 David Leigh and Ewen MacAskill, "Blair in Secret Saudi Mission", *Guardian*, 27 September 2005.

5 Ibid.

6 Rob Evans, Ian Traynor, Luke Harding and Rory Carroll, "Web of State Corruption Dates Back 40 Years", *Guardian*, 13 June 2003.

7 You can find this document at the bottom of this page: <http://www.guardian.co.uk/armstrade/story/0,,976559,00.html>. See: DESO Overview (page 2).

8 David Leigh and Rob Evans, "BAe Accused of Arms Deal Slush Fund", *Guardian*, 11 September 2003.

9 David Leigh and Rob Evans, "BAe Denies £60m Saudi Slush Fund", *Guardian*, 6 October 2004; Conal Walsh, "BAe Flies Into Storm Over Saudi 'Slush Fund'", *Observer*, 7 November 2004.

10 Leigh and MacAskill, op. cit.

11 David Leigh and Rob Evans, "MoD Chief in Fraud Cover-Up Row", *Guardian*, 13 October 2003.

12 Rob Evans, Ian Traynor, Luke Harding and Rory Carroll, "Politicians' Claims Put BAe in Firing Line", *Guardian*, 12 June 2003; Rob Evans and Ian Traynor, "US Accuses British Over Arms Deal Bribery Bid", *Guardian*, 12 June 2003.

13 David Leigh and Rob Evans, "Parliamentary Auditor Hampers Police Inquiry Into Arms Deal", *Guardian*, 25 July 2006.

14 House of Commons Defence, Foreign Affairs, International Development and Trade and Industry Committees, 3 August 2006, Strategic Export Controls: Annual Report for 2004, Quarterly Reports for 2005, Licensing Policy and Parliamentary Scrutiny <http://www.publications.parliament.uk/ pa/cm200506/cmselect/cmquad/873/873.pdf>.

15 Rob Evans and David Hencke, "Whitehall Tried to Smear Comedian", *Guardian*, 8 January 2001.

16 House of Commons Defence, Foreign Affairs, International Development and Trade and Industry Committees, op. cit.

17 Simon Basketter, "Derry Anti-War Protesters, Including Eamonn McCann, Arrested After Raytheon Occupation", *Socialist Worker*, 12 August 2006 <http://www.socialistworker.co.uk/article.php?article_id=9465>.

18 House of Commons Defence, Foreign Affairs, International Development

and Trade and Industry Committees, op. cit.

19 Criterion 2 of the EU Code on Arms Exports.

20 Foreign and Commonwealth Ofiice, Human Rights Annual Report, 2005; cited by the House of Commons Defence, Foreign Affairs, International Development and Trade and Industry Committees, op. cit.

21 Bob Graham, Michael Evans and Richard Beeston, "British Kit Found in Hezbollah Bunkers", The Times, 21 August 2006.

22 House of Commons Defence, Foreign Affairs, International Development and Trade and Industry Committees, op. cit.

23 Benjamin Joffe-Walt, "Made in the UK, Bringing Devastation to Lebanon – The British Parts in Israel's Deadly Attack Helicopters", Guardian, 29 July 2006.

24 Dominic O'Connell, "BAe Cashes in on £40bn Arab Jet Deal", Sunday Times, 20 August 2006.

25 Campaign Against the Arms Trade, Who Calls the Shots? How Government-Corporate Collusion Drives Exports, February 2005 <http://www.caat.org.uk/publications/government/ who-calls-the-shots-0205.pdf>.

26 Ibid; Evans, Traynor, Harding and Carroll, op. cit.

Asserting Our Right to Kill and Maim Civilians

1 Richard Norton-Taylor and Ewen MacAskill, "UK Refuses to Back Cluster Bomb Ban as Extent of Use in Lebanon Revealed", Guardian; 19 October 2006; Ben Russell, "Britain 'Is Blocking' Cluster Bomb Ban", Independent, 19 October 2006.

2 UNIDIR, Cluster Munitions in Albania; cited by Handicap International, Fatal Footprint: The Global Human Impact of Cluster Munitions, November 2006 <http://www.handicap-international.org.uk//files/ Fatal%20Footprint%20FINAL.pdf>.

3 Titus Peachey and Virgil Wiebe, Mennonite Central Committee, 1999; cited by Handicap International, op. cit.

4 UN Mine Action Coordination Centre for South Lebanon, September 2006; cited by Landmine Action, Foreseeable Harm: The Use and Impact of Cluster Munitions in Lebanon: 2006, October 2006 <http://www.landmineaction.org/ resources/ForeseeableHarmfinal.pdf>.

5 Handicap International, op. cit.

6 Ibid.

7 Ibid.

8 Ibid; and Landmine Action, op. cit.

9 Article 51, Protocol 1 to the Geneva Conventions, 1977.

10 Handicap International, op. cit.

11 Lord Triesman, Armed Forces: Cluster Bombs, 12 October 2006
<http://www.publications.parliament.uk/pa/ld199900/ldhansrd/pdvn/ldso6/
text/61012-0001.htm>.

12 David Cracknell and Isabel Oakeshott, "Benn Slams Cluster Bombs", *Sunday Times*, 5 November 2006.

13 Norton-Taylor and MacAskill, op. cit.

A War Dividend

1 Des Browne, Votes A 2006–7, 21 November 2006 <http://www.publica-
tions.parliament.uk/pa/cm200607/cmhansrd/
cm061121/wmstext/6112 1m0003.htm>.

2 Department for International Development, What Are We Doing to Tackle
World Poverty?, 2006 <http://www.dfid.gov.uk/pubs/files/
DFIDquickguide1.pdf>.

3 Ministry of Defence, Defence Spending, 2006 <http://www.mod.uk/
DefenceInternet/AboutDefence/Organisation/KeyFactsAboutDefence/
DefenceSpending.htm>.

4 National Audit Office, Ministry of Defence: Major Projects Report 2006,
24 November 2006 <http://www.nao.org.uk/publications/
nao_reports/06–07/060723i.pdf>.

5 Ministry of Defence, Delivering Security in a Changing World: Defence
White Paper, December 2003 <http://www.mod.uk/NR/rdonlyres/
051AF365-0A97-4550-99C0-4D87D7C95DED/0/cm6041I_whitepaper2003.pdf>.

6 Richard Norton-Taylor, "Military Alliance Battles to Reinvent Itself
As It Struggles for Credibility in First Real Combat Test", *Guardian*,
25 November 2006.

7 Ministry of Defence, Delivering Security in a Changing World: Defence
White Paper.

8 Ministry of Defence, Delivering Security in a Changing World: Future
Capabilities, July 2004 <http://www.mod.uk/NR/rdonlyres/
147C7A19-8554-4DAE-9F88-
6FBAD2D973F9/0/cm6269_future_capabilities.pdf>.

9 David Leigh and Rob Evans, "BAe Accused of Arms Deal Slush Fund",
Guardian, 11 September 2003; David Leigh and Rob Evans, "MoD Chief in
Fraud Cover-Up Row", *Guardian*, 13 October 2003; David Leigh and Rob
Evans, "BAe Denies £60m Saudi Slush Fund", *Guardian*, 6 October 2004.

10 John Kampfner, *Blair's Wars* (London: Free Press, 2004), pp. 15–16.

11 Ibid., p. 170.

12 Ministry of Defence, Defence Spending.

13 Ministry of Defence, The Defence Vision, 2006 <http://www.mod.uk/DefenceInternet/AboutDefence/Organisation/DefenceVision/>.

14 Chris Abbott, Paul Rogers and John Sloboda, Global Responses to Global Threats: Sustainable Security for the 21st Century, Oxford Research Group, June 2006 <http://www.oxfordresearchgroup.org.uk/publications/briefings/globalthreats.pdf>.

The Darkest Corner of the Mind

1 Deborah Sontag, "Video Is a Window Into a Terror Suspect's Isolation", New York Times, 4 December 2006.

2 Ibid., citing Dr Angela Hegarty.

3 Ibid.

4 Detainee Abuse and Accountability Project, By the Numbers, 26 April 2006 <http://hrw.org/reports/2006/ct0406/index.htm>.

5 Carlotta Gall, "U.S. Military Investigating Death of Afghan in Custody", New York Times, 4 March 2003.

6 Dana Priest and Barton Gellman, "U.S. Decries Abuse But Defends Interrogations", Washington Post, 26 December 2002.

7 Alfred W. McCoy, "The Hidden History of CIA Torture. Abu Ghraib Is Only the Newest U.S. Atrocity", San Francisco Chronicle, 19 September 2004.

8 Detainee Abuse and Accountability Project, op. cit.

9 Carol Costello, American Morning, CNN, 4 May 2006 <http://transcripts.cnn.com/TRANSCRIPTS/0605/04/ltm.01.html>.

10 Laura Sullivan, At Pelican Bay Prison, A Life in Solitary, National Public Radio, 26 July 2006 <http://www.npr.org/templates/story/story.php?storyId=5584254>.

11 Ibid.

12 Peg Tyre, Trend Toward Solitary Confinement Worries Experts, CNN, 9 January 1998 <http://www.cnn.com/US/9801/09/solitary.confinement/>.

13 Laura Sullivan, Making It On the Outside, After Decades in Solitary, National Public Radio, 28 July 2006 <http://www.npr.org/templates/story/story.php?storyId=5589778>.

Arguments With Power

I'm With Wolfowitz

1 Joseph Stiglitz, "This War Needs the Right General", *Guardian*, 15 March 2005.

2 Leading article, "Wolfowitz at the Door", *Guardian*, 17 March 2005.

3 See, for example, Armand van Dormael, *Bretton Woods: Birth of a Monetary System* (London: Macmillan, 1978); Robert Skidelsky, *John Maynard Keynes: Fighting for Britain 1937–1946* (London: Macmillan, 2000); and Michael Rowbotham, *Goodbye America! Globalisation, Debt and the Dollar Empire* (Charlbury, Oxfordshire: Jon Carpenter, 2000).

4 Harry Dexter White, quoted in New Economics Foundation, *It's Democracy, Stupid: The Trouble With the Global Economy – the United Nations' Lost Role and Democratic Reform of the IMF, World Bank and the World Trade Organisation* (NEF, World Vision and Charter 99, 2000).

5 Harry Dexter White, quoted in van Dormael, op. cit.

6 Joseph Stiglitz, *Globalization and Its Discontents* (London: Allen Lane, 2002).

7 Noreena Hertz, "The Poodle and the Wolf", *Guardian*, 19 March 2005.

8 Leading article, "Paul's Conversion?", *Observer*, 20 March 2005.

9 See Catherine Caufield, *Masters of Illusion: The World Bank and the Poverty of Nations* (New York: Henry Holt, 1996).

10 Ibid., quoting Robert McNamara.

11 Ibid.

12 The Bank funded a project to log 45,000 acres of lowland forest. The region has never recovered.

13 For example, the Polonoroeste scheme, initiated by the Bank in 1980.

14 The Indonesian transmigration programme, first funded by the Bank in 1976.

15 See, for example, International Rivers Network, Risky Business for Laos: The Nam Theun 2 Hydropower Project, Berkeley, California, September 2004.

16 George Soros, *On Globalization* (Oxford: Public Affairs, 2002); and Stiglitz, op. cit.

17 Clare Short, quoted by Larry Elliott, "Why the West Is Always in the Saddle", *Guardian*, 21 March 2005.

18 Martin Jacques, "The Neocon Revolution", *Guardian*, 31 March 2005.

Still the Rich World's Viceroy

1 For more about these arrangements, see George Monbiot, *The Age of Consent: A Manifesto for a New World Order* (London: HarperCollins, 2003).

2 Ngaire Woods and Domenico Lombardi, Uneven Patterns of Governance: How Developing Countries Are Represented in the IMF Review of International Political Economy 13 (3), August 2006.

3 Christian Aid, Options for Democratising the World Bank and IMF, February 2003 <http://www.christianaid.org.uk/indepth/0303options/options.pdf>.

4 Ibid.

5 Daniel D. Bradlow, The Changing Role of the IMF in the Governance of the Global Economy and Its Consequences, Annual Banking Law Update, University of Johannesburg, 3 May 2006. <www.new-rules.org/docs/imfreform/bradlow.pdf>.

6 International Monetary Fund, Draft Resolution: Quota and Voice Reform in the International Monetary Fund, 31 August 2006.

7 A. Mirkhor, Peter J. Ngumbullu and Damian Ondo Mane, Letter to African Governors Re: Draft Resolution on Quotas and Voice, 28 August 2006.

8 Bretton Woods Project, Committee Questions Independence of IMF's Evaluation Arm, 30 June 2006 <http://brettonwoodsproject.org/art.shtml?x=539118>.

9 Bradlow, op. cit.

10 Joseph Stiglitz, Globalization and Its Discontents (London: Allen Lane, 2002).

11 Leading article, "Reform at the IMF – and a Lesson for the United Nations", Washington Post, 2 September 2006.

On the Edge of Lunacy

1 David Walker, "Privatisers' Prime Thinktank Is Flush With Public Money", Guardian, 2 January 2004.

2 The DfID website <http://www.dfid.gov.uk> lists £4,097,000 of ongoing aid to Liberia, and £4,207,000 to Somalia.

3 Ed Pearce, "The Prophet of Private Profit", Guardian, 19 April 1993.

4 Alan Rusbridger, "Sense, Nonsense and the Adam Smith Institute", Guardian, 22 December 1987.

5 See <http://www.adamsmith.org/>.

6 USAID, Creating Opportunities for U.S. Small Business <http://www.usaid.gov/procurement_bus_opp/osdbu/book-information.htm>.

7 Letter and photographs from a doctor in Gondar, personal communication, 22 June 2002.

8 <http://www.dfid.gov.uk>.

9 Vision 2020, the document produced by the government of Andhra Pradesh, envisages a reduction in rural employment of between 36% and 43%. See chapter 9, at <http://www.aponline.gov.in/quick%20links/vision2020/vision2020.html>.

10 Cited in Luke Harding and John Vidal, "Clare Short in Indian GM Crops Row", Guardian, 7 July 2001.

11 <http://www.dfid.gov.uk>.

12 Christian Aid, Master Or Servant? How Global Trade Can Work to the Benefit

of Poor People, November 2001 <http://www.christian-aid.org.uk/indepth/0111trme/master2.htm>.

13 David A. McDonald, The Bell Tolls for Thee: Cost Recovery, Cutoffs and the Affordability of Municipal Services in South Africa, Municipal Services Project, March 2002 <http://qsilver.queensu.ca/~mspadmin/pages/Project_Publications/Reports/bell.htm>.

This Is What We Paid for

1 Vision 2020 can be read at <http://www.aponline.gov.in/quick%20links/vision2020/vision2020.html>.

2 Ibid., p. 96.

3 Ibid., p. 42.

4 Ibid., p. 195.

5 Ibid., p. 170. This is worded as follows: "However, agriculture's share of employment will actually reduce, from the current 70 per cent [of the population of 76 million] to 40–45 per cent."

6 Ibid., p. 158.

7 Ibid., p. 333.

8 The figures have been tabulated by Tom Huppi in the document Chile: The Laboratory Test, which can be found at <http://www.huppi.com/kangaroo/L-chichile.htm>.

9 Clare Short, Parliamentary Answer to Alan Simpson MP, *Hansard*, 20 July 2001, column 475W.

10 The full list can be read at <http://www.dfidindia.org/>.

11 Government of Andhra Pradesh, Strategy Paper on Public Sector Reform and Privatisation of State Owned Enterprises, 2002[?].

12 Department of Trade and Industry, Byers to Help UK SMEs Foster Export Links With India, Press Release, 6 January 2000.

13 Government of Andhra Pradesh, Minutes of Cabinet Sub-Committee Meeting on 10 January 2004.

14 Ibid.

15 Ibid.

16 Clifford Chance Solicitors, Vizag – Meeting with the Attorney-General, fax transmission, 3 June 1999.

17 P. Sainath, "The Politics of Free Lunches", *The Hindu*, 15 June 2003.

18 K. G. Kannabiran and K. Balagopal, Governance & Police Impunity in Andhra Pradesh: World Bank Urged Not to Make Loan, Peoples' Union for Civil Liberties and Human Rights Forum, Andhra Pradesh, 14 December 2003.

19 Government of Andhra Pradesh, Draft Report of the Rural Poverty Reduction Task Force; cited in D. Bandyopadhyay, "Andhra Pradesh: Looking

Beyond Vision 2020", *Economic and Political Weekly*, 17 March 2001.

20 P. Sainath, The Bus to Mumbai, June 2003
<http://www.indiatogether.org/2003/jun/psa-bus.htm>.

Painted Haloes

1 Leading article, "That's Enough Debt Relief", *Daily Telegraph*, 13 June 2005.

2 G8 Finance Ministers, Conclusions on Development, 10–11 June 2005
<http://www.hm-treasury.gov.uk/otherhmtsites/g7/news/
conclusions_on_development_110605.cfm>.

3 United Nations Security Council, Final Report of the Panel of Experts on the
Illegal Exploitation of Natural Resources and Other Forms of Wealth of the
Democratic Republic of the Congo, October 2002. See also: Amnesty
International, Democratic Republic of the Congo: "Our Brothers Who Help
Kill Us" – Economic Exploitation and Human Rights Abuses in the East,
1 April 2003 <http://web.amnesty.org/library/Index/ENGAFR620102003>;
Human Rights Watch, Democratic Republic of Congo – Rwanda Conflict,
4 December 2004 <http://www.hrw.org/english/docs/2004/12/04/
congo9767.htm>; International Rescue Committee, Mortality in the
Democratic Republic of Congo: Results from a Nationwide Survey,
Conducted April – July 2004, December 2004 <http://www.theirc.org/pdf/
DRC_MortalitySurvey2004_RB_8Dec04.pdf>; Global Witness, Same Old
Story – Natural Resources in the Democratic Republic of Congo, June 2004
<www.globalwitness.org/reports/download.php/00141.pdf>; All-Party
Parliamentary Group on the Great Lakes Region and Genocide
Prevention, Cursed by Riches: Who Benefits from Resource Exploitation
in the Democratic Republic of the Congo?, November 2002
<http://www.appggreatlakes.org/content/pdf/riches.pdf>; Bureau of
Democracy, Human Rights, and Labor, US State Department. Country
Reports on Human Rights Practices, 2002: Rwanda, 31 March 2003
<http://www.state.gov/g/drl/rls/hrrpt/2002/18221.htm>.

4 <http://www.unodc.org/unodc/en/crime_signatures_corruption.html>.

5 David Leigh, "Jersey Breaks Promise to Outlaw Bribes", *Guardian*,
2 June 2005.

6 Warren Nyamugasira and Rick Rowden, New Strageies; Old Loan
Conditions. Uganda National NGO Forum, Kampala, April 2002
<http://www.internationalbudget.org/resources/library/UgandaPRSP.pdf>.

7 Ibid.

8 Report of the meeting by a health ministry official, cited in Nyamugasira
and Rowden, op. cit.

9 G8 Finance Ministers, G8 Proposals for HIPC Debt Cancellation,

10–11 June 2005 <http://www.hm-treasury.gov.uk/otherhmtsites/g7/news/conclusions_on_development_110605.cfm>.

The Corporate Continent

1 The Greater Talent Network, Noreena Hertz: Global Activist and Socio-Economist <http://www.greatertalent.com/cgi-bin/speakers/db?keyword=003857&db=speakers&uid=&mh=25&sb=3&ascend=&view_ records=1&ww=1&cs=&x=46&y=5>.
2 The African Growth and Opportunity Act, H.R. 434, 2000 <http://www.agoa.gov/agoa_legislation/agoatext.pdf>.
3 Ibid.
4 <http://www.africacncl.org/About_CCA/members.asp>.
5 Corporate Council on Africa, *The African Growth and Opportunity Act: A Comprehensive Business Guide to Trading Under AGOA* (Washington DC: CCA, 2003).
6 Ibid.
7 Ibid.
8 Business Action for Africa Conference, 5–6 July, 2005 <http://www.cbcglobelink.org/cbcglobelink/events/bafa2005/Agenda.htm>.
9 Commonwealth Business Council, Private Sector to Drive New Investment Climate Facility (ICF), 13 June 2005 <http://www.sustdev.org/index>.
10 Richard Wachman, "Irish Knight Fights for Africa", *Observer*, 3 July 2005.
11 Quoted by Felicity Duncan, Easy Does It, Moneyweb, 6 June 2005 <http://www.moneyweb.co.za/specials/african_economic_summit/446897.htm>
.
12 James Hall, "Business Tapped in $550m Africa Fund", *Daily Telegraph*, 3 July 2005.
13 OECD Guidelines for Multinational Enterprises.

The Flight to India

1 Ha-Joon Chang, *Kicking Away the Ladder: Development Strategy in Historical Perspective* (London: Anthem Press, 2002).
2 Ibid.
3 Jake Lloyd-Smith, "White-Collar Jobs Under Attack: After Call Centres, Middle Management Are Next in Line for India's Onslaught", *Evening Standard*, 11 September 2003; Simon Hinde, "How We Lose Out to Call of the East", *Daily Express*, 20 February 2003.
4 Lloyd-Smith, op. cit.

5 Boyd Farrow, "Senior Jobs to Go in Rush to Cheap Asia Outsourcing", *Evening Standard*, 11 August 2003.
6 Cited in Amy Martinez, "Jobs That Won't Leave", *News and Observer* (Raleigh, North Carolina), 31 August 2003.
7 Ibid.
8 Cited in < http://www.blonnet.com/2002/08/28/stories/2002082800451700.htm >.
9 United Kingdom Office of National Statistics, personal communication, 17 October 2003. Of 73,000 workers in "call-in" call centres, 46,000 are women.
10 < http://www.rediff.com/money/2003/aug/04sld2.htm >; Luke Harding, "Delhi Calling", *Guardian*, 9 March 2001.

How Britain Denies Its Holocausts

1 Mike Davis, *Late Victorian Holocausts: El Niño Famines and the Making of the Third World* (London: Verso, 2001).
2 An order from the lieutenant-governor, Sir George Couper, to his district officers, quoted in ibid.
3 Caroline Elkins, *Britain's Gulag: The Brutal End of Empire in Kenya* (London: Jonathan Cape, 2005).
4 Mark Curtis, *Web of Deceit: Britain's Real Role in the World* (London: Vintage, 2003).
5 Elkins, op. cit.
6 Curtis, op. cit.
7 David Anderson, *Histories of the Hanged: Britain's Dirty War in Kenya and the End of Empire* (London: Weidenfeld and Nicolson, 2005).
8 Max Hastings, "This Is the Country of Drake and Pepys, Not Shaka Zulu", *Guardian*, 27 December 2005.
9 Andrew Roberts, "We Should Take Pride in Britain's Empire Past", *Daily Express*, 13 July 2004.
10 Andrew Roberts, "Why We Need Empires", *Sunday Telegraph*, 16 January 2005.
11 Prasannan Parthasarathi, "Rethinking Wages and Competitiveness in Eighteenth-Century Britain and South India", *Past and Present*, 158 (1998); quoted in Davis, op. cit.
12 John Keegan, "The Empire Is Worthy of Honour", *Daily Telegraph*, 14 July 2004.
13 Curtis, op. cit.

A Bully in Ermine

1 < http://www.parliament.the-stationery-office.co.uk/pa/ld199697/ldhansrd/pdvn/lds06/text/60313-23.htm#60313-23_unstaro >.

2 <http://www.parliament.the-stationery-office.co.uk/pa/ld199697/ldhansrd/pdvn/lds06/text/60313-26.htm>.

3 Ibid.

4 Hill and Knowlton, Client Successes: Debswana <http://www.hillandknowlton.com/index/case_studies/our_results/10>.

5 Corporate Watch UK, Hill & Knowlton: A Corporate Profile, Part 4, June 2002 <http://www.corporatewatch.org.uk/?lid=380>.

6 See <http://www.publications.parliament.uk/pa/cm/cmparty/050211/memi21.htm>.

7 See <http://www.publications.parliament.uk/pa/cm/cmparty/060210/memi19.htm>.

8 Rebaone Odirile, "Brit Engaged to Counter SI", Botswana Guardian, 10 November 2005 <http://www.botswanaguardian.co.bw/437221693156.html>.

9 Hill and Knowlton, op. cit.

10 See <http://www.survival-international.org/press_room.php?id=1357>.

11 BBC World Service News, 16 March 2006, 15.00 GMT.

12 Papua Press Agency, Meterai Kebernaran, Part D.3, The World Political Situation and the U.S. Intervention in the Case of West Papua <http://www.westpapua.net/docs/books/book1/part03.htm>.

13 Festus Mogae, 1997, quoted by Jonathan Mazower, Censorship and the Bushmen – Banning Dissent, Index on Censorship <http://www.ifex.org/fr/content/view/full/51580/>.

14 Margaret Nasha, in an interview with Carte Blanche TV, South Africa, 26 February 2002.

15 Government of Botswana, The Relocation of Basarwa from the Central Kalahari Game Reserve <http://www.gov.bw/basarwa/background.html>.

16 UN Committee on the Elimination of Racial Discrimination Sixty-Eighth Session, Concluding Observations: Botswana, 20 February–10 March 2006.

17 First People of the Kalahari, Press Release, Our People Are Being Terrorised: First People of the Kalahari On Torture in Khutse Game Reserve, 29 June 2005 <http://www.survival-international.org/related_material.php?id=219>; Survival International, Government Tries to Subvert Bushmen's Court Case Fundraising, 2 March 2006 <http://www.survival-international.org/news.php?id=1423>.

18 <http://www.parliament.the-stationery-office.co.uk/pa/ld199697/ldhansrd/pdvn/lds06/text/60313-26.htm>.

19 Watson, Survival International, personal communication, 19 March 2006.

20 John Simpson, Bushmen Fight for Homeland, BBC News Online, 2 May 2005 <http://news.bbc.co.uk/1/hi/world/africa/4480883.stm>.

21 BBC Radio 4 Today Programme, 17 March 2005.

Lady Tonge: An Apology

1 Jenny Tonge, "We Need a Proper Debate About Indigenous People", *Guardian*, 24 March 2006.

Arguments With Money

Property Paranoia

1 Andrew Oswald, "The Hippies Were Right All Along About Happiness", *Financial Times*, 19 January 2006.
2 Ibid.
3 New Economics Foundation, The Power and Potential of Well-being Indicators NEF and Nottingham City Council, 2004.
4 Richard Layard, *Happiness: Lessons from a New Science* (London: Allen Lane, 2005).
5 Ibid.
6 Daniel Defoe, *Robinson Crusoe*, 1719.

Britain's Most Selfish People

1 Richard Savill, "Village Trust to Build Houses for Locals Only", *Daily Telegraph*, 18 May 2006.
2 Office of the Deputy Prime Minister, reported by Faith Glasgow, "The Lure of a Rural Bolthole Or One in the City If That's More to Your Taste", *Financial Times*, 29 April 2006.
3 Shelter, Building for the Future – 2005 Update, Table 4, Shelter Housing Investment Project Series, November 2005.
4 Affordable Rural Housing Commission, Final Report, 2006 <http://www.defra.gov.uk/rural/pdfs/housing/commission/affordable-housing.pdf>.
5 Leader, "Second Homes and the Politics of Envy", *Daily Telegraph*, 18 May 2006.
6 Simon Jenkins, "Not Too Round, Not Too Precise: That's Why 11,000 Is a Magic Number", *Guardian*, 19 May 2006.
7 Press Association, Rural Homes Cost More Than Urban, 18 May 2006 <http://www.guardian.co.uk/uklatest/story/0,,-5829622,00.html>.
8 HACAN/Clear Skies, 2005, cited by Transport 2000 in Facts and Figures: Aviation <http://www.transport2000.org.uk/>.

9 Charles Clover, "Councils May Be Allowed to Stop Sales of Second Homes", *Daily Telegraph*, 18 May 2006.

10 Affordable Rural Housing Commission, op. cit.

11 Peter Dunn, "The Real Causes Driving Up Homelessness in Rural Communities", *Guardian*, 22 May 2006.

12 Steven Swinford, "MPs With Mansions Get Second Home Perk", *Sunday Times*, 7 May 2006.

13 Quoted by Ben Hall, "Mandelson Tells Labour It Risks Support in South", *Financial Times*, 20 May 2006.

Theft Is Property

Unfortunately I no longer have the references for this column.

Expose the Tax Cheats

1 Llew Smith et al., "A Different Way to Spend", *Guardian*, 25 September 2004; Vince Cable, Speech to the Liberal Democrat Conference, 20 September 2004.

2 Duncan Campbell, "Havens That Have Become a Tax on the World's Poor", *Guardian*, 21 September 2004.

3 In the first six months of the current financial year, the public sector deficit was £13.5bn.

4 Income tax receipts last year were £115bn <http://www.inlandrevenue.gov.uk/stats/t_receipt/table2-8.pdf>.

5 The 2004 budget costs the NHS at £81bn.

6 Nick Davies, "Poor Leadership, Missed Chances and Billions Down the Drain", *Guardian*, 24 July 2002.

7 Patience Wheatcroft, "Vodafone Brings Out Taxing Issue", *The Times*, 2 April 2004.

8 Leading article, "Levy Pays His Dues", *Daily Telegraph*, 27 June 2000.

9 Nick Davies, "The Scandal of Our Craven Tax Collectors", *Guardian*, 17 October 2002.

10 Patrick O'Brien, Press Officer, Inland Revenue, personal communication, 24 September 2004.

11 Email from Patrick O'Brien, 24 September 2004.

12 Ibid.

13 Barry Hugill, Press Officer, Liberty, personal communication, 24 September 2004.

Bleeding Us Dry

1 Table faxed by Tammy Lyons, Department of Health, 22 May 2001, Average Number of Available and Occupied Beds, 1996/7 to 1999/0 for England (Source: KH03, DoH).

2 This is contained in a series of leaked documents. To protect my source, I cannot give their titles.

3 Patrick Wintour, "Billions Lost in Contracts Failure", *Guardian*, 28 December 2000; Nick Mathiason, "Crime Pays Handsomely for Britain's Private Jails", *Observer*, 11 March 2001; Nicholas Timmins, "A Sensible Strategy for Spectacular Returns", *Financial Times*, 3 July 2000.

4 Conversation with Bill Mesquita, 4 June 2001.

5 Quoted in the *Guardian*, 4 July 1997.

6 George Monbiot, *Captive State: The Corporate Takeover of Britain* (London: Macmillan, 2000).

7 Tony Blair, Labour Campaigns on Central Issues, Labour Party Press Release, 1 June 2001.

An Easter Egg Hunt

1 Leader, "The High Price of the PFI Learning Curve", *Financial Times*, 4 May 2006.

2 House of Commons Committee of Public Accounts, *The Refinancing of the Norfolk and Norwich PFI* Hospital (London: The Stationery Office, 2006).

3 Edward Leigh, 3 May 2006, quoted in MPs Condemn "Capitalist" NHS Deal, BBC Online <http://news.bbc.co.uk/1/hi/england/norfolk/4966996.stm>.

4 House of Commons Committee of Public Accounts, op. cit.

5 In oral evidence to the Committee of Public Accounts, 16 November 2005, ibid.

6 Andrew Stronach, Press Officer, Norfolk and Norwich University Hospital NHS Trust, 5 May 2006.

7 Richard Bacon, PFI Company Walks Away With £95m As Norfolk and Norwich Hospital Struggles, 3 May 2006 <http://www.richardbacon.org.uk/parl/norfolkandnorwichpfi.htm>.

8 Richard Bacon, personal communication, 5 May 2006.

9 Treasury Press Office, 8 May 2006.

10 Ben Lewis, Press Officer, Department of Health, 8 May 2006.

A Vehicle for Equality

1 Patricia Hewitt, quoted by Michael Harrison, "Hewitt Says the Rover Directors Accused of Asset-Stripping 'Deserve Big Rewards'", *Independent*,

26 May 2004.

2 Rover Suppliers Offered £40m Aid, BBC Online, 8 April 2005 <http://news.bbc.co.uk/1/hi/business/4423181.stm>.

3 Larry Rohter, "Workers in Argentina Take Over Abandoned Factories", *New York Times*, 8 July 2003.

4 Jon Jeter, "For Argentines, a Sweet Resolve: Cooperatives Step in When Factories Fail", *Washington Post*, 24 February 2003.

5 Jesús Catania, Chairman of the General Council of the Mondragón Corporación Cooperativa, Message from the Chairman, viewed 8 April 2005 <http://www.mondragon.mcc.es/ing/index.asp>.

6 Committee for the Promotion and Advancement of Cooperatives, The Contribution of Cooperatives to Employment Promotion, 1 July 2000 <http://www.copacgva.org/idc/coops-employment.htm>.

7 Michael Kremer, *Why Are Worker Cooperatives So Rare?*, Working Paper 6118. (Cambridge, MA: National Bureau of Economic Research, 1997).

Too Soft On Crime

1 Health and Safety Executive, Michael Mungovan: Rail Companies Must Be Properly Trained and Supervised, Says the Health and Safety Executive, Press Release, 1 October 2004.

2 Health and Safety at Work Act 1974, Section 3 (1).

3 Centre for Corporate Accountability, Why Influencing the Conduct of Company Directors Is Important, viewed October 2004 <http://www.corporateaccountability.org/directors/why.htm>.

4 Health and Safety Executive, 1985; Health and Safety Executive, 1986; Health and Safety Executive, 1987; Health and Safety Executive, 1988; Loughborough and UMIST, 2003; all cited in Courtney Davis, Making Companies Safe: What Works?, 2004 <http://www.corporateaccountability.org/dl/courtreport04/makingcompaniessafe.pdf>.

5 Jack Straw, quoted in *Guardian*, 3 October 1997.

6 Jack Straw, Reforming the Law on Involuntary Manslaughter, Consultation Paper, 23 May 2000 <http://www.homeoffice.gov.uk/docs/invmans.html>.

7 Home Office, Press Release, 20 May 2003; cited at <http://www.corporateaccountability.org/Updates/manslaughter.htm#blunk>.

8 <http://www.corporateaccountability.org/Updates/manslaughter.htm>.

9 Ibid.

10 Ibid.

11 Tony Blair, Speech to TUC conference, Warwick, 13 September 2004.

12 Valerie Keating, Criminal Policy Group, Home Office, "Letter to Organisations", Annex A, 10 September 2002.

13 HSC, Corporate Responsibility and Accountability for Occupational Health and Safety: A Progress Report on HSC/E Initiatives and Measures (HSC/03/105), October 2003.
14 *Guardian*, 29 July 1997.
15 M. Wright, R. Lancaster and C. Jacobson-Maher, *Evaluation of the Good Health and Good Business Campaign*, Health and Safety Executive Contract Research Report 272 (Suffolk: HSE Books, 2000); cited in Davis op. cit.
16 Mark Lawson, "Stuff Would Still Happen", *Guardian*, 4 September 2004.

Media Fairyland

1 Quoted by Michael Massing, "Press Watch", *The Nation*, 27 September 2001.
2 "Guess Who's a GOP Booster?", *Asian Wall Street Journal*, 24 September 2004.
3 CNN, 7 June 1998. The name of the programme was Valley of Death.
4 Barry Grey, Why Did CNN Retract Its Nerve Gas Report?, 16 July 1998 <http://www.wsws.org/news/1998/july1998/cnn-j16.shtml>.
5 Ibid.
6 Greg Toppo, "White House Paid Commentator to Promote Law", *USA Today*, 7 January 2005.
7 David D. Kirkpatrick, "TV Host Says U.S. Paid Him to Back Policy", *New York Times*, 8 January 2005.
8 George E. Curry, "Armstrong Williams: No Money Left Behind", *New Pittsburgh Courier*, 17 January 2005.
9 Glen Ford and Peter Gamble, "America's Black Rightwing Forum", *Black Commentator*, issue 20, 12 December 2002.

The Net Censors

1 Jonathan Swift, *Gulliver's Travels* (1726), part 4, chapter 1.
2 Changsa Intermediate People's Court of Hunan Province, 2005, first trial case no 29; in translation at <http://www.rsf.org/IMG/pdf/Verdict_Shi_Tao.pdf>.
3 Ibid.
4 Thomas Friedman, *The Lexus and the Olive Tree* (London: HarperCollins, 1999).
5 Leading article, "U.S. Firms Help China Censor Fr**dom, D*mocr*cy", *USA Today*, 20 June 2005.
6 Google has removed the statement from its own site, but it can be read at <http://pekingduck.org/archives/001843.php>.
7 Kris Kotarski, "MSN, China Pals in Censorship", *Calgary Herald*, 29 June 2005.
8 Open Net, Internet Filtering in China in 2004–2005: A Country Study <http://www.opennetinitiative.net/studies/china/#28>.
9 Reporters Without Borders, China Report, 2005

<http://www.rsf.org/article.php3?id_article=10749>.

10 Tim Johnson, "Critics Say U.S. Companies Enable Censorship", *Miami Herald*, 24 July 2005.

11 James Kynge, "News Corp Clinches TV Deal in China", *Financial Times*, 20 December 2001.

12 Murdoch called him "a very political old monk shuffling around in Gucci shoes" (this sounds to me like a rather better description of Rupert Murdoch). Gwynne Dyer, *Canberra Times*, 29 September 2001.

13 Evelyn Iritani, "News Corp Heir Woos China With Show of Support", *Los Angeles Times*, 23 March 2001.

14 Agence France Presse, Murdoch's News Corp Looks for Further China Access After TV, 20 December 2001.

15 Quoted in *Private Eye*, 17 August 2005.

16 Lisa Sanders and Jean Halliday, BP Institutes "Ad-Pull" Policy for Print Publications, Ad Age.com, 24 May 2005; republished at <http://www.spinwatch.org/modules.php?name=News&file=article&sid=1034>.

17 Ibid.

Arguments With Culture

The Antisocial Bastards in Our Midst

1 <http://www.safespeed.org.uk/prindex.html>.

2 Andrew Gilligan, "Spooks On the Trail of 'Captain Gatso'". *Evening Standard*, 12 September 2005; Malcolm Macalister Hall, "We're MAD As Hell . . .", *Independent*, 27 April 2004.

3 UCL and PA Consulting Group, The National Safety Camera Programme: Four-Year Evaluation Report, December 2005 <http://www.dft.gov.uk/stellent/groups/dft_rdsafety/documents/downloadable/dft_rdsaf ety_610816.pdf>.

4 Jeremy Clarkson, "Hurrah for the Gatso vigilantes", *Sun*, 6 September 2002.

5 Jeremy Clarkson, "Tuf Time for Gatsos", *Sun*, 7 February 2004.

6 Jeremy Clarkson, "Beware Vicious Cycles", *Sun*, 16 July 2005.

7 Jeremy Clarkson, "We Mustn't Take Thrill Out of Our Children's Lives", *Sun*, 26 March 2005.

8 Jeremy Clarkson, "I'll Have Tony in Sights", *Sun*, 10 July 2004.

9 Jeremy Clarkson, "What Will Plod Do Now We Can Kill the Burglars?", *Sunday Times*, 5 February 2005.

10 Jeremy Clarkson, "Ecologists Can Kill a Landscape", *Sunday Times*,

24 April 2005.
11 <http://www.abd.org.uk/>.
12 David Harvey, *A Brief History of Neoliberalism* (Oxford: Oxford University Press, 2005).
13 Quoted by Don Foster MP, *Hansard*, 2 July 2003, column 407 <http://www.parliament.the-stationery-office.co.uk/pa/cm200203/cmhansrd/vo030702/debtext/30702–10.htm>.
14 Quoted by Harvey, op. cit.
15 Compiled from DfT figures by Road Block, Totnes, Devon.

Driven out of Eden

1 Sheena Stoddard, *Paradise* (London: National Gallery, 2003).
2 Simon Schama, *Landscape and Memory* (London: Fontana, 1996).
3 <http://www.nps.gov/yose/nature/history.htm>.
4 Numbers 24:17.
5 Bernhard Grzimek, Michael Grzimek, E. L. Rewald, *Serengeti Shall Not Die* (London: Collins, 1965).
6 <http://www.magicalkenya.com/default.nsf/doc21/4YGEX3ADMY6?opendocument&l=1 &e=1>.
7 <http://www.gov.bw/basarwa/background.html>.
8 Survival International, News Release: Botswana Leaves Bushmen in Desert Without Water, 22 February 2002; Survival International, News Release: Botswana Tortures Bushmen, Then Prosecutes Them, 14 February 2002; Survival International, News Release: Botswana: Government Plans to Destroy Bushman Tribes, 30 January 2002.
9 <http://www.gov.bw/tourism/foreword/foreword.html>.
10 See, for example, <http://www.nationaltrust.org.uk/places/stowegardens/index.html>.
11 Stoddard, op. cit.
12 <http://www.bbc.co.uk/nature/programmes/tv/congo/>.

Breeding Reptiles in the Mind

1 BBC/Discovery Communications, *The X Creatures*, Presented by Chris Packham, 30 September 1998.

Willy Loman Syndrome

1 British Medical Association, Child and Adolescent Mental Health – A Guide for Healthcare Professionals, June 2006 <http://www.bma.org.uk/ap.nsf/

Content/Childadolescentmentalhealth>.

2 Nuffield Foundation, Time Trends in Adolescent Well-being, September 2004 <http://www.nuffieldfoundation.org/fileLibrary/pdf/ 2004_seminars_childern_families_ado lescents_and_wellbeing001.pdf>.

3 Tom Hertz, Understanding Mobility in America, 26 April 2006 <http://www.americanprogress.org/atf/cf/{E9245FE4-9A2B-43C7-A521- 5D6FF2E06E03}/HERTZ_MOBILITY_ANALYSIS.PDF>.

4 *Business Week*, cited by Paul Krugman, "The Death of Horatio Alger", *The Nation*, 18 December 2003.

5 Cited by Alister Bull, America's Rags-to-Riches Dream an Illusion – Study, Reuters, 26 April 2006.

6 Jo Blanden and Steve Gibbons, The Persistence of Poverty Across Generations: A View from Two British Cohorts, Joseph Rowntree Foundation, April 2006 <http://www.jrf.org.uk/bookshop/eBooks/9781861348531.pdf>.

7 Learning and Skills Council, Kids Seeking Reality TV Fame Instead of Exam Passes, 13 January 2006 <http://www.lsc.gov.uk/National/Media/ PressReleases/pr336-reality-tv-fame.htm>.

8 British Medical Association, op. cit.

The New Chauvinism

1 Richard Littlejohn, "Patriotism", *Sun*, 26 July 2005.

2 Jonathan Freedland, "The Identity Vacuum", *Guardian*, 3 August 2005.

3 Tristram Hunt, "Why Britain Is Great", *New Statesman*, 1 August 2005.

4 He uses this phrase in both *My Country Left Or Right* (1940) and *The Lion and the Unicorn* (1940); both published in George Orwell, *Essays* (London: Penguin, 1968).

5 Orwell, *The Lion and the Unicorn*.

6 Leader, "Ten Core Values of the British Identity", *Daily Telegraph*, 27 July 2005.

7 You can read the transcript of Miller's speech at <http://www.cnn.com/2004/ALLPOLITICS/09/01/gop.miller.transcript/>.